THE HOLOCAUST AND HALAKHAH

THE LIBRARY OF JEWISH LAW AND ETHICS

EDITED BY NORMAN LAMM

Jakob and Erna Michael professor of Jewish philosophy
Yeshiva University   New York City

THE HOLOCAUST
AND HALAKHAH

by IRVING J. ROSENBAUM

KTAV PUBLISHING HOUSE, INC.
1976

Library of Congress Cataloging in Publication Data

Rosenbaum, Irving J
    Holocaust and halakhah.

    (Library of Jewish law and ethics; 2)
    Bibliography: p.
    Includes index.
    1. Holocaust and Jewish law. I. Title.
D810.J4R658   940.53'1503'924   76-7407
ISBN 0-87068-296-2

MANUFACTURED IN THE UNITED STATES OF AMERICA

CONTENTS

ACKNOWLEDGMENT

The most important source for Holocaust responsa, and the work most often quoted in this book, is Rabbi Ephraim Oshry's 3-volume collection, *Teshuvot Mi-Maamakim* ("Responsa from the Depths").

Rabbi Oshry is one of the few surviving rabbinical scholars of Lithuania from World War II. He now occupies the pulpit of one of the oldest and most distinguished congregations in New York City, Beth Hamedrash Hagadol. He is Dean of Yeshiva Torah Ve-Emunah; president of the Rabbinical Board of New York; and president of the Rabbis Survivors From Concentration Camps.

We acknowledge our indebtedness to Rabbi Oshry, and are grateful for his permission to quote copiously from his works.

EDITOR'S FOREWORD

"Many reeds have been broken and much ink has been spilled" on the Holocaust (to use the talmudic idiom). Yet there is so much that remains to be said—of those matters and experiences that are at all capable of articulation.

One of the significant aspects of this tragic era, which has been more deeply explored in recent years, is the epic of Jewish heroism in the face of certain defeat by an enemy possessing vastly greater supplies of arms and men, and an inexhaustible reservoir of sadism and imaginative cruelty. Jewish resistance to the Nazis and their local cohorts in the various countries of Europe constitutes a glorious chapter in the history of human courage. Rarely, if ever before, have men and women demonstrated so much bravery in the face of such hopelessness, and at the cost of such brutality and bestiality. In ghettos and in concentration camps, from forests and sewers, Jews who had been subjected to every debilitating abuse and unspeakable torture emerged to fight with whatever pitiably few arms they could muster, taking whatever toll they could from the hated enemy. They died with dignity.

But this chapter of Jewish heroism is sadly incomplete unless adequate attention is paid to those whose courage was expressed in living as well as dying with dignity, in an often quiet but always fierce resistance to the Nazi program of psychological humiliation and degradation visited with special relish upon the Reich's Jewish victims. Historians of the Holocaust, anxious to lay to rest that heartless canard that all Jews went "like sheep to the slaughter" (inspiring such callous and insensitive questions as, Why did they allow them to do it to us?), have quite understandably turned their attention to the many glorious instances of armed resistance by Jewish partisans, camp victims, and ghetto denizens. In the course of so doing, they have largely neglected the magnificent record of another kind of courage—that of believing Jews who summoned up an unbelievable and invincible dedication to God, to Judaism, and to life itself. They tapped that mysterious and mystical reservoir of the Jewish spirit which has been the Jew's surest promise of survival. The faith of the Jew in his God and his Torah and his people was pitted against the diabolical arch-enemy, whose goal of crushing Jewry, body and soul, took precedence even over the survival of the Nazi war machine against the Allied onslaught, as has been amply demonstrated by Professors Jacob Robinson and Lucy S. Dawidowicz. And this faith often—remarkably often!—triumphed over the demons unleashed in this "enlightened" century.

On the basis of his research into documents by leaders of the Third Reich, Professor Uriel Tal has suggested that the Nazis focused on Judaism no less than upon Jews as their major enemy. The theoreticians of Nazism defined their movements as a "political theology" and as a form of secular messianism diametrically opposed to the religion and messianism of Judaism, which was thus conceived as quintessentially anti-Nazi. The confrontation between Jews and Nazis was thus formulated as not only political and racial but also as ideological—indeed, theological.

Granting this thesis—and no Jew need feel anything but pride in subscribing to this polarity—it is reasonable to expect that Jewish resistance to the Nazis would be carried out on the religious and spiritual plane as well as in other areas.

Indeed, this was the case, as the present volume by Rabbi Irving Rosenbaum amply proves. Religious Jews somehow managed, here and there, to observe now one *mitzvah* and now another commandment—under the very eyes of the Nazi S. S. and their Polish, Lithuanian, Ukrainian, and Hungarian henchmen. Prayer services were held in the camps, lectures in Talmud delivered in the ghettos, an *etrog* smuggled in here and a bit of *matzah* baked there. The battle was joined in one of the most awesome and gruesome confrontations in the history of our benighted species. In the end, Judaism's religious theology emerged triumphant over the Germans' political theology, and the Nazis' secular messianism went up in flames in Berchtesgaden while Jews still proclaim their confidence in the coming Messiah.

What is most remarkable, to the point of taxing credibility, is the staggering psychological stamina and spiritual invincibility of those Jews who sought guidance in Halakhah (Jewish law) from their few remaining rabbis. Questions *(she'elot)* on fine points of Jewish law were directed to a scholarly rabbi, and answers or responsa *(teshuvot)* were offered. Dedication to Torah was expressed not in the abstract, but in the minutiae of daily life even *in extremis*. Thus, a semblance of normality was restored to the inmates of the vicious madhouses, as the norms of the Halakhah provided a minimal psychic structure of human dignity and morale. This was infinitely more than "foxhole faith" and empty consolation. As some of the questions and answers recounted by Rabbi Rosenbaum reveal, people stood ready to offer up not only their own lives but even the lives of their only surviving children if this was the decision of the Halakhah. The ancient *Akedah* motif—the sacrifice of Isaac by his father, Abraham—was played out in all its terrible magnificence.

The history of the rabbinate will always accord a special place of glory to those remarkable individuals who rose to the heights of genuine spiritual greatness in the hell of Hitler's Europe. Many of them perished, and we shall never know of them or their responsa or the consolation they offered their flocks. Some, however, did survive, and it is thanks to their recollections and subsequent recording of the questions and responsa in all matters pertaining to Jewish law, that we are enlightened today with this insight into Jewish spiritual heroism. Amongst them one may mention the late Rabbi Hirsch Meisels, who lived in Chicago after the war and published his responsa in his book *Mekadeshei ha-Shem*. But the most voluminous and wide ranging of all are the works of Rabbi Ephraim Oshry, the distinguished talmudic scholar now occupying a pulpit in New York City. Rabbi Oshry spent most of the war years in the ghetto of Kovno, where Lithuanian Fascists vied with German Nazis in the cruelty of their anti-Semitism. His responsa, which have appeared in three volumes of his *Mi-Maamakim* (De Profundis)—the fourth was published after Rabbi Rosenbaum's work was completed—cover the entire gamut of Jewish law. Questions of life and death alternate with financial law, problems of domestic relations with inquiries on the observance of Sabbath and Festivals. One can hardly overstate our indebtedness to such men upon whom destiny has thrust the awesome responsibility of deciding Jewish law for the faithful—including questions of life and death—without an adequate library, a school, or colleagues to consult.

These works, and others like them, were largely unknown to the general public. Even the rabbinic-talmudic community had not produced any major anthology of, or study, on, this unique literature of the Halakhah. It is for this reason that KTAV'S *Library of Jewish Law and Ethics* is particularly pleased to publish this volume. Rabbi Rosenbaum's work now hopefully begins to fill the lacuna in the history of Jewish heroism during World War II. The author's erudition, his felicitous style, and his critical judgment in the selection and systematization of his material, will introduce the halakhic responsa of the Holocaust period to a much wider audience. Of necessity, he has been eclectic; comprehensiveness would have required a much larger volume, or series of volumes, and the exhaustiveness might have exhausted the nonspecialist and denied the general reader this much needed glimpse into human courage and Jewish dignity.

Reading this work cannot but leave one a changed individual. That is commendation enough for any book.

NORMAN LAMM

February 19, 1976

Chapter One

Holocaust and Halakhah

It has become almost an article of faith that the Holocaust was without precedent in Jewish experience. It was not! But the mistaken assumption that it was has not only spawned an entire literature of "Holocaust theology," but also has been responsible for an almost total unawareness of the role played by the Halakhah in the lives and deaths of the Holocaust's victims. It has been estimated that more than half of the millions of Jews caught up in the Holocaust observed the *mitzvot,* the commandments of the Torah, in their daily lives prior to the advent of the Nazis.[1] Did this commitment to the Halakhah, the "way" of Jewish religious law, crumble and disintegrate under the pressures of the "final solution"? Or did the Halakhah continue to bring not only some semblance of order, but of meaning, sanity, and even sanctity into their lives?

Precisely because the Holocaust was not without precedent, and because the Halakhah had confronted, dealt with, and transcended similar situations in the past, it was able to guide and sustain those who lived and died by it during the bitter and calamitous times of the German domination of Europe. While much of its technology was novel, the Holocaust simply duplicated on an extensive and enormous scale events which had occurred with melancholy regularity throughout Jewish history. The concept of the "final solution," it may be argued, differed in kind from earlier attempts at the destruction of Jews; but this could make little difference in the reaction of its victims, who were unaware of the comprehensive nature of the plan. Pillage, psychological degradation, exclusion from society, mass murder, mass graves, burning, torture, beatings, cremation, forced labor, imprisonment, death marches, infanticide, enforced prostitution, rape, and expulsion had all been experienced by Jewish communities in the past. Long, long before the Holocaust, the Halakhah had

1

developed its theoretical "theology" and its practical course of action when confronted with such tragic events.

The Halakhah was, therefore, uniquely equipped to adjust to death and suffering as well as to life and joy. It would be blasphemous effrontery for anyone who did not himself experience the terrors and the madness of the Holocaust to speak rapturously of the supportive and sustaining power of the Halakhah during that insane and diabolical period. But the vivid and compelling testimony of survivors, the literary testaments of victims, even the eyewitness accounts of the SS and those in league with them, clearly indicate the significant and ennobling role of Jewish religious observance in the Holocaust kingdom. In the face of events which would make Job's trials seem trivial, Jews retained their confident belief in a just Creator, whose secret purposes they might not be able to fathom, but whose revealed and clear dictates in the Halakhah they were bound to observe.

But while the course of action prescribed by Jewish law under ordinary circumstances in normal times was clear to most observant Jews, even then, cases of an unusual or difficult nature required special rabbinic guidance. In such cases, especially when they had no obvious precedents or analogies in Talmudic or later Rabbinic literature, a *she'elah* (pl. *she'elot*)—a question—was directed to a rabbi whose halakhic competence was respected. His *teshuvah* (pl. *teshuvot*)—responsum—delineated the course of action he believed to be demanded by Jewish law.[2]

Thus, from the very beginning of the drastic changes in Jewish life instituted after the adoption of the Nuremberg Laws in Germany, *she'elot* began to proliferate. Incredible as it may seem, even in the death camps of Auschwitz and Dachau, and under the guns of the SS *Einzatzgruppen* [3] in the ghettos of Kovno and Warsaw, believing Jews inquired of their religious leaders as to what the Halakhah required of them.

The spectrum of their inquiries is as broad as the Halakhah itself. In this volume we shall examine a considerable number of these *she'elot u'teshuvot*, as well as the varying Holocaust matrices out of which they emerged. We shall also study anecdotal material concerning the tenacious adherence of observant Jews to halakhic norms under circumstances where no formal *she'elah* and *teshuvah* were possible—where the unspoken inquiry was directed to one's own tormented soul, and the response was received from the same source.

A study of this material cannot help but bring about not only an awareness of the all-embracing character of the Halakhah, which can speak to even the most bizarre and unimaginable aspects of the human condition, but also a recognition of the majesty of a system which elicited obedience in the face of events which seemed to question the justice, if not the very existence, of its Author.

Perhaps the mind "set" out of which the *she'elot* of the Holocaust arose may be more clearly understood through the study of a moving episode described by Rabbi Zvi Hirsch Meisels in the foreword to his responsa volume, *Mekadeshei ha-Shem*.[4] Rabbi Meisels was the scion of a distinguished Hasidic and rabbinic family and was the *rav* of the city of Veitzen in Hungary. Before being transported to Auschwitz he had already achieved a considerable reputation as a halakhic scholar and was the author of a volume of responsa. After the liberation he was appointed chief rabbi of Bergen-Belsen and of the British sector; and was instrumental in clarifying the halakhic approaches permitting the remarriage of those whose spouses had been killed in the Holocaust.

He tells of the events which took place in Auschwitz on the eve of Rosh Hashanah in 1944. The Nazi commander of Auschwitz had determined to keep alive only those boys between the ages of fourteen and eighteen who were big enough and strong enough to work. The others would be sent to the crematorium. In the large "parade ground" behind the camp blocks some sixteen hundred boys who had hitherto managed to escape a *selektion* were assembled. The commander directed that a vertical post with a horizontal bar affixed at a predetermined height be planted in the ground. Each of the boys was forced to pass under the bar. Everyone whose head reached the horizontal bar was to be sent to a work detail. Those who were not tall enough were to be destroyed. Some youngsters, knowing what was intended, tried to stretch on their tiptoes to reach the bar and were bludgeoned to death on the spot. At the end of the *selektion,* the fourteen hundred boys who had not passed the "test" were imprisoned in a special cellblock under the guard of the Jewish *kapos*.[5] They were to receive no further food or drink, and it was understood that they would be sent to the crematorium the next night. Generally, the crematoria at Auschwitz were operated only during the night hours.

The next morning, the first day of Rosh Hashanah, fathers or other relatives who had heard of the fate that awaited the children, tried to persuade the *kapos* to release them. The *kapos* replied that an exact count had been taken of the boys, and they would have to pay with their own lives if even one were to be found missing. Some of the relatives still had valuables concealed in their clothing or on their bodies, and they offered them to the *kapos* in return for the lives of their children. Even those who had absolutely nothing with which to redeem their sons somehow managed to secure small valuables from other prisoners who wished to help. All that day of Rosh Hashanah the Jews clustered outside the doors of the cellblock bargaining with the *kapos*. Succumbing to greed, the *kapos* agreed to release some of the prisoners. But, they warned, for each prisoner released they would have to seize some other Jewish boy who had escaped the *selektion* or had managed to reach the bar, so that the count would be full when the block's inmates were taken to the crematoria.

Although they knew that their sons' lives would be spared only at the cost of others, fathers made whatever deals they could to save their own children. All this bargaining went on in full view of the camp inmates. The SS guards, Rabbi Meisels writes, generally remained at the periphery of Auschwitz and allowed the *kapos* to maintain control of the inner blocks. While he was observing this mad trafficking in human life, Rabbi Meisels was approached by a Jew from Oberland who said, "Rabbi, my only son is in that cellblock. I have enough money to ransom him. But I know for certain that if he is released, the *kapos* will take another in his place to be killed. So, Rabbi, I ask of you a *she'elah le'halakhah u'lema'aseh* (a question which demands an immediate response to an actual situation). Render a judgment in accordance with the Torah. May I save his life at the expense of another? Whatever your ruling, I will obey it."

Rabbi Meisels replied, "My beloved child: How can I determine the Halakhah in such a grave matter under these conditions? Even when we possessed the Holy Temple, a capital matter such as this required determination by a Sanhedrin. Here I am in Auschwitz, without any halakhic source books, with no other rabbis with whom to consult, and without the necessary clarity of mind because of these dreadful circumstances." Rabbi Meisels reasoned that if the *kapos* were first to release the ransomed boy and then capture another in his place, the Halakhah might possibly permit the father to redeem his child. This, because the *kapos,* who, after all, were Jews, however degraded and corrupt, might somehow relent after releasing the first child and not attempt to take another. Where it is not absolutely certain that saving the one life will cost another, the Halakhah might not forbid the ransom attempt. But the *kapos,* fearful that the SS might come at any time and hold them responsible for the full count, made certain to seize another victim before they would release the first. So, unable to give halakhic permission to the father, and unwilling to deny it, Rabbi Meisels continued to implore the Jew from Oberland not to ask his *she'elah*.

But the distraught father refused to accept Rabbi Meisel's evasions and said, "Rabbi, you must give me a definite answer while there is still time to save my son's life." Rabbi Meisels replied, "My dear and beloved Jew, please, I beg you, desist from asking me this *she'elah*. I cannot give you any kind of answer without consulting sources, especially under such fearful and terrible circumstances." The father responded, "Rabbi, this means that you can find no *heter*—permission—for me to ransom my only son. So be it. I accept this judgment in love." The rabbi continued to implore the man not to rely upon him. "Beloved Jew, I did not say that you could not ransom your child. I cannot rule either yes or no. Do what you wish as though you had never asked me." After much entreaty, the father finally said, "Rabbi, I have done what the Torah has obligated me to do. I have asked a *she'elah* of a *rav*. There is no other *rav* here. And if you cannot tell me that I may ransom my child, it is a sign that in your own mind, you are not certain that the Halakhah permits it. For if you were certain that it is permitted, you would unquestionably have told me so. So for me your evasion is tantamount to a *pesak din*—a clear decision— that I am forbidden to do so by the Halakhah. So my only son will lose his life according to the Torah and the Halakhah. I accept God's decree with love and with joy. I will do nothing to ransom him at the cost of another innocent life, for so the Torah has commanded!" [6]

In spite of the rabbi's importuning, the father persisted in his decision. All that day of Rosh Hashanah, Rabbi Meisels writes, the Jew from Oberland went about murmuring joyfully that he had the merit of giving his only son's life in obedience to the will of the Creator and His Torah. He prayed that his act might be as acceptable in the sight of the Almighty as Abraham's binding of Isaac, of which we are reminded in the Rosh Hashanah Torah reading and prayers.

Throughout this tragic interchange of question and answer, neither Rabbi Meisels nor the father raised the one question which to those outside the world of the Halakhah would seem to be the most urgent and demanding: "Shall not the Judge of all the earth do justly?" [7] Indeed, in almost all the halakhic literature of the Holocaust there is hardly any attempt at questioning, let alone vindicating, the justice of the Almighty. To some extent this avoidance of theodicy may be explained by the apothegm attributed to the great spiritual leader of East European Jewry, Rabbi Israel Meir Hacohen, the *Ḥafetz Ḥayyim* (d. 1933): "For the believer there are no questions; and for the unbeliever there are no answers." But the more essential reason was that personal and national tragedies had long since prompted the raising of all the possible questions. They are strewn throughout the Bible, the Talmud, the Midrash, and the post-Talmudic literature. The answers, however unconvincing or unsatisfying or even contradictory they might be, were well known to anyone at all familiar with Jewish tradition. The Halakhah maintained that the only tenable response of the believing Jew to the chastisements of God—deserved or not—was that of Moses himself, who, after describing God's outpouring of wrath upon His people, declared, "The secret things belong unto the Lord our God, but the things that are revealed belong unto us and to our children forever, *that we may do all the words of this law"* (Deut. 29:28). The one course of action which remained mandatory under even the most calamitous circumstances was the fulfillment of the *mitzvot.*

This basic principle was applicable no less to the Holocaust than it was to every personal and national tragedy that preceded it. It was clearly enunciated in the second century in the response of the Sages to the apostacy of Elisha ben Abuyah. Observing that the consequences of the fulfillment of the commandments of *shiluah ha-kan* (not taking fledglings in the presence of the mother bird) (Deut. 22:6) and *kibbud av* (parental honor) (Exod. 20:12) were not, as the Torah promised, "well-being and length of days," but, at least on one occasion, violent and untimely death, Elisha concluded *let din ve'let dayyan* ("there is no justice and no Judge"), and abandoned the Halakhah. Rabbi Jacob, however, declared that the "well-being" and "long life" promised by the Torah to those who observed its commandments were not necessarily to be enjoyed in this world, but in the next.[8] As Rabbi Yannai summed it up, "It is not in our power to explain either the prosperity of the wicked or the afflictions of the righteous" (*Avot* 4:19). Whether one met with sorrow and suffering or happiness and rejoicing, he was still obligated to praise and bless God (*Berakhot* 48b).

But a Jew did not need to be a Talmudic or Rabbinic scholar to know that the Halakhah provided for and was operative in death and pain as it was in life and joy. The beloved and well-known texts of the *siddur* (prayerbook), the *tehilim* (Psalms), the *humash* (Pentateuch), the *selihot,* (penitential prayers) and the *kinot* (elegiac prayers for Tisha b'Av) had familiarized him with the lot which had befallen pious Jews in the past with no consequent impairment of their piety. It may be said that in a very real sense this daily, albeit vicarious, experience of suffering prepared the observant Jew for the agonies of the Holocaust. Conversely, the "culture shock" of the alienated and emancipated Jew of the Western world was infinitely greater when he was confronted with the actual experience of the Holocaust, or even with a mere historical account of its events. The Jew who lived by the Halakhah, reciting the 137th Psalm each weekday before saying grace, was aware that the ancient Babylonians had dashed Jewish infants to death upon the rocks. In the daily *taḥanun* (petitionary) prayers he proclaimed, "Our soul is shrunken by reason of the sword and captivity and pestilence and plague and every trouble and sorrow. . . . O God, sunken is our glory among the nations, and they hold us in abomination, as of utter defilement."[9] On fast days, in the *avinu malkenu,* he recalled the Roman persecutions or the medieval massacres of the First Crusade, or the Chmielnicki decimation of East European Jewry in 1648, or the more recent Czarist pogroms or Petlura riots—"Our Father our King, have compassion upon us and upon our children and our infants; do it for the sake of them that were slaughtered for Thy holy name; do it for the sake of them that were slaughtered for Thy unity; do it for the sake of them that went through fire and water for the sanctification of Thy name; avenge before our eyes the blood of Thy servants that hath been shed; do it for Thy sake if not for ours. . . ."[10]

On Mondays and Thursdays, after the reading of the Torah, he joined in the prayer, "May it be the will of our Father who is in heaven to have mercy upon us and upon our remnant, and to keep destruction and the plague from us and from all His people, the house of Israel. . . . As for our brethren, the whole house of Israel, such as are given over to trouble or captivity, whether they be on the sea or on land, may the All-Present have mercy upon them and bring them forth from trouble to deliverance, from darkness to light and from subjection to redemption, now, speedily, and very soon, and let us say, Amen."[11]

On most Sabbaths of the year he recited the *av haraḥamim,* composed after the First Crusade in 1096, when the Jewish communities of the Rhineland were annihilated: "May the Father of Mercies who dwelleth on high, in his mighty compassion remember those loving, upright, and blameless ones, the holy congregations who laid down their lives for the sanctification of the Divine Name, who were lovely and pleasant in their lives; and in their death were not separated. . . . May God remember them for good with the other righteous of the world and render retribution for the blood of his servants which hath been shed. . . ."[12]

In the *selihot* prior to and on Rosh Hashanah and Yom Kippur, he chanted the harrowing accounts of many Jewish martyrdoms. Even if he were barely literate, he was familiar with the account of the Ten Martyred Scholars of the Hadrianic persecutions (135 C.E.) and the question placed by the poet of the *mahzor* in the mouths of the *Seraphim* when they saw the rabbis tortured and murdered: "Is this, then, the reward for the Torah?" The response of the Almighty, as the *mahzor* has it, was also known to him: "It is a decree from before Me. . . . accept it, all of you who love the Law!" [13]

The *kinot* recited on Tisha b'Av, the Book of Lamentations, the *tokhahah* in Deuteronomy (28:15–68), all provided graphic descriptions of the starvation, torture, death, exile, madness, and degradation which had been, or might be, the lot of the Jewish people. Halakhic Judaism had not obliterated the memory of these tragedies. On the contrary it had reinforced them, so that at least on a subliminal level, and generally on a conscious level as well, Jews who observed the Torah and its commandments were aware that the Halakhah had enabled their predecessors to survive, and even to surmount, the enemies and afflictions of earlier times. Thus, in the ghettos of Kovno, Warsaw, and Lodz, in the concentration camps of Auschwitz, Bergen-Belsen, and Mauthausen, they were able to face life with dignity, death with serenity—and sometimes even ecstasy.

To be sure, there must have been thousands of observant Jews who did ask Abraham's question, "Shall not the Judge of all the earth do justly?" and who found the conventional answers wanting. They could find no sin heinous enough to warrant the punishment they were receiving, and no promised bliss in the hereafter adequate to outweigh the hellish tortures they were suffering in this world. They abandoned and rejected the Halakhah at the same time that they denied God. But there were thousands more to whom the *mitzvot* were as important, perhaps more important, during the Holocaust as they were in normal times. For them the Rabbinic observation, "Since the day the Temple was destroyed, the Holy One, blessed be He, is only to be found in the 'four cubits' of Halakhah" (*Berakhot* 8a), became almost literally true. Their one sure link with the Divine was the performance of His commandments. The one universe in which they could be certain He was to be found was the universe of Halakhah. It is these men and women, who lived in the Holocaust and Halakhah kingdoms at the same time, with whom this volume is concerned.

The Origins of Holocaust Responsa

A brief examination of the methodology of the Nazis in attempting to achieve the "final solution" of the "Jewish problem" is necessary to an understanding of the halakhic response to the Holocaust.[14] The first stage of an anti-Jewish activity was from the accession of Hitler to power on January 30, 1933, until the outbreak of World War II in 1939. During this period the aim of the Nazi policy was to make Germany and German-controlled areas free of Jews. Using "legal" means to eliminate Jews from the German state and society, the Nazis sought to make life unbearable for Jews and to force them to emigrate. Jews were eliminated from citizenship, public office, the professions, and the intellectual and artistic life of Germany. The Nuremberg Laws (September 1935) were but the forerunners of a series of "legal" measures designed to achieve Hitler's purpose. These "legal" steps were accompanied by acts of degradation and violence, deportation and destruction, culminating in the demolishing of German synagogues on *Kristallnacht,* November 9, 1938. In the short period of six and one-half years, the German Jewish community, numbering 500,000 in 1933, was uprooted and reduced to a group of some 220,000 outlaws.

Until the latter part of this period, the primary effect of the Nazi persecutions on Jewish religious observance concerned the slaughtering of kosher meat—*shehitah.* On the pretext of a concern for cruelty to animals, the Germans outlawed *shehitah* unless the animal had previously been stunned by an electric shock. The pre-stunning of the animal raised grave questions since it could very easily cause lesions which would render the animal *terefah*—unfit for kosher use—even if it were slaughtered in kosher fashion after the stunning. After a time the Nazis also banned the importing of kosher meat from other countries. In any event, by virtue of their difficult financial straits, German Jews were unable to purchase such meat. By 1934, confronted with a situation in which not only individual Jews but also Jewish communal institutions, orphan homes, hospitals, and homes for the aged, which had previously adhered to strict standards of *kashrut,* would be compelled to use *terefah* meat if they did not comply with the regulations concerning *shehitah,* Rabbi Jehiel Jacob Weinberg, head of the department of Talmud and Codes at the *Bet Midrash Le'Rabbanim* in Berlin, and an acknowledged halakhic authority, prepared an exhaustive treatise on the subject. In it he found some warrant for permitting *shehitah* of electrically stunned animals—

particularly under the difficult conditions which obtained in Germany, and especially for those who were ill, aged, or infirm. A number of other German rabbis agreed with him. However, the leading scholars of Poland and Lithuania, to whom he traveled personally, and with whom he corresponded, could not countenance this drastic change in the method of *shehitah*. They were concerned not only about the grave halakhic difficulties which it raised, but also with the impression which might be conveyed to Jews and their enemies that the Germans had been successful in causing Jews to abandon their religious practices. They felt, too, that permitting such questionable *shehitah* in Germany would set a precedent for the adoption of such practices in other countries by those who were concerned with cruelty to animals.[15]

Still another *she'elah* was directed to Rabbi Weinberg during this early period, when Jews were forbidden to appear, or were fearful of being present, in places of public assembly, such as concert and lecture halls. Was it permissible to conduct lectures and concerts in the synagogue, or would such programs be considered as violating its sanctity? Rabbi Weinberg concluded that lectures were permitted, as were concerts of sacred music. However, discussion periods after lectures (because of the likelihood of unseemly or irreligious controversy) and secular concerts were forbidden.[16]

With each succeeding year, the *teshuvot* of the period begin to take on a more foreboding and ominous note. Rabbi Menaḥem Mendel Kirschboim, who was the rabbi of the *Kehilah ha-Kelalit* in Frankfurt-am-Main, was perhaps one of the first to be confronted with the harsh realities of the German plans for the Jews. In 1934 he too had traveled to Eastern Europe to discuss the problems of *shehitah* with the rabbis of that area. He was one of the authorities who sought to find some solution to the problem. In 1938, after the *Kristallnacht* episode, thousands of Jews were imprisoned in concentration camps. Many of them were killed, and their bodies were cremated by the Germans. In that still "civilized" period, the Nazis sent the ashes back to the victim's family for burial. A number of halakhic questions arose concerning the observing of mourning practices and the disposition of the ashes. Rabbi Kirshboim, on January 4, 1939, issued a four-page decision covering all these matters. Since it was forbidden to print Hebrew works in Germany, he sent it to his brother in Cracow, who arranged for its publication. His *teshuvah* concluded that the *shivah* mourning period was to begin upon notification of death from the authorities. The chest in which the ashes reposed was to be borne to the cemetery in the same manner as the coffin usually was. If possible, the ashes were to be buried in a coffin. In any event, a *tallit* and *takhrikhin* were to be wrapped around them as a confident indication of the belief in immortality and resurrection.[17]

Undoubtedly a great many more *she'elot u'teshuvot* relating to conditions during this early period have been lost. Rabbi Weinberg points out that he was compelled to leave hundreds of his *teshuvot* behind when he was expelled from Berlin by the Gestapo in 1939.[18] These were destroyed, as were those of the other rabbinic leaders of Germany. There are, however, a number of responsa from the satellite countries of Hungary and Slovakia dating from 1941 and 1942, when the conditions of the Jewish community there were roughly comparable to those of the last pre-1939 years in Germany.[19] Two *teshuvot* from this period are cited in *Mekadeshei ha-Shem,* vol. 1, pp. 150–151. These *she'elot* reveal the difficult, but not yet desperate, situation of Hungarian Jews. The first, dated Tamuz 5701 (July 1941), is from Rabbi Yitzhak Weiss of Werbau, who was asked, "Since Tisha b'Av falls this year on Saturday night, and since there is a decree from the *goyim* that Jews are not allowed on the streets after 8:00 P.M., how will we recite the *ma'ariv* evening service and the Book of Lamentations?" Was it permissible to advance the time of *ma'ariv* until just after *pelag ha-minha* (about one and one-quarter hours before sunset), at which time the Jews would still be allowed to be outside? According to Talmudic practice this is permissible in time of emergency. Or should we follow the *Magen Avraham* in *Orah Hayyim* 292, who rules, according to the *Maharshal* and the *Bah,* that even though the Talmud permits it, one should not do so, since reciting the *ma'ariv* service before the Sabbath is over at nightfall would cause wonderment and perplexity among the public? While the *Shakh* (*Yoreh Deah* 247) says that one may render such a decision, despite the "wonderment" it may cause, if the reason for the decision is made known, others do not agree.

Further, because of the principle "we do not hasten the approach of trouble" (*Megillah* 5a), it may not be proper to recite *ma'ariv* early, thereby ushering in the Tisha b'Av fast before it should really begin. After considering all these issues, Rabbi Weiss ruled that it would be improper to recite *ma'ariv* early because of the reservations about this practice expressed by the *Magen Avraham*. To begin the fast and to recite the Book of Lamentations publicly after *pelag ha-minhah* would contravene the principle of "we do not hasten." Therefore, he proposed that the Jews of his community recite *ma'ariv* at home privately after the conclusion of the

Sabbath at nightfall. They should also read the Book of Lamentations privately at that time. However, in order to fulfill the requirement of a public reading of Lamentations, it should be read at the synagogue on Tisha b'Av morning, although it is not customarily read then. This procedure would satisfy the requirements of the *Levush (Orah Hayyim* 559), who insists on a public reading of Lamentations, as well as the *Hayyei Adam* (402), who accepts a private reading as valid.

The second *she'elah* is dated the eve of *shabbat ha-gadol*, 5702 (March 28, 1942). It was directed to Rabbi Weiss by Rabbi Yitzhak Friedman of Tirnau. He writes that because of the decree prohibiting Jews from being outside after 6:00 P.M., a difficulty had arisen for women whose ritual immersion in the *mikveh* fell due on a Friday night. This immersion ordinarily must be performed after nightfall after the counting of seven "clean days," but because of the curfew regulations they were unable to go to the *mikveh* on both Friday night and Saturday night. While in case of emergency the Halakhah permits ritual immersion during the day after the seven-day period, they would not be able to go until Sunday morning. However, this undue delay in the opportunity of fulfilling the commandment of "be fruitful and multiply," and the denial of the opportunity for marital relations, goes counter to the letter and spirit of the Torah concerning marriage. Since the *Hokhmat Adam*, 118:5, rules that in emergency situations it is permissible to visit the *mikveh* on the seventh day during the daylight hours (in this case on Friday), provided the husband is unaware of this, and provided marital relations are not had until after nightfall, Rabbi Friedman asks whether we may allow this procedure and permit ritual immersion on Friday during the day for the women affected. After considerable searchings of heart, and of the sources, Rabbi Weiss reluctantly indicated that such permission might be granted on an individual, rather than a general, basis, and records that he had heard that such a decision had also been rendered in one of the large cities of Hungary.

Another *she'elah* apparently from this period, although it is undated, appears in the collection of responsa *Yerushat Pelatah*, pp. 8 ff. In the face of a government decree requiring Jewish-owned shops to be opened on *shabbat*, Rabbi Pinhas Tzimetboim of Grossvarden was asked if it was permissible for the shops to remain open, since the penalty for not doing so was the total shuttering of the stores by the government. Such action would be disastrous, resulting in a total loss of livelihood for the many Jews affected. After exploring the possibilities of keeping the shops open on the *shabbat* by having a non-Jew handle all transactions, Rabbi Tzimet-boim writes,

> And even if one can find a *heter,* permission, to open the shops on *shabbat* during this time of persecution by having a non-Jew handle all buying and selling, it is necessary to make an important *takanah* that each person so doing give his solemn word (*t'kiat kaf*), staking his share in the world to come in the presence of a *rav* or a *bet din,* that he will not personally sell on the *shabbat* and that he will renounce any profit from these Sabbath transactions. Even so, it may be advisable for no official ruling to be issued, but for each person to determine his own course of action and not be able to point to an official *heter* from a *bet din.* It is necessary to take counsel with the "great ones of the generation" on this matter and for a general ruling for the entire country to be decided—whether it is *le'issur* or *le'heter,* so that some rabbis do not rule one way and others another.

While the problems raised in these *she'elot* of the early Nazi period are by no means inconsequential, they cannot compare in poignancy and tragedy with those which arose during the second period of the Nazi campaign against the Jews, which began with the invasion of Poland in September of 1939. During this period, from September 1939 until April 1942, a systematic process of physical destruction was launched in Greater Germany and the Polish areas annexed to Germany. Jews were deprived of elementary human rights, including freedom of movement; robbed of their properties and businesses; dismissed from the professions; crowded in restricted quarters under outrageous conditions; forced to wear the yellow badge; compelled to work at forced labor without remuneration, and subjected to starvation and savage brutality. Synagogues were burned, Torah scrolls desecrated, and rabbis taunted and tormented. This, then, was the Nazi-created ghetto.

The ghetto was both an instrument of physical and psychological warfare against the Jew and a control device designed to facilitate his ultimate destruction. The isolation of the Jewish population behind barbed wire and high walls did succeed in reducing their number through starvation, debilitating forced labor, disease, and overcrowding. The concentration of the Jews in the ghetto also made it a superb waystation for the assembly and transfer of Jews to labor and extermination camps.

Yet while it would be fatuous to minimize the severe psychological trauma which ghettoization must have had upon the Jewish population, it did not at all fulfill the Nazi expectation that it would crush the Jewish spirit. Despite the appalling circumstances of ghetto life, Jews managed to maintain a remarkable level of human dignity and sanity—even sanctity, *kiddush ha-ḥayyim.*[20] They organized employment and established welfare institutions. There were public soup kitchens for children, the aged, and the needy. Clinics and hospitals were maintained. In many cases a network of elementary, secondary, and even higher schools functioned—most of them illegal. Public prayer and religious studies did not cease despite their strict prohibition, and underground *yeshivot* were set up. Scholars, poets, writers, and artists continued their work; and historians compiled documentation to supply evidence of Jewish suffering and heroism for future generations.

It is from this ghetto milieu that most of the responsa in this volume are drawn. The largest number come from the ghetto of Kovno (Kaunas), Lithuania. During the period of Nazi occupation—from June 24, 1941 until August 1, 1944—Rabbi Ephraim Oshry, one of the few halakhic authorities of Kovno who remained alive, was asked many *she'elot* by the Jews of that city, long noted for its scholarship and piety. He committed his responsa to writing on whatever scraps of paper he could find, and buried them in the ground, confident that someday redemption would come. He was in a unique position to determine the requirements of the Halakhah, not only because of his scholarship, but also because he was appointed for a time by the Nazis as one of the custodians of the warehouse of Jewish books which they had set up in Kovno. Rabbi Oshry thus had access to at least some of the major works of Rabbinic literature necessary in formulating his *teshuvot.* He indicates in his three-volume publication of these responsa that, except for an occasional passage or citation, they appear precisely as he prepared them during the Nazi occupation.[21] Other *teshuvot* from the ghettos are not as complete as those of Rabbi Oshry. In some instances they are a simple yes or no ruling; in others they are a *"teshuvah* of the deed," where the halakhic response to a particular situation is evident not from a literary fragment, but from an eyewitness account of what was actually done. It would also appear that the halakhic decisions of some rabbis either were not rendered in written form or, if they were, did not survive the war.[22]

With the German invasion of the Soviet Union in June of 1941, the process of the physical destruction of the Jews was accelerated. While ghettos were set up in large Jewish population centers, such as Kovno and

Vilna, at the same time the immediate liquidation of vast numbers of Jews was begun. In the Soviet areas the shooting and occasional gassing of Jews by the *Einsatzgruppen* (special-action groups) reached gigantic proportions. There were two waves of intensive extermination; the first from June through October, 1941. The second, after stabilization of the Russian front, began in January of 1942.

In Poland, mass murder centers had begun operation in November of 1941. Perhaps the most infamous of these was Auschwitz. Opened in May of 1941, the extermination operation began there in March of 1942. Auschwitz II (Birkenau), with its extensive gas installations and crematoria, was opened on November 26, 1941 and continued in operation until the end of 1944. Like many other camps, Auschwitz was a multi-purpose installation. It was used for the execution of non-Jewish Poles, the physical destruction of sick and debilitated inmates—particularly Jews—shipped from various other camps, and also for medical experiments. However, it was primarily the site of the destruction of the countless Jews transported there, gassed either immediately upon arrival or after a period of debilitating work in the widespread military-industrial installations in or near the camp.

It is from the Jews working at forced labor in Auschwitz or similar camps that most of the *"teshuvot* of the deed" in this volume are drawn. While many of those who were at the gates of the gas chamber and crematorium demonstrated a remarkable fidelity to the Halakhah until the very last moment, their *she'elot* were essentially reducible to one—how to die as a Jew. However, for those who worked under conditions of semi-starvation and degradation in the camps, the question of how to live as a Jew had many halakhic aspects. Their responses to this question while not formal responsa, have much to say about the Holocust and Halakhah.

Translation

The presentations of the *she'elot u'teshuvot* in this work are neither literal translations nor totally free renditions. In the case of the *she'elot,* I have attempted to capture the flavor of the original without retaining much of the florid rabbinic style, which weakens rather than enhances their emotional impact when put into English. The resultant style is hardly elegant, but it is, I believe, eloquent. I have often retained descriptive material in the *she'elah* that is not directly related to the halakhic issues, but sheds light on the Jewish condition at the time. In the *teshuvot* I have attempted to retain the major halakhic arguments of their authors, generally in the sequence which they themselves set up. Occasionally, for the sake of clarity, I have been compelled to present their arguments in an order different from the original.

It may be argued by some that it is next to impossible to present the subtleties of the legal reasoning of a *teshuvah* in English translation with any degree of success. This may, indeed, be so. I believe, however, that it is worth the attempt. Simply to give the *she'elah* and then the decision in the case, without the sources on which it is based and the reasoning which led to it, fails to convey an understanding of the halakhic process. Since in large measure Halakhah *is* process, such a presentation would be of little value. In a number of *teshuvot* I have condensed the treatment of some fine points of Jewish law, but I have attempted to retain, in all cases, the major arguments and issues.

Not all the *teshuvot* that were available have been included in this volume. I have attempted, however, to present a representative sampling covering the widest array of Holocaust cases. In addition, a number of responsa dealing with the immediate post-Holocaust period are discussed. However, the large number of post-Holocaust responsa dealing with the problem of *agunot* are not included. This material is an entire literature in itself and deserves treatment in a separate volume.

The anecdotal and eyewitness material—the *"teshuvot* of the deed"— were selected, for the most part, because the protagonists consciously took account of halakhic principles in determining their observance of the *mitzvot* under Holocaust conditions. Much more material might otherwise have been included. In translating these accounts, I have attempted to be faithful to the meaning and spirit of the originals without being limited to an excessively literal renditon.

Chapter Two

Matters of Life and Death

Murder—"Whose Blood is Redder?"

It is an axiom of the Halakhah that human life is precious. Except for the three grave sins of murder, sexual crime (e.g., incest or adultery), and idolatry, every commandment of the Torah may be violated to save a life.[1] But what if one life can be saved only at the risk of, or the cost of, another? Does the Halakhah offer guidance in this most terrible of dilemmas? We have seen that Rabbi Zevi Hirsch Meisels, in Auschwitz, refused to render a halakhic judgment in one such case.[2] However, other rabbis did express their opinions. Two teshuvot were given during the Holocaust and were le'halakhah u'lema'aseh—meant to serve as guides to action for the participants in the events themselves. Two others were written after the Holocaust, but are no less significant for the understanding of the attitude of Jewish law on this subject.

Two different, although closely related, questions were discussed in these she'elot. The first: May one, or must one, risk his own life to save that of someone else? The second: May one endanger the life of someone else in order to save his own life? While the teshuvot are based for the most part on the same Talmudic and Rabbinic sources, they do not arrive at identical conclusions.

Let us examine two treatments of the first question: May one, or must one, risk his own life to save that of another? One responsum, written by Rabbi Ephraim Oshry, describes a problem which came before him in the early stages of the German occupation of Kovno.[3]

At the very beginning of the occupation, on the twenty-eighth of Sivan, 5701 (June 23, 1941), the Nazis began their campaign of destruction against the Jews of Kovno. Each day they organized "actions" in which they seized numbers of Jews and took them to the "Seventh Fort,"[4] where their fate was determined. In this work the Germans were assisted by

17

Lithuanians who delighted in being able to oppress and persecute the Jews whom they had hated for so long. They welcomed the chance to trouble, to kill and destroy them, for they had anxiously been awaiting just such an opportunity.

"Anyone who oppresses Jews becomes a leader."[5] There were some among the Lithuanians who distinguished themselves by their cruel acts toward the Jews in an attempt to find favor in the eyes of their German masters—so much so that the Germans appointed a number of Lithuanians as supervisors of the roundups of Jews, confident that they would do their work enthusiastically and effectively because of their poisonous hatred for the Jews, which had been concealed beneath the surface for generations. Indeed, these Lithuanians robbed and murdered Jews in a measure no less heinous than the Germans. Hundreds of Jews were seized in those days, taken captive while walking in the streets, or even dragged out of their homes. Among those taken captive were a number of *yeshivah* students.

In that terrible time Rabbi Oshry was requested by Rabbi Abraham Grodzinsky, the dean of the Slobodka *yeshivah,* to ask Rabbi David Itzkowitz, the secretary of the *Agudat ha-Rabbanim,* to approach the Lithuanians who were in charge of the rounding up of Jews, and with whom he was well acquainted since before the war, to attempt to persuade them to free the *yeshivah* students who had been seized.

The *she'elah* which confronted Rabbi Oshry under these circumstances was whether, from the point of view of Jewish law, it was permissible for Rabbi Itzkowitz to approach the Lithuanians to get them to free the *yeshivah* students. Since the Lithuanians might seize him just as they had the other Jews, he would be placing his own life in danger. Was it permitted for him to endanger his own life in order to save another?

In his *teshuvah* Rabbi Oshry refers to the Talmud (*Sanhedrin* 73a), which declares, "Whence do we know that if a man sees his companion drowning, or being mauled by a wild beast, or attacked by bandits, that he is obliged to save him? The Bible says, 'Neither shalt thou stand idly by the blood of thy neighbor' (Lev. 19:16)." He then cites another passage in *Sanhedrin* 74a, in which a certain man is recorded as having come before Raba saying, "The governor of my town has ordered me, go and kill so and so; saying if you do not kill him, I will kill you." Raba answered, "Let him rather kill you, but you may not kill the other man. Who can say that your blood is redder than his? Perhaps his blood is redder than yours."

There is, Rabbi Oshry points out, an apparent contradiction between the two passages. For the implication of the first passage is that one must attempt to save his neighbor, even at the risk of his own life. But the implication of the second passage is that any man (except where he is being forced actually to murder another) can say, "How do we know that the blood of my neighbor is redder than mine? Perhaps mine is redder than his?" Since mortals cannot know which life is the more valuable, we cannot compel one man to risk his life for another. Accordingly, we must conclude that when the Talmud says a man must save his neighbor from drowning, and so forth, it refers to a situation where he is not risking his own life in the process.[6]

Rabbi Oshry finds support for this opinion in *Tosafot, Yevamot* 53b, who declare,

> Only in the case where a man is being forced to murder another by a direct action on his part do we say he must not; because of "how do we know whose blood is redder?" However, where the death of another might take place through no direct action of his, but only by his refraining from taking action; on the contrary—he may say, "how do we know that my neighbor's blood is redder than mine?" There is no *mitzvah* to save his neighbor at the cost of his own life . . .

It would appear at this point that in the present case it would be forbidden for Rabbi Itzkowitz to approach the Lithuanians to release the *yeshivah* students, for he would be saving their lives by endangering his own. Yet this may not be so. For the previous citations deal with cases where the would-be rescuer is involving himself in a situation of "certain danger." Perhaps only in such cases do we say he is not obliged to do so. But where his neighbor is in a situation of "certain danger," and in his rescue attempt he places himself only in a position of "possible danger," it may be that the Biblical commandment of "thou shalt not stand idly by the blood of thy neighbor" does apply. In our case the *yeshivah* students are in "certain danger," since they are already in the power of the Lithuanians; Rabbi Itzkowitz is only risking "possible danger," since we do not know for certain, but only fear, that the Lithuanians will seize him.

Indeed, the *Kesef Mishnah,* in his commentary to the Rambam (*Hilkhot Rotzeah* 1:14), cites a passage from *Hagahot Maimuni* based on the Palestinian Talmud, which states specifically that a man must risk a "doubtful danger" in order to save his neighbor from a "certain danger." However, the *Or Someah* points out that the Rambam himself, in *Hilkhot*

Rotzeaḥ 7:8, appears not to follow this point of view of the Palestinian Talmud and to deny the obligation to incur even a "possible danger" to save another.

Rabbi Oshry adds that all the great codifiers—the *Shulḥan Arukh,* the *Alfas,* the *Rosh,* and the *Tur*—omit reference to the passage in the Palestinian Talmud cited by the *Kesef Mishnah,* and apparently hold that it is not of binding force. The *Pitḥei Teshuvah, Ḥoshen Mishpat* 426:2, cites authorities who explain this omission of the passage as due to its conflict with the Babylonian Talmud. In such cases we follow the ruling of the Babylonian Talmud—not the Palestinian.

Therefore, it is certainly not incumbent upon Rabbi Itzkowitz to risk his life to save those of the *yeshivah* students. However, Rabbi Oshry continues, the *Arukh Hashulḥan, Ḥoshen Mishpat* 426:4, writes,

> While the codifiers omit the Palestinian Talmud's dictum that a man must risk "possible danger" to save his neighbor from "certain danger" (because the Babylonian Talmud disagrees), each case must be decided on its own merits, and one should weigh the matter carefully, and not be overly protective of his own welfare. Concerning this it is said, "To him that ordereth his way aright, I will show the salvation of God" (Ps. 50:23) and "He who saves a single life is as if he had saved an entire world."[7]

In addition, in his *Emek She'elah,* 129:4, the *Netziv,* in explaining a difficult passage in *Tosafot* to *Niddah* 61a, concludes that while there is no obligation to incur even a doubtful danger to save another, it is nonetheless permissible for one who wishes to do so and is a *midat ḥasidut,* a mark of special piety.

Accordingly, Rabbi Oshry concludes, the Halakhah does not *demand* that Rabbi Itzkowitz approach the Lithuanians, but if he is "a man of strong character and his spirit moves him to risk his life to save the *yeshivah* students, certainly we may not attempt to deter him; and one may rely upon the *Netziv* and the *Arukh Hashulhan* quoted above. This is especially so in this case, where the very existence of Torah depends upon students of the *yeshivah,* who consecrate their lives to its study. Particularly is this important in times such as these, where the primary intent of the enemy is to destroy not only the body but the soul of our people."

Rabbi David Itzkowitz heard and acceded to Rabbi Oshry's request.

Courageously, he went to the Lithuanians and succeeded in persuading them to free the *yeshivah* students and was apparently not harmed. However, Rabbi Oshry ends his *teshuvah,* "May the Almighty remember this unto him for good and avenge his pure blood, which was later spilled in the concentration camps of murder and destruction."

Another responsum which addresses itself to the same question of whether it is permitted, or even obligatory, to risk one's life to save another, is found in *Ḥelkat Ya'akov* by Rabbi Mordecai Ya'akov Breish (London, 1959). In volume 2:143, responding to an inquiry from Rabbi Abraham Israel, he discusses the issue from a viewpoint somewhat different from that of Rabbi Oshry. Rabbi Israel's *she-elah* concerned an event which took place during the closing days of World War II. The Nazis, fleeing before the advancing American Army, had emptied one of the concentration camps of its remaining prisoners. These prisoners were being forced to accompany their captors in their attempt to escape the Americans. They were marched at a rapid pace far beyond the capacity of their already weakened bodies to endure. Those who could not keep up with this "death march" were shot on the spot by the SS guards. From time to time the Germans would allow the prisoners to rest for a few moments at the side of the road. If one of them dozed off or fell asleep and did not spring up the moment the command was given to resume the march, the guard, without saying a word, would kill him. To protect themselves the prisoners set up a "buddy system," so that when they stopped to rest, one would be responsible to wake the other.

Ater the war, one of these former prisoners came to Rabbi Israel with this account. He was marching together with his younger brother. When they were allowed to rest, he said to his brother that it would be all right for him to sleep for a bit, and that he would be sure to wake him when the command to resume marching was given. But the rest period was somewhat longer than usual, and he, too, fell asleep. Suddenly he was awakened by the shouted order to march. Half-asleep and confused as he was, he dashed into the line of march with his fellow prisoners. In the moment or two it took for him to become aware of the situation, it was no longer possible for him to return to get his brother without himself risking being killed by the Nazis. His younger brother was never heard from again, and he was certain that he had been killed at that time. In the almost thirteen years which had passed since the event, he had constant pangs of conscience concerning his responsibility. He inquired of Rabbi Israel as to whether what he had done was sinful, and if so what kind of atonement it was necessary for him to make.

In his *teshuvah* Rabbi Breish examines two issues. The first: Is the older brother culpable for having forgotten to wake his younger brother? He concludes that he cannot be held responsible, since his failing to do so was caused by his own falling asleep and his consequent confusion upon awakening. His falling asleep was not, under the circumstances, an act of negligence, but rather an *ones,* an event beyond his control. Rabbi Breish cites a number of sources who would agree that no atonement is needed for this act.

It is, however, the second issue which is similar to that raised in Rabbi Oshry's *teshuvah* to Rabbi Itzkowitz. That is: Was it wrong for the older brother not to have risked his own life and returned from the line of march to wake his younger brother? Should he not have placed himself in a situation of "possible danger" in order to save his brother, who was in "certain danger"?

Rabbi Breish concludes that there is no obligation for him to have done so. Like Rabbi Oshry, he cites the *Kesef Mishnah's* quotation from the Palestinian Talmud, which declares that a man is so obligated. However, unlike Rabbi Oshry he examines the original text (*Terumot* 8), and demonstrates that it is by no means certain from that passage that such an obligation exists. Rabbi Simeon ben Lakish's rescue of Rabbi Imi from bandits at the risk of his own life, described in that passage, does not necessarily set a standard of action for all men. It may have been an act of special piety on his part, or due to his renowned physical strength and courage, or because he possessed special information about the bandits on the basis of his own early associations with such people.[8] In addition, the Halakhah ordinarily is decided according to Rabbi Yohanan, who disapproved of his action.

In any event, Rabbi Breish also concludes that since the great codifiers did not include this obligation in their works, for whatever reason, it is not required to risk one's own life to save another.

He, too, cites the *Netziv* and his interpretation of the *Tosafot* to *Niddah* 61a. While he takes issue with the *Netziv's* approach, he concurs in his conclusion that while risking one's life is not obligatory it is permissible as a *midat hasidut*—an act of piety. However, he also makes reference to the *Teshuvot Ridvaz* 3:625, who declares that risking one's life to save another is not a *midat hasidut*—an act of piety—but rather the action of a *hasid shoteh*—a pious fool. A number of other authorities who look askance at taking such risks are adduced by Rabbi Breish, who then declares:

> Were it not for the *Ridvaz,* who terms such an act that of a *hasid shoteh,* it would seem more reasonable to term it the act of a *kadosh* —a saintly person. Especially since a consequence of the *Ridvaz's* point of view would be that any coward could say he was afraid of possible risk and refuse to rescue another when he should. These matters must be weighed in just scales, and one ought not to pervert the law only for his own benefit without carefully heeding the obligation to save the life of the other.

Without ever referring to the *Arukh Hashulḥan* (*Ḥoshen Mishpat* 426:4) cited by Rabbi Oshry, Rabbi Breish comes to almost the same conclusion. However, in the present case he rules that the brother need not be troubled by his conscience since he certainly acted within the law. He cautions further that "he ought not to fall into melancholy, for that is an even greater sin which prevents him from serving the Almighty who must be served in joy." He suggests that an appropriate form of atonement and penance for the possible taking of life—although none is really required—would be to engage in the performance of such *mitzvot* as are concerned with the perpetuation of life. For example: to take extraordinary care to avoid embarrassing anyone publicly—since the Talmud likens this to the spilling of blood; in addition, if it is possible for him to do so, to fulfill the commandment of "be fruitful and multiply," for he who refrains from it is destroying life; or to raise an orphan in his home; or to support those who study Torah."Above all, let his heart be joyous to fulfill the commandments of God."

A related halakhic question as to whether one may risk his own life, not to save that of another, but simply to strengthen and encourage him in time of crisis, was answered in a *"teshuvah* of the deed" by the last three rabbis of the Warsaw ghetto. According to Rabbi David Shapiro,[9] a proposal suddenly came from the highest ranks of the Roman Catholic hierarchy to save Rabbi Menaḥem Zemba, Rabbi Samson Stockhamer, and himself. They were to be concealed in a safe hiding place. The proposal was submitted to the three men, and they now had to decide whether to accept it or reject it. They had to make the decision quickly; no time could be lost since the Nazis constantly kept asking members of the *Judenrat* whether there were still any rabbis in the ghetto.

Rabbi Shapiro opened the discussion by saying, "I am the youngest among you, and therefore my words are not binding on you. We already know that we cannot help our people, but by staying with them and by not abandoning them, we encourage them and strengthen their hopes, and this is the only encouragement we are able to give the last Jews. I simply do not have the strength to abandon these wretched people." His colleagues agreed with his position. Rabbi Zemba and Rabbi Stockhamer ultimately were killed. Rabbi Shapiro survived as the "last Warsaw rabbi."

The searching of conscience, the emotional turmoil, and the clash of the instinct for self-preservation with the demands of morality, are unquestionably present in the cases treated in the previous two *teshuvot*. There the question was only whether one needed to risk his own life to save that of another. How much more agonizing must the decision be to someone who views himself as a religious person, or simply a decent one, when it comes to saving one's own life at the cost of the life of another innocent human being.

One *teshuvah* dealing with this problem was prepared by Rabbi Oshry during the occupation of the Kovno ghetto. While it is contemporaneous with the events described, it appears clear that he was not asked in advance for his opinion in the matter. He merely recorded his own observations as to how the Halakhah would view the actions of those involved. Another *teshuvah,* by Rabbi Shimon Efrati in *Mi'gei ha-Haregah* (Jerusalem 1961), discusses an episode which took place in a bunker somewhere in Europe during the Holocaust. In this instance, as in the *she'elah* addressed to Rabbi Breish, the questioner wishes to know if his past actions are permitted or condoned by the Halakhah. If not, what acts of penance must he do in order to atone for his sin?

Rabbi Oshry and Rabbi Efrati both use the same basic texts in arriving at their decisions. Yet their conclusions are altogether different. Let us first examine the incident described by Rabbi Oshry.[10]

On the twenty-third of Elul, 5701 (September 15, 1941), the German supervisor of the Kovno ghetto (Jordan) provided the *Aeltestenrat (Judenrat)*[11] five thousand "white cards" to be distributed to workers and craftsmen in the ghetto and their families. Only those having "white cards" would be allowed to remain. At that time there were about thirty thousand souls in the ghetto, of whom about ten thousand were such workers and their families. In consternation, those workers who were the strongest forcibly seized "white cards" for themselves from the *Aeltestenrat*. Rabbi Oshry perceived two halakhic questions involved in the matter. The first:

Was it permissible for the *Aeltestenrat* to accept the cards and distribute them? The second: Was it permissible for a worker to snatch a card for himself, even though by so doing he would certainly be causing the death of another—since there were only five thousand cards for ten thousand workers?

It appears from the style of this *teshuvah*, compared to most of his others, that the considerations were more theoretical than practical. This is to say, neither the *Aeltestenrat* nor the workers came to Rabbi Oshry in advance to ask if what they were doing conformed with the Halakhah. Rabbi Oshry simply sought to find some justification in Jewish law for what had already been done.

Presumably, Rabbi Oshry was not privy at the time to the discussions which took place within the *Aeltestenrat* concerning the morality of its course of action. Leib Garfunkel, a member of the *Aeltestenrat,* in his *Kovno Ha-Yehudit be-Ḥurbanah,* reveals some of the events and considerations (of which Rabbi Oshry was not aware) that prompted the *Aeltestenrat* to cooperate in the distribution of the "white cards." Here is Garfunkel's account:

> On the fifteenth of September, 1941, toward evening, Kaminski [a Nazi officer] came to the office of the *Aeltestenrat* and handed over a written order from the *Gebietz-Kommissar* of Kovno together with five thousand white certificates. On each certificate there was printed in German: "Certificate of Jewish Artisans. *Gebietz-Kommissar* of Kovno. Signed, Jordan, *Hauptsturmführer* S.A."
>
> The order of the *Gebietz-Kommissar* directed the *Aeltestenrat* to complete the distribution of the documents to the artisans of the ghetto and their families in one day—the sixteenth of September. When Kaminski was asked what the meaning of these documents was, he answered that there would be extra rations for those receiving them, and that the general economic conditions in the ghetto would be much improved.
>
> The next morning the *Aeltestenrat* began to distribute the certificates through a special committee of its labor office in accordance with the instructions it had received from Kaminski. Even though the entire matter raised many suspicions, they did not at first perceive any indication of impending destruction. In the early hours the distribution of the certificates proceeded in an orderly fashion and with relative calm. To be sure it was difficult to determine who was

really an artisan, because many who had no experience at all had registered as skilled workers in the lists of the *Aeltestenrat*. Moreover, it was difficult to determine the actual number of family members of each artisan. Nonetheless, attempts were made to overcome these problems. The situation changed completely after noon, when the *Aeltestenrat* began to receive written requests from the German supervisors of establishments in the city in which Jewish workers from the ghetto were employed to give "their Jews" a number of "life-permits" [*Lebensscheinen*]. Immediately the true meaning of the white certificates was understood and the reason for the German directive for their distribution. It was clear that the Germans had decided to allow to remain alive only five thousand Jews of the entire ghetto—those workers and their families who could be of use to them. The remaining twenty-four thousand were to be destroyed. Then the Jews understood what Kaminski had meant when he said, "the economic conditions in the ghetto would be much improved."

The news spread like lightning throughout the ghetto, which in any event was in a terrible state of tension and nervousness. By the thousands, men stormed the offices of the *Aeltestenrat* demanding to receive the white cards. . . . Thousands of fear-crazed men and women pleaded, screamed, threatened, fought amongst themselves and cursed those who had distributed the cards. It is not difficult to understand the feelings of those who had had placed upon themselves the bitter responsibility of distributing the certificates—that is, determining who should live and who should die. Who was the man wise and discerning enough to find the fitting and proper criterion according to which one person merits remaining alive and another does not. . . . According to the order, the certificates were to be distributed only among the artisans and workers. Was it possible to reconcile oneself to the destruction of all other classes, including all the intellectuals? At every moment fearful and tragic questions of conscience arose which it was impossible to answer. Should one give a certificate to every member of a family—or only to one, or two, or three? To women, to children, to chronically ill people?

In the *Aeltestenrat* a radical proposal was made: To return all the "Jordan certificates" to the Germans and to let them know that the *Aeltestenrat* saw no possibility of distributing them. There were those who went further and suggested that all the white certificates should be burned. Those who made these proposals maintained that if the decree had gone forth to destroy the Jews of Kovno, it was not morally justifiable to say that a sixth of them should be singled out and spared because they were of some use to the Germans. If we were destined to be destroyed, let us all be destroyed together. It became known in the ghetto that the *Aeltestenrat* was considering these proposals, and many artisans and workers began to protest sharply and vigorously, "What right do you have to deny us and our families the right to remain alive?" They demanded that they be given the certificates which they "had coming." Moreover, some of the ghetto workers had already received certificates in the early distribution as a result of the requests of their German employers. After long and wearying discussions, the *Aeltestenrat* came to the opinion that it had no moral right to consign to destruction the five thousand Jews whom it was possible to save at this time. The *Aeltestenrat* decided, however, that it would distribute some of the certificates to persons other than workers and take upon itself the responsibility for so doing. . . .

On the sixteenth of September, it was not possible to complete the distribution of the white cards. . . . So on the seventeenth, by six o'clock in the morning, violent masses of ghetto residents surrounded the *Aeltestenrat* offices, demanding the certificates. . . . In the early hours of the morning, the *Aeltestenrat* lost control of the situation. The climax came when the news spread that the Germans had set up machine guns around the ghetto and that German troops and Lithuanian partisans had already entered the ghetto and that the *Aktion* had begun. At that point, Jews began to grab hold of the white certificates and pull them out of the hands of the members of the *Aeltestenrat* and its workers, and in a matter of moments, there were none left. But the disappointed masses, the majority of whom were left without certificates, refused to believe that they were all gone. They broke into all the offices screaming hysterically; they shattered desks and files and broke windows. The chairman of the *Aeltestenrat,* Dr. Elkes, suffered a heart attack and fell unconscious. Another member of the *Aeltestenrat,* Goldberg, was pushed to the floor by the mob and did not recover consciousness for some time. . . .

For a number of reasons, the Germans suspended the *Aktion* against those who did not possess "white cards" at midpoint, and postponed its partial implementation until the end of October. It was presumably during this interval that Rabbi Oshry formulated his *teshuvah*. While it seems evident that his perception of the facts was somewhat different from that of the members of the *Aeltestenrat,* the halakhic considerations involved are still relevant.

The thrust of Rabbi Oshry's argument is that neither the *Aeltestenrat* nor the workers were halakhically justified in their actions. The *Aeltestenrat* should not have agreed to the German directive; and once the cards were issued, the workers had no right to seize them. However, at the very end of the responsum, Rabbi Oshry does find some warrant for the actions of the *Aeltestenrat.*

The Talmudic precedent which is first cited is found in the *Tosefta* of *Terumot* 7:13.

> A company of men is confronted by non-Jews. They say, "Give us one of your number whom we will kill. If you do not, we will kill all of you!" Even though all of them will be killed, let them not deliver a single Jewish soul into their hands. However, if they specified a single individual, as for example in the case of Sheva ben Bikhri (2 Sam, 20), then they may deliver him up and not themselves be killed. Rabbi Simeon ben Lakish said, "This is so only when that person is guilty of a capital offense, as was Sheva ben Bikhri." Rabbi Yohanan, however, said, "He may be delivered up, even though he is not guilty of a capital offense."

The Rambam (*Yesodei ha-Torah* 5:5) determines that the Halakhah follows the opinion of Rabbi Simeon ben Lakish, and they may deliver up only such a specified person as was guilty of a capital offense. And even then we do not *ab initio* recommend this action. While there are problems raised by the commentators on Maimonides as to his preferring Rabbi Simeon's view over that of Rabbi Yohanan (whereas standard practice is to decide according to Rabbi Yohanan), these are reconciled on the assumption that the Rambam had a reversed reading of the passage in his edition of the Palestinian Talmud. Since later authorities agree with the Rambam's decision *(Taz, Yoreh Deah* 157:1), it is clear that this point of view is binding.

If so, then in our case, inasmuch as those who were not workers and craftsmen were not guilty of capital offenses according to either the Torah or the laws of the country, it was forbidden for the *Aeltestenrat* to distribute the cards. For this would have had the effect of delivering up to death, all those over the number of five thousand. And while this might be the equivalent of "specifying an individual," as in the Talmudic case, the individuals so specified were, unlike Sheva ben Bikhri, guilty of no crime.

The second question—the permissibility of seizing a card and saving one's own life at the expense of another—also has precedents in Jewish law. The first is found in the *Shakh, Ḥoshen Mishpat* 163:11, who cites an earlier authority to the effect that if the ruling power has decreed that two unspecified members of the Jewish community are to be seized and killed, it is permissible to make efforts to exempt specific individuals from the decree, even though it is evident that if they are excluded, two others will be taken in their place. However, Rabbi Oshry rejects this as a precedent for our case, since the *Shakh's* decision applies only when the men have not yet been seized. Then it is permissible to try to prevent them from being taken, even though others would suffer as a result. However, the *Shakh* would most probably rule that if two men were already in custody, it would not be permitted to attempt to free them; for it would then be inevitable that two others would be taken in their stead. In the Kovno ghetto situation, one could say that the entire community was already "taken prisoner." If so, the decision of the *Shakh* would not apply, and it would be forbidden for the workers to seize the "white cards."

Yet it might be held, Rabbi Oshry continues, that in our case it would still be permissible. For as the *Yad Avraham, Yoreh Deah* 157, points out, it is only forbidden for *others* to try to rescue the imprisoned men when this will simply lead to different victims being seized. However, it is certainly not forbidden for the prisoner *himself* to attempt to escape even though someone else will suffer.[12] So too, here, the worker who seizes the card is saving *himself,* not another. But upon close examination this analogy proves imperfect. For the *Yad Avraham* is referring to a case where his action does not directly cause another to die. It is simply that if he escapes another is imprisoned in his place. Though the second man may ultimately die because of this, his death is not directly resultant from the act of the first. But in the Kovno ghetto, the seizure of the card by one workman would directly result in the death of one who was denied a card by his action.

It is possible to support this distinction between direct and indirect action from the classic case in the Talmud, *Baba Metzia* 62a.

If two men are traveling on a journey [far from civilization] and one has a pitcher of water, if both drink they will both die, but if one only drinks, he can reach civilization. Ben Patura taught: "It is better that both should drink and die, rather than that one should behold his companion's death." Until Rabbi Akiba came and taught: "'that thy brother may live *with* thee' (Lev. 25:36), thy life takes precedence over his life."

As Rabbi Oshry explains Ben Patura's point of view, it is the drinking by the one man that causes the death of the other. The saving of his own life is, thus, the direct cause of his fellow's death. Ben Patura does not believe that the injunction of "and live by them" (Lev. 18:5)— not die by them—applies if one gains his own life by not attempting to save his comrade's. And though Rabbi Akiba disagrees with Ben Patura, it is only in this case of the two travelers, where the one takes no direct physical action to injure his fellow, but simply refrains from giving him water, that Rabbi Akiba would sanction his behavior. However, in our case, where as a result of the direct action of seizing the card, a fellow workman will be delivered over to the murderers, it is quite possible that Rabbi Akiba would agree with Ben Patura and forbid the action.

Rabbi Oshry considers the possibility that since the cards were assigned to all the workmen in the ghetto, each is therefore a partner in the ownership of them; and accordingly, no one could be censured for seizing what is partially his property. However, he points out that this very argument works against any leniency in the matter. At the time of the publication of his *teshuvah,* it was called to his attention that the *Maharsha,* in *Baba Metzia* 62a, asserts that if the pitcher of water were the property of both men, Rabbi Akiba would certainly agree with Ben Patura that one had no right to drink at the expense of the life of the other, who had equal claim to the water.

At the end of the *teshuvah,* Rabbi Oshry returns to his original consideration of whether the *Aeltestenrat* had the right to distribute the cards altogether. Perhaps, he says, it was incorrect to say that this case was analogous to the one in the *Tosefta,* where the threat was made that if one of the company was not delivered up, the rest would die. In that case the intent of the attackers was to spare the lives of all except the one they sought. The others were thus buying their own lives at the cost of one of their number. In the case of Kovno, however, there was certainly no intent on the part of the Germans to spare the lives of anyone, even those who distributed the cards. They too would soon be put to death. If so, then the distribution of the cards was actually a means of saving a portion of the community—mandatory according to the Halakhah. Afterwards, Rabbi Oshry writes, he heard from Rabbi Abraham Shapira, the chief rabbi of Kovno, that when the Germans decreed that all the Jews should assemble in the *Demokratia-Platz* for a *selektion* on October 26, 1941, they directed the *Aeltestenrat* to post notices to this effect. Its members, in turn, came to Rabbi Shapira to ask him whether this was permissible according to the Torah, since they knew that many of those who assembled would be taken out to their deaths. After serious consideration he replied, "If the decree to destroy an entire Jewish community has been determined by the enemy, and through some means or other it is possible to save part of the community, its leaders are obliged to summon up their spiritual strength and take upon themselves the responsibility of doing whatever needs to be done to save a part of the community." And so too in our case, it appears that the accepting and the distribution of the "white cards" was also a method of saving part of the community. If so, not only were the members of the *Aeltestenrat* permitted to do so, but they were obligated to accept and distribute them.[13]

Rabbi Oshry's *teshuvah* concluded that those who had allocated the "white cards" and thereby indirectly condemned others to die had acted contrary to the Halakhah. His ruling was based on the *Tosefta, Terumot* 7:23, in which it is held that a group of threatened individuals may not deliver one of their number unto death unless he has been specifically named and is guilty of a capital offense. Rabbi Efrati, on the other hand, using the same text, comes to the opposite conclusion in a case of direct homicide.[14]

Here is the *she'elah* which came to him: During the Holocaust period, a group of Jews were hiding in a bunker from the Nazis, who were conducting a "search and destroy" operation. It was certain that they would all be killed if the Germans discovered their hiding place. Suddenly, an infant, who was among those concealed in the bunker, began to cry. It was impossible to quiet him. If the Nazis heard his cries, they would be discovered and all would be lost. While they were wondering whether it would be all right to stifle the cries with a pillow, since the child might suffocate, one of the men in the bunker seized one and covered the child's face. After the Germans had left and they were safe, they removed the pillow and found, to their dismay, that the infant had suffocated.[15] Rabbi Elfrati was asked: Was this man's action permissible, since it was done to save the lives of others? And if it was not permissible according to the

Halakhah, even though the death was caused unintentionally, must he accept upon himself some type of penance through which he might atone for his sin?

While Rabbi Oshry was content to accept the decision of the Rambam (*Yesodei ha-Torah* 5:5) that it is forbidden to deliver up anyone to those who will murder him unless he is deserving of death, as was Sheva ben Bikhri, Rabbi Efrati goes back to the original text of the *Tosefta* (*Terumot* 7:23) on which it is based. He suggests a most ingenious interpretation of the *Tosefta*, which leads not only to a significant practical halakhic ruling, but also resolves many of the difficulties raised by the commentators on the Rambam.

The *Tosefta,* unlike the parallel passage in the Palestinian Talmud, contains the following material:

> Rabbi Judah says, "When does this apply [that they may not deliver up a specified victim]?—if the murderers are outside the city, and the victims inside. But if the murderers and the threatened group are both inside the city [and, therefore, there is no possibility that any of them will escape, cf. *Minhat Bikkurim*], since both the named individual and the entire group will certainly be killed, they *may* give him up." And thus Scripture says, "Then the woman went unto all the people in her wisdom . . ." (2 Sam. 20:22). She said to them, "Since he will be killed and you will be killed [if you do not give him up], give him up and do not be killed." Rabbi Simeon said, "What she said to them was, 'He who rebels against the rule of the House of David is guilty of death.'"

Rabbi Efrati perceives a meaning in the statement of Rabbi Judah which he believes was also understood by the Rambam. Rabbi Judah is emphasizing that in the case of Sheva ben Bikhri there were *two* factors which made it permissible for him to be killed. The one, that he was deserving of death. The other, that it was certain he would be killed by the forces of Joab even if he were not given up by the residents of the city where he had taken refuge. As Rabbi Efrati understands it, Rabbi Judah is saying that if *either* of these conditions exist, it is permitted to deliver up the specific individual. The recurring use by the *Tosefta* of the expression "like Sheva ben Bikhri" can be construed to mean that whether the person is deserving of death like Sheva ben Bikhri, or is certain to be killed in any event, again like Sheva ben Bikhri—his life may be sacrificed to save the others.

One section of Rashi's commentary on a passage in *Sanhedrin* 72 appears to bear out this point of view. In connection with the principle there enunciated of *en dohin nefesh mipenei nefesh* ("one life is not set aside in favor of another"), Rashi says:

> And if you will ask about the case of Sheva ben Bikhri where his head was tossed over the city wall to Joab, that was because, even if they had not handed him over, he would have been killed in the city when Joab seized him; and they would have been killed with him. But if in that case he would have been saved even though they would have been killed, they would not have been permitted to save themselves by sacrificing him.

So, Rabbi Efrati points out, in the matter which came before Raba (*Sanhedrin* 74a), where he forbade the killing of one man by the other ("who can say whose blood is redder?"), there was a reasonable possibility that the intended victim might escape if he did not carry out the governor's order. That is why he was not allowed to kill him to save his own life. If it had been certain that the designated victim would have been killed in any event, Raba would have ruled differently.

Rabbi Efrati seeks to demonstrate that the Rambam, in spite of the fact that it is difficult to read this meaning into his words, is, in fact, deciding the Halakhah according to Rabbi Judah. Since this is the accepted practice when Rabbi Judah disagrees with Rabbi Simeon, many of the questions raised by commentators are thus resolved. He finds further evidence for his point of view in the *Sefer Hahinukh* 296, and the commentary of the *Ran*.

In our case, therefore, since the crying child would certainly have been killed together with the others if his voice had been heard, it is comparable to that of Sheva ben Bikhri (who would also certainly have been put to death). All Jews were under sentence of death by the Nazis and no one would have escaped. Therefore, it was permissible for them to attempt to quiet the child even though there was a possibility that he would die as a result.

Rabbi Efrati adds that there is still another halakhic principle which is relevant in this case. A *rodef,* one who pursues an innocent victim with intent to kill him, may be killed by anyone in order to save the life of the pursued (*Rambam, Hilkhot Rotzeah* 1:7). Since the crying child was endangering the lives of the others, he might be considered a *rodef.* While there is a distinction between a *rodef* who is intent upon killing of his own free will, and one who is an *ones*—a *rodef* by compulsion, Rabbi Efrati maintains that here, too, if both the *rodef* and his intended victim will certainly die unless the *rodef* is killed, the *rodef* may be killed. The principle of *en dohin nefesh mipnei nefesh* ("one life may not be set aside for another") applies in the case of a *rodef* by compulsion only if one life will be saved—even if it be that of the *rodef*. But in our case, unless the child—*rodef*— is silenced, no life, not even his, will be spared. Therefore the full provisions of an ordinary *rodef* apply to him, and it is permissible to kill him to save the others.

Accordingly, both on the grounds of Rabbi Efrati's interpretation of the *Tosefta,* and of the laws of *rodef,* the person who silenced the child was justified in his action. There is a practical difference, Rabbi Efrati says, arising from which of the two grounds are used. In the case of the *Tosefta,* the Rambam rules that while the person may be delivered up, we do not *ab initio* adivse those concerned that this is the law. In the case of a *rodef,* it is a *mitzvah* to slay him. While Rabbi Efrati concedes that this probably is true only in the case of a *rodef* who is acting of his own free will, and not in the situation of a *rodef* acting under compulsion, he maintains that it is certainly permissible, if not mandatory, to slay him. And we would so rule, even *ab initio.*

However, if a victim does not wish to exercise the right to slay a *rodef* under the circumstances in our case, he is performing a special act of piety and may be considered a *kadosh*—a martyr. Thus, those who did not wish to silence the child and save their lives in this fashion were fulfilling the commandment of the sanctification of God's name. There were, Rabbi Efrati writes, those in his own family who gave up their lives rather than suffocate a Jewish child. However, the man who did so need have no pangs of conscience, for what he did was in accordance with the law, since his act was intended to save Jewish lives. He concludes with the observation,

> The great commentator who explained the verse in Obadiah 1:10, "For the violence done to thy brother Jacob, shame shall cover thee" properly explained it to mean, "Esau thou needs be ashamed for that thou brought thy brother Jacob to perform deeds of violence." For it is only because of Esau that Jacob was compelled to do such deeds as are described in this *teshuvah.* May the Almighty revenge the blood of His servants which has been spilt.

Justifiable Suicide

The Halakhah, it would appear at first glance, has a clear and unequi-vocal position on suicide—it is forbidden. The passage in Genesis 9:5, "For your life-blood, too, I will require a reckoning," was interpreted by the Talmud (*Baba Kamma* 91b) as a prohibition not only of suicide, but also of any self-inflicted injury. The Midrash (*Genesis Rabbah* 34:13) recognized that there were exceptions to the general prohibition against suicide, and cited as an example the suicide of King Saul, described in I Samuel 31:3–5,[16] which Scripture records without condemnation.

But while later Rabbinic literature debated in some detail the Midrash's justifications for considering Saul's suicide permissible, these discussions concerned only the question of whether full burial honors and mourning rites might be allowed in a specific case of suicide which had already taken place. Under normal circumstances it was highly unlikely that a would-be suicide would approach a rabbi in advance with a *she'elah* as to whether his contemplated act of self-destruction was permissible. But during the Holocaust this did become an actual halakhic issue.

Perhaps there were many such *she'elot* from believing Jews, asking whether the Halakhah would permit, or at least condone, self-destruction. Certainly there were numerous suicides in Germany and Austria even before the Nazi plans for the "final solution" were put into effect. But the only recorded *teshuvah* we have on this subject is that of Rabbi Oshry,[17] who writes that on the sixth of Heshvan, 5702 (October 27, 1941), two days before the great slaughter of the Jews of the Kovno ghetto, he was approached by the head of one of the distinguished Jewish families of the city with a *she'elah*. Ten thousand men, women, and children of the ghetto had already been taken away in preparation for the slaughter. Those who were left were simply waiting until the cruel hand of the Nazis would reach out for them. The householder declared to Rabbi Oshry that he was convinced from what he had heard that the sadistic SS troopers would not simply kill him when he was taken, but would first torture and slay his wife, children, and grandchildren before his eyes. He did not believe he would be able to withstand such torture; his heart would certainly fail him and he would surely die. His *she'elah,* then, was: "Is it permissible to hasten his end, to set his own hand against himself, even though it not be lawful? This, so that his own eyes not see the destruction of his family. And so that he himself not die a violent death after unspeakable tortures by the 'cursed murderers, may their name be blotted out'; and so that he might have the merit of being given a proper Jewish burial in the Jewish cemetery of the Kovno ghetto."

The essential issues confronted by Rabbi Oshry in his *teshuvah* are these: Under what types of duress is a person who kills himself not considered a *m'abed atzmo la-da'at* ("one who destroys himself while of sound mind")[18] and, hence, not a true suicide from the viewpoint of the Halakhah? And, further, are there degrees of duress so intense that the Halakhah would not only permit full burial honors and mourning rites to be observed for a suicide resulting from them, but also permit, or at least not prohibit, the very act of suicide itself?[19]

Rabbi Oshry begins his *teshuvah* by citing the categorical prohibition against suicide derived from Genesis 9:5, and the Midrashic extension of the verse (*Genesis Rabbah* 34:19) to include not only suicide where blood is shed, but also self-destruction by strangulation. This *de'oraitah* (Biblical) prohibition against suicide, he emphasizes, is applicable only when the person is of sound mind. The relevant passages in the Talmud (*Baba Kamma* 91b) and the Rambam (*Hilkhot Hovel u'Mazik* 5:1) are cited.[20]

That suicide is a grave sin (although obviously not punishable by earthly courts) is clear from the oft-quoted dictum that "he who commits suicide while of sound mind has no share in the world to come."[21] Rabbi Oshry cites the *Maharit*, who ingeniously demonstrates this from a passage in *Ketuvot* 103b, as well as others who attempt to prove it from *Sanhedrin* 90a, which declares that Ahitofel, who committed suicide (2 Sam. 17:23), has no share in the world to come.

Other authorities (*Tur, Yoreh Deah* 345; *S'dei Hemed* 18; *Darkei Mosheh* 345) are quoted on various aspects of the heinousness of suicide. The Rambam (*Hilkhot Evel* 1:11) and the *Shulhan Arukh* (*Yoreh Deah* 345:1) prohibit full mourning rites for a suicide. While the Rambam disagrees in some particulars, the general practice is to follow the decision of the *Shulhan Arukh*. However, in accordance with the *Rashba* (*Teshuvot* 763) it is customary, Rabbi Oshry notes, to bury a suicide in the usual shrouds and in the Jewish cemetery, except that this grave is separated from the others and placed at the edge of the cemetery. Such was the practice in Lithuania and Germany.

Yet, Rabbi Oshry notes, when suicide is for the "sanctification of the name" (martyrdom) it is permitted and encouraged. Thus the *Ritva* (*Avoda Zara,* chap. 1) writes in the name of *Rabenu Tam,* "An Israelite who is afraid that he will be forced to abandon Judaism and violate its commandments, and kills himself, is not denied any burial or mourning rites. This was the reason that during the persecutions [of the Crusades] fathers slaughtered their children with their own hands." This view would give sanction, however, only to one who committed suicide because he was afraid of being forced to apostatize.

But then a passage of critical importance to his *teshuvah* is examined by Rabbi Oshry. It is taken from the *Be'somim Rosh* (sec. 345), and goes far beyond the *Ritva* in its lenient attitude to suicide committed under duress. Rabbi Oshry recognizes that many authorities question whether this work was in reality written by *Rabenu Asher ben Yehiel,* the great scholar and codifier of the thirteenth century. He cites in detail the authorities who dispute its authenticity. But he also marshals an array of reputable scholars who defend it. The text in question describes a *she'elah* which was directed to Rabenu Asher concerning a man living in grinding poverty who declared in the presence of two witnesses that life was detestable to him, and thereupon killed himself. Since the man was a suicide, were his relatives permitted to observe the customary mourning practices, which are denied in the case of a willful suicide? He ruled that it was unthinkable to judge this man unfavorably.

> For already in the *Midrash Rabbah* on the verse, "For your lifeblood, too, I will require a reckoning," the Midrash says, "You might thing that even one in the plight of Saul is meant: the Torah teaches us by the use of the word *akh* [a limiting particle] that the case of Saul is specifically excluded." And Saul committed suicide only because he was afraid that the Philistines would make sport of him. And do not say that only in his case, where he was fearful that he would be put to great shame, and the Philistines would boast of their defeat of Israel, and there would be a desecration of God's name, does this exception apply. No! In any case of suicide because of a multiplicity of troubles, worries, pain, or utter poverty, there is not the slightest reason to deny mourning rites. Indeed, our sages denigrated King Zedekiah for not having killed himself rather than see his sons slain before his very eyes. And even Aḥitofel, who is counted as one who will not receive a share in the world to come, is so included because he rebelled against King David, and not because he was a suicide. What then is a real case of suicide? It is one who is an ingrate and complains even though things are good; who hates the world as do certain of the philosophers who defy the

Almighty and rebel against God. But a tormented soul who can no longer endure his troubles; who indeed commits the act in order that he may prevent himself from sinning (for "trouble and poverty cause a man to violate his own conscience and the will of his Creator")— in his case there is no prohibition.

It is, of course, on this issue of what constitutes a "justifiable suicide" that the *teshuvah* hinges. Apart from the problems concerning the authenticity of the passage from the *Be'somin Rosh,* there are eminent authorities who disagree with its conclusions. Some (*Bedek ha-Bayit* 157; *Yam Shel She'lomo, Baba Kamma* 59) do not agree that King Saul's suicide was justified because he was afraid of torture—but rather because he was afraid he would be forced to abandon Judaism. Only in the case of the danger of forced conversion, and under no other type of duress, they maintain, would a person who killed himself be held not culpable.

Rabbi Oshry, after giving due consideration to all these views, does not accept them. The plain meaning of the text concerning Saul is that he was fearful of being made sport of—demeaned, degraded, or tortured—by the Philistines.[22] The Rambam accepts this view, as do many others. After citing the case of King Zedekiah, who also, according to the Midrash, sought death rather than see his sons slain (*Yalkut,* 2 Kings 25), Rabbi Oshry concludes that in this parallel case in Kovno, suicide would be permissible. He cautions that this applies

> if the person who kills himself out of fear of affliction and pain is a God-fearing man. In his case especially one may judge his intentions favorably. Not so, however, in the case of those who have learned from the gentiles and who commit suicide because of trivial matters, and who do not believe in a God who nourishes and sustains all, or in the immortality of the soul.
>
> Therefore, in our present case, where certainly he will be horribly tortured as King Saul would have been, it appears that it would be permissible for him to commit suicide.

Rabbi Oshry's understandably great reluctance to permit suicide even under the excruciatingly painful conditions of the Kovno ghetto becomes evident in the final sections of his responsum. Here, once again, he cites a number of authorities who do not sanction suicide because of fear of physical pain, or, as in the present case, because of a desire to fulfill a *mitzvah*—in this instance that of being buried according to Jewish law.

Yet ultimately he rejects the arguments advanced by them. The Talmudic account of the martyred Rabbi Ḥanina ben Teradyon *(Avodah Zara* 18a), who refused to accelerate his death even though he was being burned alive,[23] is cited by the *Ḥatam Sofer* as proof that one may not commit suicide because of torture. Rabbi Oshry answers that Rabbi Ḥanina was not setting a standard for ordinary men, but only for himself, because of his great saintliness and piety.

In his concluding sentences, Rabbi Oshry indicates that while he permitted suicide in this case, he prohibited his decision from being widely publicized at the time. It would have given aid and encouragement to the Nazis, who often taunted the Jews of Kovno for not committing suicide as did so many of the Jews of Berlin. Such mass suicides would be a desecration of God's name, for it would indicate that the Jews had no trust in the mercy of God, who would rescue them from the impure and cursed hands of the Nazis. This would then fulfill the wish of the murderers, whose goal was to infuse the Jews with a spirit of despair and to extinguish within them any spark of hope for God's salvation. He goes on,

> It is worth noting, with pride, that in the entire ghetto of Kovno there were only three cases of suicide by people who had lost all hope. But the remainder of the ghetto inhabitants believed with perfect faith that the Almighty would not forsake His people, and would say to the Destroyer—"enough!" They believed in the coming of the Messiah and awaited his coming each day.

Rabbi Oshry's observation about the rarity of suicide in the Kovno ghetto is corroborated by Leib Garfunkel, a member of the *Aeltestenrat.* He writes:[24]

> . . . there were hardly any suicides. From any rational point of view there were more than enough reasons to warrant putting an end to one's afflictions and tortures. Yet it is worthy of note that from the time of the outbreak of the war between the Soviet Union and Germany through the period of the establishment of the ghetto—except for the very last days—there were no more than two or three suicides of Jews. Only in the last week, when it became known for certain that the ghetto and its labor camps were to be destroyed and the remain-

ing Jews transported to Germany—there almost certainly to be slaughtered—only then did the number of suicides in the ghetto increase. But even in that week, the number was relatively small.

In his Warsaw diary, Chaim Kaplan attempts to explain this phenomenon of the low rate of suicide among the Jews of Eastern Europe.[25]

A certain invisible power is embedded in us, and it is this secret which keeps us alive and preserves us in spite of all the laws of nature. . . This secret power works wonders in us; as evidence, we don't have cases of suicide. German Jewry collapsed and fell. Its vital strength disappeared immediately. It was gripped by fear. When no way for salvation was found through conversion, it condemned itself to death. Without strength to live, thousands of individuals found sanctuary in the abyss. The same with Austrian Jewry. Each new decree sacrified thousands of victims on its altar. Entire families voluntarily wiped themselves out when the world became too narrow for them. Proud, filled with self-esteem, thousands of German and Austrian Jews put an end to their lives.

Not so with the beaten-down, shamed, broken Jews of Poland. They love life, and they do not wish to disappear from the earth before their time.

The fact that we have hardly any suicides is worthy of special emphasis. Say what you wish, this will of ours to live in the midst of terrible calamity is the outward manifestation of a certain hidden power whose quality has not yet been examined. It is a wondrous, superlative power with which only the most established communities among our people have been blessed.

We are left naked, but as long as this secret power is still within us we do not give up hope. And the strength of this power lies in the indigenous nature of Polish Jewry, which is rooted in our eternal tradition that commands us to live.

"Be Fruitful and Multiply"— Birth Control and Abortion

In Kovno as well as in other Nazi-created ghettoes, for a time at least, men and women attempted to create some semblance of normality in an obviously deranged world.[26] Marriages took place; husbands and wives lived together and perhaps even looked forward to the birth of children in a society which would be free from the German terror. However, on the twentieth of Iyar, 5702 (May 7, 1942), the Nazis promulgated a decree stating that any Jewish woman found to be pregnant would be put to death immediately. Rabbi Oshry was asked whether it was permissible, under these circumstances, for Jewish women to prevent conception by using a diaphragm during intercourse.[27]

Students of Jewish law are familiar with the wide divergence of opinion among the earliest as well as the later authorities on the permissibility of such a birth-control device being used by the woman when conception would involve a threat to her health. (For a full and complete discussion of this subject, see David M. Feldman's *Birth Control in Jewish Law,* New York University Press, New York, 1968.) Rabbi Oshry cites the Talmudic passage in *Yevamot* 12b, which discusses the use of a *mokh* (the ancient equivalent of a diaphragm or pessary), and considers the varying interpretations of this text given by Rashi and *Tosafot.* It is these differing interpretations which form the basis for the subsequent halakhic controversies on the subject. Rabbi Oshry evaluates the opinions of those who forbid the use of a *mokh* under almost all circumstances, those who rule that the woman *may* use it in cases of a threat to health, those who insist that it *must* be used where there is a hazard to her health. He concludes that in the present case, where the danger to life is external, and does not arise out of the natural biological processes of birth and conception, all authorities would agree that a *mokh* may be used. He points out, further, that since it is certain in this case that not only would the woman be endangered, but the foetus would never see the light of day (since it would be destroyed with her), the halakhic prohibitions against "destruction of the seed" do not apply—for this is a "seed" which could never bear fruit. To these factors he adds the consideration that the wrath of the SS, once it was kindled against pregnant women, might also be let loose upon the rest of the community and lead to further slaughter. He therefore permitted the use of a diaphragm unconditionally as long as the Nazi decree was in force.

Another *she'elah* which arose as a result of the SS decree against pregnant women was brought to Rabbi Oshry on the twenty-sixth of Av, 5702 (August 9, 1942). He was asked whether a woman who had already become pregnant might have an abortion in order to save her life. In his *teshuvah*[28] he cites the Mishnah in *Ohalot* 7:6, "If a woman is in difficult labor [and may die if labor continues], we may cut up the child in her womb and remove it piecemeal; for her life takes precedence over its life." He further adduces the *Shulḥan Arukh, Ḥoshen Mishpat* 452:2: ". . . therefore when a pregnant woman is in difficult labor, it is permissible to destroy the foetus whether chemically or manually, for the foetus is [has the legal status of] a 'pursuer' [*rodef*]." (In order to save the life of an innocent victim, bystanders may kill a *rodef* who is in hot pursuit, even though the *rodef* has not yet murdered the victim, and there is no absolute certainty that he will, indeed, do so.) An array of later authorities—Rabbi Akiba Eiger, the *Tiferet Yisrael,* the *Bet Yitzhak,* the *Ma'haram Schick,* and the *Maḥnei Ḥayyim*—all agree that the mother's life takes precedence over that of the still unborn child; and that where her life can be saved only at the expense of the life of the foetus, the foetus may be destroyed.

Rabbi Oshry concludes that in this case, where there is no question that both mother and child will die if the mother continues to carry the child, but that the mother will live if she aborts, the abortion may pe performed.

Still a third *she'elah* came before Rabbi Oshry as a result of the German decree against pregnancy. On the twentieth of Iyar, the day it was first promulgated, Rabbi Oshry was in the vicinity of the hospital in the Kovno ghetto. An SS trooper, who became enraged when he saw a pregnant Jewish woman, fired at her. She fell to the ground, dead. Bystanders hurriedly brought her into the hospital. A Jewish physician in attendance proposed that an immediate Caesarian be performed on the dead woman. He was convinced that this procedure had an excellent chance of saving the life of the child. Rabbi Oshry was asked if this was permitted. Presumably he was familiar with the basic halakhic issues involved. Certainly there was no time to consult sources! He gave immediate assent to the doctor's request. A Caesarean was performed and a viable child was delivered.

In his *teshuvah* Rabbi Oshry discusses the issues he considered in arriving at his decision.[29] The first was the prohibition of *nivul ha-met* (disfiguration of the dead). Cutting open the body of the dead woman might be construed as being prohibited for this reason. The second was the possibility that if the woman were not actually dead, but simply near death, the operative procedure might, in fact, actually kill her. The basic text on which Rabbi Oshry founded his decision is in *Arakin* 7a:

> Rabbi Naḥman says in the name of Samuel, "If a woman be on the birth-stool and dies, on the Sabbath one may bring a knife and cut her womb open to take the child." Is this not self-evident? All he is

doing is cutting the flesh [which is permitted on the Sabbath]. Rabbah answers that it is permitted to fetch the knife through a public thoroughfare on the Sabbath [ordinarily forbidden]; and he is teaching us that even in the case of a doubtful saving of life [since the child may already be dead], it is permitted to violate the Sabbath.

This text would appear to indicate that in a case quite comparable to the one before him in Kovno, there was no concern about either *nivul ha-met* or hastening the death of the mother.

However, Rabbi Oshry points out, there is a basic disagreement between Rashi and *Tosafot* which might affect the decision in the instant case. *Tosafot* appears to hold—since the Talmud speaks of a woman being "on the birth-stool"—that only where the process of labor has already begun do we assume that it is possible for the foetus to survive the mother and, hence, permit cutting open her womb. Rashi, on the other hand, indicates that especially where the mother has died a violent death (as in our case), we may assume that it is possible for the foetus to survive her even if labor has not begun. Therefore, it is only Rashi who would permit the Caesarean in the present instance.

After copious references to authorities who support Rashi's point of view, Rabbi Oshry cites the *Shulḥan Arukh, Oraḥ Hayyim* 330:5, "If a woman on the birth-stool dies, we may carry a knife on the Sabbath through a public thoroughfare to cut open her womb and take out the child who may yet be alive." The *Rama* in his note on this passage adds, "And the reason we are not accustomed to do this even on a weekday is that we are not expert enough to determine that the mother is actually dead." On which the *Magen Avraham* comments, "Perhaps she is simply in a coma, and if she is operated on, she will die. And if we do wait long enough to be certain that she is certainly dead, the foetus will have already died in any event."

Rabbi Oshry concludes that in our case, since the physician is expert enough to determine whether the mother is alive or dead, and confident there is a strong possibility that the child is still alive, the Caesarean must be performed. There is no question of *nivul ha-met,* since this prohibition does not apply where there is some benefit to be derived—especially where there is saving of life. For these reasons he directed the doctor to perform the operation.

His *teshuvah,* however, concludes on a sad note:

But to our great sorrow we were unable to bring our good intentions to fruition. For the cruel murderers who kept the "books of the living and the dead" with typical German exactness, and who kept precise records of all those who were killed by them—these murderers returned to the hospital to complete their cruel work. They wished to record the name of the dead woman in their books, as was their practice. When they came to the hospital for this purpose and saw the child who had been removed alive from her womb, their anger flared up within them. One of them seized the infant and dashed its brains out against the wall of the hospital room. Woe to the eyes which have seen such as this. May God remember these evil days to the children of these monsters, and to their children's children, so that they receive their just reward for what they did unto us . . .

Conversion

During earlier persecutions of Jews by the Church, Jews had available to them the option of saving their lives by converting to Christianity. But during the Crusades and the Inquisition, in conformity with the Halakhah, tens of thousands chose martyrdom and death in preference to apostasy. In the Nazi period, of course, no such choice was available to the Jew. Even practicing Christians of the Jewish "race," as defined by the Nuremberg Laws, met the same fate as did the most pious Jews.

However, because of their physical appearance or language facility or educational background, some few Jews, given the proper documentation, could pass for Christians and save themselves. Was this permitted by Jewish law? The *she'elah* was asked during the period in Hungary when the satellite rulers of that country exempted certain classes of Jews with Christian documents from anti-Semitic legislation. It was asked again in Kovno during the Nazi occupation. If the conversion was only apparent, and if it was meant to save one's life, should it not be permitted—even encouraged?

On Nisan 1, 5602 (March 19, 1942), Rabbi Oshry was asked whether it was permissible for a Jew to save himself by purchasing a forged baptismal certificate if by so doing he would be able to pass as a Christian, flee to the forests, and join the partisans.[30]

Rabbi Oshry replied unequivocally that this was forbidden. He cites the Rambam in *Sefer ha-Mitzvot*:

He commanded us to sanctify His name in the verse "I will be sanctified in the midst of the children of Israel" (Lev. 22:32). The import of this *mitzvah* is that we are commanded to publicly proclaim this true faith in the world, and that we not be afraid of any kind of threat or danger. Even though someone attempt by force to compel us to abandon our faith, we must not listen to him, but rather deliver ourselves unto death. We must not attempt to deceive him [the non-Jew] into thinking that we have apostatized, even though in our hearts we actually believe in Him.

After emphasizing the categorical nature of the Rambam's statement, Rabbi Oshry points out that in the present case the sole purpose of the baptismal document is to deceive the gentiles into believing that the bearer is not a Jew. Accordingly, to follow such a procedure would be in violation of the *mitzvah* of *kiddush ha-shem*, sanctification of God's name; and, according to the Rambam, this is an instance of *ye-horeg ve'al ya'avor* —"let him be killed rather than violate the Torah."

Our case is not comparable to the one cited by the *Nimukei Yosef* (*Baba Kamma, ha-Gozel*) in which he rules that while a Jew is forbidden to make a direct statement saying that he is an idolator, he is permitted, when his life is endangered, to make one which is couched so that it can be interpreted to mean this by a gentile—even though the Jew really means something quite different. Although the *Rama* (*Yoreh Deah* 157: 2) rules in accordance with this opinion of the *Nimukei Yosef*, he, too, emphasizes that this permission is valid only when what the Jew says, even to save his life, is ambiguous.[31]

But in the instant case there is only one possible interpretation of the baptismal certificate—that the possessor of it has forsaken the "Rock whence he is hewn" and become a traitor to the people chosen by God. This is certainly forbidden, even if in his heart he still believes in Israel's God and Redeemer. The commandment of *kiddush ha-shem* demands that he die rather than cause the gentiles to believe that he has really denied the God of Israel.

To further buttress his position, Rabbi Oshry cites the *Hafetz Hayyim* (*Nidhei Yisrael* 6), who maintains that one must risk death rather than even simply say, "I am not a Jew." All the more so in our case, where even if he acquires the baptismal certificate there is no certainty that it will save his life. Even if he reaches the forests, he may die from violence or starvation. There is, therefore, no possible permission for acquiring such a document, but rather he is commanded to sanctify the name of God, as it is written, ". . . but I will be sanctified in the midst of the children of Israel."

Rabbi Isachar Teichthal of Hungary was presented with a somewhat similar problem during one of the periods when the possession of a baptismal certificate would exempt a Jew from being affected by the anti-Semitic decrees of the Hungarian satellite government.[32] His *teshuvah*, undated, reads:

> When I was still occupying my position, I was asked by the *bet din* of Pressburg [Bratislava] what my opinion was concerning their procedure of not allowing anyone who had purchased such a baptismal certificate to receive an *aliyah* to the Torah. This had caused much controversy in their community. I replied to them that immediately after the ugly practice of purchasing these certificates had become widespread in order to avoid the rigorous decrees, I publicly proclaimed the gravity of the prohibition of so doing. I declared it to be forbidden and in the category of *ye-horeg ve'al ya'-avor*, since with such a document one accepts a non-Jewish faith, and this is as if he says explicitly that he is an idolator.

He then cites the same text of the Rambam from *Sefer ha-Mitzvot* quoted by Rabbi Oshry. He goes on to make the same distinction between an ambiguous utterance and a definitive one that was made by Rabbi Oshry, and also concludes that a baptismal document is not ambiguous, even if the Jew possessing it was never really converted and never performed any act of Christian worship.

Having concluded that the act of purchasing such certificates is forbidden, Rabbi Teichthal, nevertheless, does not believe that those who have acquired them should be ostracized by the Jewish community or denied religious privileges if they seek them.

Chapter Three

Prayer, Study, and Martyrdom

In Chapter Two we examined some of the implications of the halakhic principle *ye-horeg ve'al ya'avor,* "be killed, and do not transgress," where the choice was one between murder and martyrdom. But more often than not the choice confronting Jews living under the Nazis was not as drastic as that. It involved the determination of what risks, if any, should or might be taken to observe *mitzvot,* other than the three (murder, sexual crime, idolatry) for the violation of which martyrdom is mandatory. The Rambam codifies the Talmudic discussions on this subject in *Hilkhot Yesodei ha-Torah,* 5:1–4. His conclusions may be summarized as follows:

1. In the case of all other commandments, if the non-Jew compelling the Jew to violate them is doing so for his own personal benefit, advantage, or pleasure, then the Jew should violate them rather than be killed.

2. If the non-Jew's purpose is not some personal advantage for himself, but to compel the Jew to violate the ordinances of his religion, and if this took place privately and ten fellow Israelites are not present,[1] the Jew should commit the transgression and not suffer death.

3. If the attempt to coerce the Jew to violate the ordinances of his religion was made in the presence of ten Israelites, he should suffer death and not transgress; thereby fulfilling the commandment: "and I will be sanctified in the midst of the children of Israel."

4. *All the foregoing applies to a time free from religious persecution. But at a time when decrees are issued against Israel with the purposing of abolishing its religion or any of the precepts, whether the coercion is in private or public, then it is the Jew's duty to suffer death and not violate any of the commandments.*

47

5. If one is enjoined to transgress rather than be slain, and chooses death instead, he is as guilty as if he himself had committed a capital offense (*mithayev be'nafsho*).
6. If one is enjoined to die rather than transgress, and chooses death, he has sanctified the name of God.
7. If one is enjoined to suffer death rather than transgress, but commits the transgression and so escapes death, he has profaned the name of God. Still, since the transgression was committed under duress, he is not punished by earthly courts.

While this formulation of the Rambam's is lucid and firmly based upon Talmudic citations,[2] there are two areas of possible disagreement, or differences of interpretation, which were relevant during the Holocaust. The first concerned whether martyrdom was obligatory in the case of positive as well as negative commandments. There was no question that the Nazis were intent on the destruction of the Jewish faith, so the provisions of Rule 4, above, applied. It was necessary to suffer death rather than violate any of the commandments. But does "violate" (*ya'avor*) refer only to the transgression of a negative commandment, that is, doing something forbidden by the Torah? Is it under these circumstances that one must suffer death? (For example, die rather than be forced to eat on Yom Kippur.) Or does this also mean that in time of religious persecution one must seek to fulfill the positive commandments of the Torah and risk death in the attempt? (For example, teach the Torah, pray publicly, or don the *tefillin* when such acts are punishable by death.) Rabbenu Nisim (*Shabbat, Ba-meh Tomnin*) is of the opinion that one is *not* obliged to suffer death in order to fulfill a *mitzvat aseh,* a positive commandment. He argues that since it is in the power of the idolator to prevent the Jew from fulfilling the commandment by measures short of death—for example, imprisonment—the provision of *ye-horeg v'al ya'avor* does not apply. This too is the viewpoint of the *Sefer Ha-ḥinukh,* 296. The Rambam, apparently, but not certainly, holds that the obligation to incur martyrdom exists in the case of all types of commandments.[3]

The second area of disagreement concerns the halakhic view of the individual who suffers martyrdom when he is not required to do so. The Rambam condemns him and declares him to be "guilty of a capital offense." Others (*Ran,* and *Sefer Haḥinukh*) believe him to be praiseworthy and declare such action a *midat ḥasidut,* a measure of special piety. However, even they hold that it is not given to every man to arrogate to himself the privilege of martyrdom when it is not demanded by the Halakhah. Thus the *Sefer Haḥinukh,* 296, writes:

> Those instances where we are told of individuals who suffered death rather than not fulfill a positive commandment [*bitul mitzvat aseh*], as in (*Mekhilta, Yitro*) the episodes of one who was stoned for circumcising his son, and another who was crucified for carrying the *lulav,* deal with great and wise men who saw that the generation needed such examples. If they had not been great and wise men they would not have been permitted to sacrifice their lives, for it is not permitted every ordinary man to give himself over to death where the Sages did not obligate him to do so.

Thus, during the Holocaust, a Jew who sought guidance as to whether he should risk death in the fulfillment of such positive commandments as Torah study and prayer might theoretically receive any of the following *teshuvot:* (1) You must risk death (if we rule that abandonment of even a positive commandment is forbidden in time of religious persecution). (2) You need not risk death (if we rule that it is not forbidden to refrain from fulfilling a positive commandment during time of religious persecution), but (3) you may choose to risk death if you wish, even if you are an ordinary or average person, or (4) you may only exercise this option if you are a great and wise man and your example will be of benefit to others in your generation, or (5) you must not under any circumstances risk death to fulfill a positive commandment even in time of religious persecution (if we rule that positive commandments are not included, and if we agree with the Rambam that anyone undergoing unnecessary martyrdom is to be condemned [*mithayev be'nafsho*]).

In practice, many Jews simply went ahead and risked their lives to fulfill the commandments without asking any *she'elah.* The simple meaning of the Rambam's code and the Talmudic passage on which it is based (*Sanhedrin 74b*)—". . . if there is a decree of religious persecution one must incur martyrdom rather than transgress even a minor precept . . . what is meant by a 'minor precept' ?—Raba said in Rab's name: even to change the manner of lacing one's shoe. . . ."—would be taken by most knowledgeable laymen to demand at least taking the risk of martyrdom to fulfill any Biblical commandment. As we shall see in this and succeeding chapters, Jews in the ghettos, the transit camps, the labor camps, and the death camps intuitively chose this interpretation of the Halakhah. Accordingly, they prayed and studied, sounded the *shofar*, carried the *lulav*, donned their *tefillin,* dwelt in the *succah,* and carried out other *mitzvot aseh* at the risk of, and sometimes at the cost of, their lives.

There is one formal *she'elah* on this subject which was addressed to Rabbi Oshry.[4] In it he examines all the halakhic points referred to above. He also records what the actions of the Jews in Kovno were in the light of, or in spite of, his *teshuvah.*

On the thirteenth of Elul, 5702 (August 26, 1942), the Nazis issued an order prohibiting the Jews of Kovno from assembling in synagogues and houses of study for public prayer and the study of Torah. Until the issuance of this edict, the synagogues of the ghetto, large and small, had been the major sources of hope and encouragement to many. After a day of forced labor, they would come to the synagogue for study or prayer, or to listen to words of comfort and consolation from rabbis or *darshanim* and to their assurances that the Almighty would wreak revenge on the oppressors. At the beginning of the Nazi occupation, Rabbi Oshry writes, he continued to give his regular lectures in Talmud at the famous *bet midrash* known as Abba Yehezkel's *Kloiz.* When the Nazis turned it into a prison, he moved his lectures to the *Halvayas ha-Mes Kloiz* and to the synagogues on Vitna Street and on Varena Street. He was particularly dedicated to his daily class with the young men of the *Tiferet Baḥurim* association,[5] and records that

> with the aid of He-who-dwells-on-high, I strengthened the faltering spirits of these young men of Israel and of the mass of the people. I tried to impart to them understanding and wisdom, so they would understand that "just as one blesses God for the good, so he must bless him for the evil," [6] and that it was incumbent upon us to wait in silence for the help of God and His salvation; for the Almighty is good to those who hope unto him and who await his kindness; "He is near to those that call upon Him; to those that call upon Him in truth;" [7] and that we must arm ourselves with faith, and trust, to bear the burden gladly and willingly, for there is "hope for our latter end." [8]

It came, then, as a tremendous blow when the Nazis decreed that those attending public worship or study would do so under penalty of death.

At that time Reb Naftali Weintraub, the *gabbai* of Gafinovitz's Synagogue, came to Rabbi Oshry and asked whether he was obligated by the

Halakhah to risk his life in order to go to pray morning and evening in his accustomed synagogue, and whether one is in fact required to sacrifice his life rather than abandon the commandments of study of Torah and prayer.

In his *teshuvah* Rabbi Oshry makes a distinction between the teaching and study of Torah, and public prayer. After an examination of the sources, he concludes that ordinarily we are required to sacrifice our lives only to avoid violation of any of the three commandments prohibiting idolatry, sexual crimes, and murder; at a time when the purpose of such forced violation is to destroy or denigrate the religion of Judaism, however, we may give our lives in defense of any of the other commandments. This is particularly true about the teaching of Torah, for the goal of the Nazis was to destroy the people of Israel and its Torah. Certainly, to foil their desire and thwart their plot, it would be incumbent upon a God-fearing person to risk his life to teach Torah, as did Rabbi Hanina ben Teradyon at the time of the Roman decree forbidding the study of Torah *(Avodah Zara* 18a).[9]

As regards the obligation to undergo martyrdom for the sake of prayer, Rabbi Oshry draws upon the episode in Daniel 6:7, in which Daniel risked his life in order to pray three times daily.[10] He cites a number of authorities who question Daniel's justification for risking his life in a situation where the Halakhah does not call for such sacrifice. Thus, he might have prayed privately, and not publicly. Moreover, he was not being asked to abandon his faith and worship idols. Some commentators justify Daniel's action only on the assumption that he was, in fact, being asked to worship idols, by abandoning prayer to the God of Israel. Others, however, point out that Daniel was not obligated to risk his life for the sake of prayer, but that as an act of special piety, in order that his generation might be given the necessary insight into the great importance of prayer, he had the option of doing so.

Rabbi Oshry concludes that in a time of persecution, when the intent of the enemy, by denying the opportunity of prayer, is to destroy the Jew's belief and his faith, it is permitted to risk one's life even for the sake of public prayer. However, he cautions that he could not tell Reb Naftali Weintraub or others that they must risk their lives for the sake of teaching Torah or for public prayer. For one cannot know which person is in the category of Daniel and his companions, whose purity of motive was beyond question and who are, accordingly, permitted to do so. On the other hand, he could not prohibit Reb Naftali Weintraub or others from risking martyrdom, for the *din* requires that "we leave the matter to the determination of each individual according to the degree of his sensitivity, and the measure of his love and reverence for God. And, of a certainty, the just and compassionate God will show him His way—the way of life."

Rabbi Oshry relates that the Jews of Kovno did continue to pray and study together. On Rosh Hashanah of 5703 (September 12, 1942), they sounded the *shofar* without fear even though the Germans might hear it; and not only did they assemble in the synagogues to pray, but they even organized services in the ghetto hospital. The leaders of this endeavor, in fact, were the "assimilated" doctors, who paid no attention to the German decree and were willing to risk their lives for the *mitzvah* of prayer.[11]

Rabbi Oshry continued his daily classes. The *Tiferet Baḥurim* refurbished a building at 8 Kaklo Street, painted and cleaned it, installed electricity and a secret room in which to hide during German searches, and continued their studies under the guidance of their devoted teacher.

The same tenacious adherence to study and prayer marked the behavior of the Jews in the other ghettos established by the Germans. Not simply on the *Yomim Noraim,* the Days of Awe, of Rosh Hashanah and Yom Kippur, when the overpowering urge to pray with one's fellow Jews could not be repressed by internal or external forces (see below pp. 108–113), but also on the weekdays and Sabbaths, Jews in Vilna, Warsaw, Kletzk, Lodz, Kolomayo, and other ghettos, risked their lives for the sake of prayer. In bunkers, or cellars, or underground tunnels and specially constructed hiding places (*malinehs*), they assembled to pray in spite of the German interdict against public worship.[12] If there were no *siddurim,* someone would write one from memory or from a torn and tattered copy which was still to be found. One Moshe Berkowitz from Zhelikov, whose entire family was destroyed, was hidden in a bunker near Warsaw for some time. His companion there writes that Berkowitz spent months in laboriously writing a *siddur* so that, "God forbid, the world should not remain without a *siddur*." In the *siddur* he also inscribed the names of his lost loved ones so that, "God forbid, the world should not remain without a remembrance of those who gave their lives for *kiddush ha-shem*."[13] Not only in the ghettos but in many of the labor and death camps, daily *minyanim* for prayer were conducted morning and evening (see below).

At the Eichmann trial, Zalman Kleinman testified to an incident indicating the interpretation of *ye-horeg ve'al ya'avor* as it applied to prayer, which was given, not by the *Sefer ha-Ḥinukh's* "great and wise man," but by a young boy at Auschwitz.

> One day I was lying down on my bunk in the children's block at Auschwitz, and I saw one of the officials of the block coming with a thick rubber truncheon to beat someone. I jumped off my bunk to see whom he was going to beat. Beatings were given for every "sin," and the number of blows was according to the severity of the crime. This was the first time the rubber truncheon was used. Generally they would use a stick, which often would break in the middle of the beating. . . . I wanted to see how the rubber truncheon worked; perhaps someday I would meet up with it myself. The official approached one of the bunks. The boy who was there already knew what was in store for him. . . . He bent over and the beating began. The rest of us watched and counted. The boy neither cried nor screamed, he did not even sigh. We wondered, we did not understand what this meant. The count passed twenty-five—this was the usual maximum number of blows. When the count reached forty, he began to beat the boy on the head and feet. The boy neither sobbed nor cried out—a fourteen-year-old boy—and he didn't cry.
>
> The official finished fifty blows and left wrathfully. I remember a tremendous red welt on the boy's forehead made by the rubber truncheon. We asked him what he had done to incur the beating. He replied, "It was worth it. I brought some *siddurim* to some of my friends so they could pray. It was worth it!" He said not another word. He got up, returned to his bunk and sat down.[14]

The continued study of Torah was an even more remarkable phenomenon during the Holocaust. The emphasis on prayer is perhaps explainable, even in non-halakhic terms, as a natural human reaction to terror and trial. But the persistence of Torah study in the ghettos and concentration camps is understandable only within the framework of halakhic Judaism. In the halakhic system, study is a form of worship. But more than that, it is at the same time the ground on which the Jew walks, and the air which he must breathe in order to stay alive as a Jew. The abandonment of Torah study is, to the halakhic Jew, tantamount to a denial of his God and a rejection of his people. Saadia Gaon's dictum that "we Jews are a people only by virtue of the Torah"[15] was an operative principle to the

Jews in the Holocaust. There was no point in national survival—or perhaps even in individual survival—if the Torah should perish.

There was perhaps, too, an awareness that, historically, attempts to destroy the Jew had almost always been accompanied by the proscription of Torah study.[16] It was the refusal to comply with such decrees which had kept the Jewish people alive. Hence, the way not only to defy the Nazis, but to outlive them, was to persist in the study of Torah.

This the Jews did in strange, and fearful, conventional and unconventional fashion. In the Vilna ghetto, for example, the Jews established a regular school system. In the religious schools, Numbers 1 and 2, children up to the age of twelve studied Hebrew reading, Bible, and some arithmetic. In the *yeshivah ketanah,* boys from the ages of twelve to sixteen studied *mishnayot* and *gemara.* In the *yeshivah gedolah* students who had studied in various *yeshivot* before the war, sat and studied Talmud. Altogether there were about two hundred students in this school "system." From time to time public examinations would be given to the students. The rabbi sat in the center of the room and examined them on the material they had covered. Guests who had been invited were also allowed to ask questions of the students. During one such examination in Talmud, when the students were vigorously discussing a complicated subject, *ye'ush shelo mi-da'at,* thirty meters away from the examination stood an SS guard unaware of what was going on.[17]

In the Dautmorgan camp in the south of Germany there was a group of *yeshivah baḥurim* who would get together at night to study *mishnayot.* Like the rest of the camp inmates, they were bone-tired from the work in the clay pits, close to starvation, covered with vermin because they had not been able to wash for months. Yet one of them, a thin, white-faced lad from Navorodok, would recite out loud chapter after chapter of *mishnayot* from memory, and the rest of them would repeat each saying.[18]

In Garelitz, one of the camps in the Gross-Rosen complex, Yankel Pick studied Talmud during the daily march from the "block" to the machine factory where he worked. The distance was about six or seven kilometers. Each day he would declaim in a strong and vigorous voice the *she'ur be'halakhah* (Talmud lesson) which he had selected from the vast store of Talmudic material in his memory. He would arrange for some of the other inmates of Block 6, also former students of Torah, or *ḥasidim,* to march alongside him each morning en route to the factory and each evening on their return. Their feet marched to the melody of the

Talmud study. It was if the *niggun,* the melody, was a marching song.[19]

In the labor camp of Plaszow, the Germans set up a factory for the manufacture of brushes. In it they employed the skilled Jewish craftsmen of Cracow, who managed to set up a *she'ur* in the *daf yomi* (a lecture on the page of the Talmud assigned for daily study). This is how it was done. A pocket-sized *Horev* edition of the Talmud was concealed in the box in which the brushes were packed. The workmen all sat alongside the long table at which they fabricated the brushes. The "foreman" sat at the head of the table and read the page of Talmud aloud so that all could hear. He also held ready at hand a half-completed brush, so that it would appear that he was working if the Nazi inspectors should come in suddenly. While they were not able to maintain the regular *daf yomi* schedule, since they had only one volume of the Talmud, they did manage to conduct the "class" almost on a daily basis.[20]

In the Warsaw ghetto, it was not a brush factory but a cobbler's shop which served as the house of study. In his diary of the Warsaw ghetto, Hillel Seidman describes the scene on Hoshanah Rabbah (the seventh day of the Succot festival), October 2, 1942.

> Now, here I am in Schultz's "shop." The people are driving in nails and saying *Hoshanot* [prayers]. Here are assembled, thanks to the aid of one of the directors, Abraham Hendel, the elite of the Orthodox rabbis, religious scholars, Orthodox social workers, and well-known *Ḥasidim.* Here you see sitting at the wooden block and mending shoes (the work mostly consists of pulling out nails with pliers) the *Kozieglower rebbe,* Yehuda Arieh Former, the former *rosh yeshivah* of the *Yeshivat Hakhmey Lublin.* This Jew is sitting here, but his spirit is soaring to other worlds. He does not stop studying from memory and his lips keep moving all the time. From time to time he addresses a word to the *Pleaseczna rebbe,* the author of *Ḥovat Hatalmidim,* who is sitting just opposite him. And then a quiet discussion on religious subjects follows. *Gemarot* and biblical texts are quoted, and soon there appear on the shoe block, or rather in the minds and mouths of the *geonim,* the *Rambam,* the *Rabad,* the *Tur, . . .* and who cares now about the SS men, about the *Volksdeutsch* supervisor, or about hunger, misery, persecutions, and fear of death! Now they are soaring in higher regions, they are not in the "shop" at 46 Nowolipie Street where they are sitting, but in lofty halls . . . ! [21]

Schultz's "cobbler's shop" was not the only house of study in the Warsaw ghetto. There are at least ten known locations where such illegal
study groups met regularly, in addition to many other underground study
cells concerning which documentation is fragmentary. Similar groups
existed in the ghettos of Cracow and Lodz. One group of young *Hasidim*
in the ghetto of Cracow sat night and day in a cellar, absorbed in study.
Following the liquidation of the Cracow ghetto, they were forced out of
the cellar and killed by the Gestapo.²²

Leib Garfunkel, a member of the *Aeltentestrat* of the Kovno ghetto,
writes that the Talmud was studied regularly and enthusiastically in the
two remaining synagogues of Kovno, as well as in temporarily organized
minyanim. The study sessions were led by former *yeshivah* students and
learned laymen.

> The principal study time was in the evenings, when the men had re-
> turned from the forced-labor details, starving and frozen . . . In the
> ghetto there were some who could not under any circumstance recon-
> cile themselves to not studying Torah all the day long, so they con-
> cealed themselves in various hiding places in order not to have to go
> to the forced labor. The labor office of the *Aeltentestrat,* which had
> the responsibility of providing the quota of workers, ultimately
> allowed these people to be free from fulfilling their forced-labor
> obligations.

That there were books in the Kovno ghetto in which pious men could
pursue their studies was due to the fact that in July and August of 1941,
when the Jews were being crammed into the ghetto, they had, under the
most difficult of circumstances, transported with them some 100,000
volumes into their new quarters. Early in 1942 the *Institut zur Erforschung
der Judenfrage,* the pseudo-scientific Nazi "research" organization under
the direction of Alfred Rosenberg, became aware of the fact that Slobodka
had been the location of a famous *yeshivah* with a valuable collection of
books. In their desire to add to their collection, the Nazis ordered, on
February 18, 1942, that the Jews of the ghetto must turn over to them
all Hebrew books in their possession.

Working with desperate haste, the young men of the ghetto, particularly
the Zionist youth, managed to salvage a considerable number of books
and hide them in various places in the ghetto. In one night, at the risk of
their lives, they succeeded in hiding not only many bound volumes but

also a considerable number of *sifrei-torah*, which were also included in the Nazi decree. But the vast majority of the books were gathered in a central storehouse for examination by the staff of the Rosenberg institute. A special emissary, a certain Dr. Benkard, was sent to supervise the classification of the books.

This situation presented Rabbi Oshry with a very different kind of *she'elah* concerning the teaching of Torah.[23] It also raised the question of whether one should give up his life for the teaching of Torah. But in this instance the problem was whether the Halakhah required one to suffer martyrdom rather than teach Torah to a non-Jew.

Rabbi Oshry was in charge of the religious-book warehouse in the ghetto, and accordingly Dr. Benkard, together with Jordan, the commandant of the ghetto, asked him to find some very ancient edition of the Talmud and explain to them what was written in it. Rabbi Oshry selected the Talmudic tractate *Zevahim*. Benkard and Jordan then asked Rabbi Abraham Gerstein to read and translate the text of the first page for them. Rabbi Gerstein asked Rabbi Oshry if it was permitted for him to comply with their request and thus be in the position of teaching Torah to these Nazis.

In his *teshuvah* Rabbi Oshry cited the Talmudic passage in *Hagigah* 13a: "One does not teach Torah to a non-Jew, for it is said, 'He hath not dealt so with any nation; and as for his ordinances, they have not known them' (Ps. 147:20)." The Talmud also declares, in *Sanhedrin* 59a, that "an idolator who engages in the study of Torah is deserving of death, and he who teaches him Torah violates the commandment of 'thou shalt not place a stumbling block in the way of the blind.' "

After an examination of the commentaries on these and related passages, Rabbi Oshry concludes that many authorities (although by no means all), such as the *Maharatz Hayyes* (*Sotah* 35b) and the *Meishiv Davar* (*Yoreh Deah* 77), agree that the prohibition of teaching Torah to a non-Jew applies only to the oral law, and not to the written Torah. However, in the instant case, it was the Talmud, the oral law, which he and Rabbi Gerstein were being asked to expound. This would be prohibited—were it not for two other important conditions which alter the ruling. These are the temporary nature of the instruction, and the element of danger involved in not complying with the request of the Nazis.

The *Turei Even,* in his *hiddushim* (novellae) on *Hagigah* 13a, raises a question from a passage in *Avodah Zarah* 44b. There the Mishnah tells us that Rabban Gamaliel, when challenged by the heathen Proclos as to why he bathed in the baths of Aphrodite (an act which Proclos assumed would be forbidden to a believing Jew), replied, "We may not answer 'questions relating to Torah in a bath" (because of the nudity of those present). When they emerged from the bathhouse, Rabbi Gamaliel said, "I did not come into her domain, she has come into mine [the bath existed before the image of Aphrodite was set up in it]. Nobody says the bath was made as an adornment for Aphrodite. . . . Aphrodite was made as an adornment for the bath. Another reason . . . this statue of Aphrodite stands by a sewer and all people urinate before it. In the Torah (Deut. 7:16, 12:2) it is only stated 'their gods'—that is, what is treated as a deity is prohibited, what is not treated as a deity is permitted."

The *Turei Even's* question is, How was it possible for Rabban Gamaliel to teach these points of Jewish law to the heathen since the Talmud in *Ḥagigah* prohibits this? He answered that since the prohibition of teaching Torah to a non-Jew is only Rabbinic and not Biblical (the Biblical verse cited in *Ḥagigah* is an *asmakhta*), the instruction is permitted if it is not on a regular, continuing basis, but only a single or occasional instance. Rabbi Oshry concludes that since the Nazis asked to be taught only a single page of the Talmud, it would be permitted. All the more so, since there was a question of actual danger to life if he did not comply.

He further proves this point—that where there is danger to life, it is permitted to teach Torah to a gentile—from a passage in *Baba Kamma* 88a.

> Our Rabbis taught: the government of Rome had long ago sent two commissioners to the sages of Israel with a request to teach them the Torah. It was accordingly read to them once, twice, and thrice. Before taking leave they made the following remark: "We have gone carefully through your Torah, and found it correct with the exception of this point, viz., your saying that if an ox of an Israelite gores an ox of a Canaanite there is no liability, whereas if the ox of a Canaanite gores the ox of an Israelite . . . compensation has to be paid in full. In no case can this be right. . . . We will, however, not report this matter to our government."

Tosafot on this passage asks how it was permissible for the sages to teach these Roman emissaries the Torah, since the Talmud, in *Ḥagigah* 13a, prohibits teaching Torah to a non-Jew. *Tosafot* replies that the sages were compelled to do so by the Roman government; and there is no obligation to give up one's life rather than violate the Rabbinic dictum prohibiting the giving of such instruction.

Rabbi Oshry was further asked by the Germans to explain some hand-written marginal notes in the Talmud volumes of Rabbi Isaac Elḥanan Spektor, the former chief rabbi of Kovno, whose entire private library had been consigned to the ghetto storehouse. He was also asked to explain one of Rabbi Spektor's responsa, which had been bound together with the tractate *Berakhot*. They then requested that Rabbi Oshry read to them from the *sifrei-torah* which were also stored in the warehouse. He complied with all these demands of the Nazi "cultural experts" in accordance with his opinion that, on a temporary basis or where life is endangered, it is permitted to teach a non-Jew Torah—even a Nazi.

Chapter Four

"How Does One Bless?"

"Just as one is obliged to bless the Almighty for the good, so is he obliged to bless Him for the evil." [1] This demanding principle seems less often to be questioned in the halakhic literature of the Holocaust than is the appropriate form of a particular benediction under a given set of circumstances.

One who lives outside the halakhic universe may find this impossible to understand. Those who see in it only a casuistic concern with minutiae and trivia will often be impatient with Jews to whom the Halakhah is the voice and will of God, and to whom no divine injunction can be trivial or unimportant. Yet even the unsympathetic and remote observer must feel some degree of admiration, and even awe, at the style and consistency of halakhic Jews in the face of death itself.

Every *mitzvah*—divine commandment—which a Jew fulfills must be preceded by a benediction. In it he praises God, the "Ruler of the universe, who has sanctified us by His commandments and commanded us to . . ." The completion of the benediction describes the particular *mitzvah* which he is about to perform. Now *kiddush hashem*, the sanctification of God's name through noble behavior by His people—through martyrdom if necessary—is a *mitzvah*. As such, one must recite a benediction before fulfilling it.

The Holocaust added a new dimension to the concept of the *mitzvah* of *kiddush ha-shem*. In past persecutions the Jew most often had the option of choosing life by abandoning Judaism. The victim of the Holocaust had no such option. Nonetheless, it was the universal rabbinic opinion, as formulated by Rabbi Shimon Huberband of Warsaw, that "a Jew who is killed, though this be for reasons other than conversion, but simply because he is a Jew, is called *kadosh*" [holy] and has fulfilled the *mitzvah* of *kiddush ha-shem*.

61

But the martyr of the Holocaust, without life options before him and contrary to the expectations of his murderers, did indeed have a choice—the manner in which he would accept and prepare for his death. Freedom to choose between one's life and one's religious faith was converted to the option of "going to one's death degraded and dejected as opposed to confronting death with an inner peace, nobility, upright stance, without lament and cringing to the enemy. This new option became . . . another attribute to *kiddush ha-shem* during the Holocaust." [2]

Rabbi Neḥemya Alter, keynoting a meeting of rabbis in Lodz, emphasized the imperative of *kiddush ha-shem,* which may assume various forms. However, central to the *mitzvah* is "not to degrade ourselves before the *goyim*" [gentiles]. Eyewitness accounts of the preparation for *kiddush ha-shem* of such ḥassidic leaders as the *Brezner, Grodzisker,* and *Zaloshizer rebbeim* reflect the calming influence upon terrified Jews as they themselves faced death with dignity. Other descriptions of *kiddush ha-shem* actually include instances of confronting death with the ecstasy appropriate to the fulfillment of the final and ultimate *mitzvah.* With a Torah scroll in his hands, Meir Ofen, a kabbalist and *ḥassid* of the *Dzikover rebbe* led hundreds of Jews during their march to a mass grave reciting Psalm 33:1, "Rejoice in God, righteous ones!" The *Grodzisker rebbe,* prior to entering the gas chamber in Treblinka, urged the Jews to accept *kiddush ha-shem* with joy and led them in the singing of *Ani Ma'amim* ("I Believe"). The *Spinker rebbe* danced and sang in the death wagons to Auschwitz, especially the prayer, *Vetaher libenu l'avdekha b'emet* ("Purify our hearts so that we may serve You in truth").

The *Piazesner rebbe* observed:

> he who is slaughtered in *kiddush ha-shem* does not suffer at all . . . since in achieving a high degree of ecstasy, stimulated in anticipation of being killed for the sanctifying of His Name, blessed be He, he elevates all his senses to the realm of thought until the entire process is one of thought. He nullifies his senses and feelings, and his sense of the material dissolves of itself. Therefore he feels not pain but rather only the joy of fulfilling the *mitzvah.* [3]

To achieve the heights of *kavanah* (proper intention) for the *mitzvah* of *kiddush ha-shem* as described by the *Piazesner* was perhaps beyond the power of most Jews. But many were able to die with dignity in the confident belief that theirs was the *zekhut* (privilege) of fulfilling this great commandment. The *she'elah* concerning the proper benediction for *kiddush ha-shem,* described by Rabbi Oshry, is compelling testimony to this fact.[4]

On the eighth of Ḥeshvan, 5702 (October 29, 1941), a day known to Kovno Jews as "the Black Day," the Germans commanded that all the Jews from the ghetto, under penalty of death, assemble in the *Demokratia Platz* for a *selektion.* Some thirty thousand men, women, and children stood before the Gestapo "selector," Raukah, on a stormy, gray day. Snow and rain mixed together fell on the faces of the victims and mingled with their tears. No one knew whether he or his loved ones would return alive.

In the crowd of Jews, a certain Reb Elyah from Warsaw, a refugee who had futilely thought to escape the Germans by fleeing to Lithuania from Poland, approached Rabbi Oshry. He knew, he said, that many thousands of those who stood there that day would be killed on the morrow. He, too, might very well be included in their number. And so he asked what was the proper and precise form of the benediction to be recited before sanctifying the name of God through martyrdom. Was it *al kiddush ha-shem*—"who has commanded us *concerning* the sanctification of the Name"? Or would it be more correct to say *le'kadesh et ha-shem* —"who has commanded us *to sanctify* the Name"? Reb Elyah wanted to know the correct benediction not only for his own sake. He proposed— as perhaps his last *mitzvah* on earth—to pass among the throng of Jews packed into the *Demokratia Platz* and teach it to others so that they, too, might recite the benediction which the *din*—the law—required.

Rabbi Oshry instructed Reb Elyah to recite the benediction as it is found in the *Shenei Luḥot ha-Brit (Sha'ar ha-Otiot* 1), *le'kadesh et shemo ba'rabim*—"who has sanctified us by His commandments and commanded us to sanctify His name in the presence of the many." He indicated that according to the *Riva,* the use of the word *al* in a benediction is restricted to commandments that could be performed on one's behalf by an agent. Since *kiddush ha-shem* was obviously not such a *mitzvah,* it would require the use of the infinitive with the *lamed—le'kadesh.* Reb Elyah repeated the proper form several times, and then went through the crowd teaching it to others so that if and when the time came for them to die as martyrs, they would have the merit of having recited the proper benediction.

Somewhat later that same day, Reb Elyah returned to Rabbi Oshry and informed him that Rabbi Naftali Wasserman, who was among those present in the *Demokratia Platz,* had been taught the same version of the blessing by his father, the great gaon, Rabbi Elhanan Wasserman.[5] He in turn had been taught this by the Hafetz Hayyim. Rabbi Joshua Levinsohn, a grandson of the Hafetz Hayyim, confirmed the fact that his grandfather had instructed his students, during the Petlura pogroms in Russia after World War I, that they should recite this blessing if they were fated for martyrdom.

In his *teshuvah* Rabbi Oshry also cites a longer version of the benediction attributed to Rabbi Asher of Frankfurt. It is quoted in the *Yosef Ometz*, 483.

> Those who are about to undergo martyrdom are obliged to recite the benediction: "Blessed art thou, O Lord our God, Ruler of the Universe, who hast sanctified us with His commandments and commanded us to love the revered and awesome Name, which was, is, and will ever be, with all our hearts and all our souls; and to sanctify His name among the multitude. Blessed art thou, O Lord who sanctifies His name amidst the many." Let them say, "Hear O Israel . . ." and give up their lives for the sanctification of His name.[6]

Yet another *she'elah* concerning benedictions came before Rabbi Oshry.[7] This one did not concern the proper form of the *be'rakha* but whether, in fact, it should be recited at all. Early on, in the daily morning service, as one of the series of benedictions of praise and thanksgiving to the Almighty for having satisfied one's personal needs as well as those of the people of Israel, the observant Jew recites the *be'rakha*: "Blessed art Thou, O Lord our God, Ruler of the universe, who hast not made me a slave."

After presenting a graphic description of the burdens of their forced labor, the pervasiveness of fear, and the utter powerlessness of the ghetto dwellers of Kovno, Rabbi Oshry tells of a confrontation between one Reb Avraham Yosef and the Almighty concerning this benediction. Reb Avraham Yosef was reciting the morning benedictions as the reader for the congregation with his customary reverent piety. When he reached the *be'rakha* "who hast not made me a slave," he cried out bitterly, "How can I recite this lie when we bear the yoke of slavery on our backs. How can a slave recite the blessing of a free man when he is enchained and sated with a diet of gall and wormword! Only an imbecile or a lunatic could say this blessing now. When we pray, do we not have to mean what we pray? I cannot recite this *be'rakha*. My heart is not in it."

Others joined him in his plaint. Rabbi Oshry was then asked whether it was indeed proper to refrain from reciting this blessing. Was it not even forbidden to recite it, since it would be praying a lie? Or perhaps, on the other hand, even under these circumstances, we ought not to change the form of prayer, which was set by our sages.

This very question, Rabbi Oshry reminds us, had already been discussed by the great authorities of earlier times. The *Abudraham* (s.v. *shavui*) considers whether a Jew who is a captive (either being held for ransom or in actual servitude) ought to recite, "who has not made me a slave." He writes that the blessing was not instituted by the sages to thank God for having relieved one of the burdens of physical labor, but rather to praise Him because one had not been born with the status of a Canaanite slave. A Canaanite slave does not have the privilege of fulfilling the commandments. But a Jewish captive does, and he is, accordingly, obligated to recite this *be'rakha*.

We see, then, that it is not slavery of the body but of the spirit that this benediction refers to. And while a Jew who is in captivity may be forcibly prevented from fulfilling the commandments, or some of them, he is still in the category of a "commandment observer," and as such is obliged to recite the *be'rakha* though he be in the sore straits of physical captivity or servitude. Therefore, Rabbi Oshry declared to those who made inquiry of him,

> Heaven forfend that they should abolish the saying of this benediction, which was instituted by the great sages of old. On the contrary, especially at this time is the obligation upon us to recite this benediction; in order that our enemies and oppressors recognize that, in spite of the fact that we are in their power to do with as their evil desires dictate, we still see ourselves not as slaves, but as free men, temporarily in captivity, whose salvation will speedily come and whose redemption will soon be revealed.

Still another *teshuvah* on the recitation of a *be'rakha* reveals not only Rabbi Oshry's insights into the Halakhah, but also his understanding of the spirit of the residents of the Kovno ghetto.[8] After the destructive German *aktion* of the thirteenth of Ḥeshvan, 5702 (November 3, 1941), in which some ten thousand Jews were killed, a *she'elah* was directed to him by some of those who had escaped and who had not been slaughtered in that particular *aktion*. Were they obligated to recite the benediction of *ha-gomel* ("Blessed be Thou, O Lord our God, Ruler of the universe, who doest good to the undeserving, and who hast dealt kindly with me"), which is recited publicly by those who have escaped from danger, or been released from prison, or recovered from serious illness? Or, since they were still confined to the ghetto, which was surrounded by an electrified fence and guarded by troopers who would shoot on sight anyone attempting to escape, and thus could be said to be in the category of prisoners not yet released, was there no obligation to recite the blessing? Or might it be argued, since, after all, they had been rescued from death, while thousands of others had perished, that they should recite the blessing of thanksgiving even though their total deliverance had not yet come?

In his *teshuvah* Rabbi Oshry discusses the Talmudic passage (*Berakhot* 54b) which is the source for the benediction of *ha-gomel*. "Rabbi Judah said in the name of Rav, 'Four must give thanks to God; those who go down to the sea, travelers in a wilderness, a sick person who has been healed, and a prisoner who has been freed.' " By a close reading of the text, Rabbi Oshry attempts, at first, to show that those who may still be in a present danger must, nonetheless, offer thanks for having escaped from a previous one. For the Talmud speaks of "a sick person who has been healed" and a "prisoner who has been freed"—both of these have a present status which is completely different from their previous one. Yet in the case of seafarers and wilderness travelers, it does not say "seafarers who have come into safe harbor," or "travelers who have reached settled territory." One might, therefore, assume that the Talmud means to tell us that the sailor who has escaped one storm offers thanks while still at sea, even though another may await him; and the traveler gives thanks after having escaped brigands, even though other mishaps are likely to occur on his journey.

Rabbi Oshry acknowledges, however, that both the Rambam (*Hilkhot Be'rakhot 10:8*) and the *Shulḥan Arukh* (*Oraḥ Ḥayyim* 219:1) specifically state that sailors and travelers recite the benediction only when they have returned to port or reached a settlement, respectively. Nonetheless, Rabbi Oshry is still puzzled by the difference which the Talmudic text seems to make between freed prisoners and healed sick people, on the one hand, and seafarers and travelers, on the other. He is inclined to believe that an additional reason for the distinction may be that in the case of seafarers and travelers, even if no specific danger has occurred while they were en route, they must still recite the benediction on their return since they had traversed a generalized area of danger.

The *Yad Ha'melekh (Be'rakhot* 10:8) supports the first part of Rabbi Oshry's thesis that if a sailor or wayfarer has been rescued from some danger en route, he must recite the benediction immediately and not wait until he reaches dry land or settled territory. But he differs in the second part and holds that if no incident of danger occurred during the journey, he need not recite the benediction at all when he reaches his destination. The *Elyah Rabbah* (219:1) disagrees with the *Yad Hamelekh* as well as with Rabbi Oshry's textual deduction, and rules that sailors and wayfarers do not recite the benediction until they are completely out of danger and have reached dry land or settled territory.

Inasmuch as the *Sedei Hemed (Asefat Dinim, Ma'arekhet He* 38), the *Orhot Hayyim,* 219, and the *Mishnah Be'rurah* all concur in the ruling that sailors and wayfarers do not recite the benediction until they are completely out of danger, and since the *Mishnah Be'rurah* also offers a different and equally plausible explanation for the textual difference which he had remarked, Rabbi Oshry concludes that one who is not completely out of danger ought not to recite the *ha-gomel* benediction. Therefore, the survivors of this *aktion* should not recite the *be'rakha.*

He writes,

> It is quite possible that the cruel murderers had already condemned these who had escaped that particular *aktion* to death. The reason they let them remain alive was because they deliberately conducted their murderous operation in "cat and mouse" fashion, always allowing some Jews to remain alive for a time. They did this in order to delude them with false hopes so that their despair might be all the greater when the truth became known to them.
>
> Time after time they would lead the ghetto residents astray with all sorts of false rumors of salvation and deliverance in order to instill in them the vain hope that the destroyer's hand had finally been stayed. So, too, when they took them out to be killed, the Germans would lead them to believe that they were simply being transported from one point to another so that the Jews should not try to escape or resist.

Rabbi Oshry advances an insight into the psychology of the Jews of the Kovno ghetto as a concluding and conclusive reason for not reciting the *ha-gomel* benediction.

Therefore, one certainly ought not to instruct those who escaped to recite the *ha-gomel* after having been saved from destruction in this one *aktion*. For these unfortunate ones may begin to imagine that the threat of death is truly over and that salvation is at hand. In this fashion we would be helping the cursed murderers in their foul plot and would simply be making it easier for them to destroy our sisters and brothers. Therefore, I ruled that they must not recite the *ha-gomel,* even without the *shem u'malkhut*.[9] And even those who had been saved from many such actions, so long as they were still confined in the ghetto, still had not experienced a complete deliverance which would warrant the recitation of the *be'rakha,* as I have already explained.

"Magnified and Sanctified"—The *Kaddish*

It may be, as some maintain, that the recitation of the *kaddish* by mourners is in the tradition of Job's affirmation of adamant faith: "The Lord hath given, and the Lord hath taken; blessed be the name of the Lord." The mourner does not rail against the justice of the Almighty; he submits to the will of God. He does not curse Him. He blesses Him! To thus glorify the Almighty when He has just snatched away the life of a loved one demands a faith of the highest order.

Though this is what the mourners' *kaddish* has come to signify for many, it was originally concerned with the dead—not the living. Jewish folklore had it that the wicked are punished in *gehinnom* for a period of no more than twelve months after death. According to a late Midrashic legend, Rabbi Akiba discovered that the recitation of *kaddish* by a son could mitigate the torments suffered by his father in the hereafter. It is on the basis of this essentially aggadic teaching that the Halakhah, quite uncharacteristically, without any basic source in Talmudic or Geonic literature, incorporated the practice of the mourner's saying of *kaddish*.[10]

Who would dare to speculate what was in the minds of the bereaved parents and children who uttered the *kaddish* at Auschwitz or in the Kovno ghetto? One could assume that though their plight was infinitely worse than that of Job, they still reacted as he did, saying, "Blessed be the name of the Lord." The actuality was undoubtedly far more complicated. But whatever mystery or poetry or theology or emotional catharsis the *kaddish* provided the Holocaust victims, the prescriptions for its recitation were subject to the rigorous examination of halakhic logic. That examination was made, not with a view to what solace the *kaddish* might provide for the living, but with a view to what relief it might bring to the dead. If the role of the *kaddish* is to alleviate the sufferings of the dead in the afterlife, then what of those who cannot possibly be imagined as undergoing punishment? What of children or infants, who certainly could not be held responsible for their acts? What, too, of *kedoshim,* martyrs, whose very act of martyrdrom, we are told on good authority, is atonement for any and all sins they may have committed in their lifetime? Is it necessary, or even proper, to recite the *kaddish* for children and *kedoshim?* Both of these *she'elot* were presented to Rabbi Oshry in the ghetto of Kovno under tragic circumstances.

Still another *she'elah* concerning the recitation of the *kaddish*—one of quite a different order—was propounded to Rabbi Oshry after the liberation of the ghetto. It concerned the propriety of reciting the *kaddish* for a Christian woman who had risked her own life to save those of a number of Jews whom she had kept hidden during the Nazi occupation.

In his three *teshuvot* on the subject of *kaddish,* Rabbi Oshry demonstrates not only a mastery of what the Rabbinic authorities have to say on how *kaddish* may be of benefit to the dead, but also a keen psychological insight into what the recitation of the *kaddish* might do to maintain the spirit of the living. As we shall see, despite the sometimes considerable weight of authority ruling that *kaddish* need not be said, Rabbi Oshry invariably accepts the other point of view—guided, one may reasonably assume, not only by concern for the dead undergoing the torments of hell in the afterlife, but also by compassion for the living, suffering them in the hell of the Kovno ghetto.

On the eleventh of Ḥeshvan, 5702 (November 1, 1941), the third day after the Nazis had taken more than ten thousand Jews from the ghetto—men, women, and children—to the Ninth Fort to be put to death, a young man who had managed to escape returned to the ghetto and recounted the terrifying details of the cruel slaughter. The Germans had ordered the victims to strip off their clothing and jump into large trenches which had already been prepared. Then they fired on them with machine guns, and when they had finished they filled the trenches with earth, covering the living and the dead alike. Many had only been wounded by the machine-gun fire and were still alive.

There was no house in the ghetto which did not mourn its dead. Brother wept bitterly for brother, husbands for wives, parents for their children, wives for their husbands. The ghetto was shrouded in sorrow and mourning. Then one Berchik the Glazier, the *gabbai* of the *Ḥevrah En Ya'acov* of the *Halvayas ha-Mes Kloiz,* came to Rabbi Oshry and asked whether the Halakhah required mourning to be observed for those who had died as martyrs for the sanctification of God's name, and whether *kaddish* should be recited for them.

In his *teshuvah,*[11] Rabbi Oshry quotes the *Maharil (She'elot u'Teshuvot* 99), who was asked the question of whether it is necssary to say *kaddish* for those who gave their lives for the sanctification of God's name. The person raising the question proposed that it not be required to mourn for martyrs. In his response, the *Maharil* says,

> I have heard from my teachers that, during the persecutions in
> Prague, there were those who wished to say that it was not necessary
> to mourn for martyrs; yet they finally decided that they should
> mourn. And this point of view seems correct to me. For even though
> they are the holy ones of the Almighty, on a level so exalted that
> no other creature can approach them, nonetheless one must still
> mourn them.

The *Yalkut Yosher,* 1:115, writes concerning Rabbi Israel Isserlin, the author of the *Te'rumat ha-Deshen,* that he fasted on the ninth of Nisan, his mother's *yahrzeit,* even though she was a martyr, slain during the Austrian persecutions, thus indicating that mourning rites were to be observed for *ke'doshim.* Moreover, all the great authorities of his time agreed that one must mourn and recite *kaddish* even for *ke'doshim.* Therefore, Rabbi Oshry ruled that the martyrs of the Ninth Fort should be mourned and *kaddish* recited for them. He concludes his responsum with a terse yet moving description of the "fearful and awesome sight of all who still remained alive in the ghetto reciting *kaddish* in one voice for their beloved and precious dear ones."

On the third and fourth days of Nisan, 5704 (March 27–28, 1944), the Germans conducted a mass murder of Jewish children which they called the *Kinder Aktion.* They destroyed some twelve hundred infants, whom they snatched from their mothers' bosoms and killed without mercy. The bereaved parents of these infants asked Rabbi Oshry whether they were obliged to recite *kaddish* for their children; and, if so, how old must the child have been to require the *kaddish* to be said.

In his *teshuvah* [12] Rabbi Oshry explores the references concerning the recitation of *kaddish* by mourners found in the *Or Zarua;* the *Kol Bo*

114; the *Rivash* 115; and the *Rama, Yoreh Deah* 376:4. These sources themselves cite various and somewhat obscure Midrashic references explaining the supposed origins of the custom. All these authorities agree, however, that the purpose of the mourner's reciting the *kaddish* is to mitigate the punishment of the dead in the hereafter. The merit of a son's reciting *kaddish* accrues to the benefit of his deceased parent.

If so, Rabbi Oshry suggests, there should be no obligation to recite *kaddish* for anyone under the age of twenty, since the Talmud (*Shabbat* 89b; *Moed Katan* 28a) indicates that the heavenly tribunals do not punish a man for the sins he commits before he has reached that age. (So too the Palestinian Talmud, *Bikkurim* 2.) The Rambam, in his *Perush ha-Mishnayot* to *Sanhedrin,* chap. 7, categorically states, "The Holy One, blessed be He, does not apply the punishment of *karet* to anyone under the age of twenty; and there is no difference in this matter between males and females."

However, the *Ḥakham Tzvi,* sec. 49, writes that at thirteen years of age one already becomes liable for punishment for his sins, since at that age he becomes obliged to fulfill the commandments. The *Nodah Be'Yehudah* (*Oraḥ Ḥayyim* 8) also writes that a thirteen-year-old may be punished for violating those commandments which involve *karet*—that is, divine retribution.

To reconcile this difference, one is compelled to say that when the Talmud speaks of being free from heavenly punishment until reaching the age of twenty, it refers only to punishments which one would receive in this life. However, it might well be, Rabbi Oshry speculates, that one would be punished after death for sins committed any time after he reached an age where he was able to distinguish between right and wrong. It is such punishment *after death* to which the *Ḥakham Tzvi* and the *Nodah Be'Yehudah* refer. Rabbi Oshry finds support for this point of view in the Talmud (*Sanhedrin* 55b), which implies that even a three-year-old girl may bear some measure of responsibility for sins in which she was involved of her own volition. He suggests that perhaps there is a distinction between an adult, who understands the nature of sin as an offense against God, and hence is punished even in this life, and a child, who is aware that what he is doing is wrong, but does not clearly comprehend the full import of his act. The child, therefore, is not punished in this life, but he may be in the next.

He further cites the *Da'at Ze'kenim* of the *Ba'alei Tosafot, (Parashat Vayeshev),* who write in the name of Rabbi Yehudah he-Ḥasid that responsibility for sin is not dependent upon age, but upon the individual child's mental ability; for there are children even less than thirteen years old who are able to distinguish between right and wrong.

Still, Rabbi Oshry is hard put to find warrant for the recitation of *kaddish* as expiation for sins committed by infants. Indeed, the *Sedei Ḥemed, Avelut* 151, writes, "It is the universal custom that one does not recite *kaddish* for a person less than twenty years old." However, the *Yeshurei Taharah,* 100:74, writes that the kabbalists rule that one should say the *kaddish* for someone less than twenty years old, for through this the soul of the departed becomes elevated to a higher status. If this is so, and the reason is not simply to mitigate the punishment of the departed, but to aid his soul to rise to higher spheres, then in any event *kaddish* should be said for an infant who lives more than thirty days. (Before thirty days have elapsed from birth, the Halakhah views the child as not having full legal status as a person.)

Rabbi Oshry then adduces evidence from other sources that *kaddish* ought to be recited for infants, and that the reason for such recitation is not the alleviation of suffering for sins committed while the deceased was alive. The *Sefer Ha'orah,* attributed to Rashi (edition Buber, 225), and the *Maḥzor Vitry,* 245, the *Or Zarua, Avelut* 428, and the *Issur Va'heter,* 139, all discuss the case of a child who died when it was twelve days old. The father was declared exempt from observing mourning rites and from reciting *kaddish.* The implication is, says Rabbi Oshry, that if the child had died after having attained the age of thirty days, the father would have been required to say *kaddish.*

While the *Shulḥan Arukh* does not specifically discuss the question of reciting *kaddish* for a child, it is possible to deduce from another provision that it would rule that *kaddish* should be said. In *Yoreh Deah* 263, the *Shulḥan Arukh* holds that an infant who dies before the eighth day of his birth, when he would normally be circumcised, is circumcised just prior to his burial and is given a name so "that he may be shown mercy from Heaven and participate in the resurrection of the dead."

If this act is performed, Rabbi Oshry asserts, so that "he may be shown mercy from Heaven," then certainly the same logic would apply to the recitation of *kaddish.* While the *Levush* ascribes a different reason for the circumcision of an infant who has died prior to the eighth day, still, according to the *Shulḥan Arukh's* view that such an infant also needs the "mercy of Heaven," the recitation of the *kaddish* is of similar effect.

For all the above reasons, Rabbi Oshry instructed the parents of infants more than thirty days old who had been slaughtered in the *Kinder Aktion* to recite the *kaddish* for them.

The third *teshuvah,* concerning *kaddish* for a Christian woman, is prefaced by Rabbi Oshry with a moving account of the unusual nature of her heroic acts.[13] He writes,

> In those evil and wrathful days, when the sword reigned without and fear within, when the cursed Germans murdered without mercy young and old, infants and children, they were aided in their work by the local non-German residents. These people, among whom the Jews had lived for hundreds of years, gave assistance to the Germans in the work of murder and pillage. They ferreted out Jews wherever they were hiding—in bunkers, in tunnels, in cellars, in caves. When they found them, they took delight in turning them over to the Germans to be tortured and oppressed.
>
> But in spite of the burning spark of hatred of the Jews which was in the hearts of these Lithuanians, and which the Germans developed into a raging fire, there were a few precious individuals among them in whom the spark of humanity had not yet been extinguished. They could not bear to see the cruelties which the Germans were inflicting upon the Jews, and they felt that they must do something to help them and save them from their oppressors. And though it was at the risk of their very lives (for the Germans immediately killed any gentile who was suspected of aiding Jews), a small number of them did everything in their power to save Jews.
>
> Now in the year 5705 [1944], shortly after we had lived to see the salvation of the Lord, who in His mercy destroyed the arm of the wicked and brought His people Israel out of darkness into great light, Reb Moshe Segal approached me with a *she'elah* of great concern to him. His life had been saved by a gentile woman, who at great risk had hidden him and about ten other Jews in her cellar during the Nazi occupation. She had managed to get food and water to them, as well, until the "days of wrath" were over. After the liberation, the Jews whom she had saved wanted to make known publicly this great act of heroic kindness and mercy, and somehow to repay her for what she had done for them. To their sorrow, they discovered that she had died shortly after the liberation. They then determined that something must be done to honor her memory, and so they arrived at the idea that one of their number should recite

the *kaddish* for her. They selected Reb Moshe Segal to fulfil this obligation, and he came before me to ask if it was permissible for him to do so or whether it might just possibly be forbidden.

In his *teshuvah* Rabbi Oshry first discusses whether *kaddish* may be recited for a *mumar,* an apostate from Judaism. After citing the *Shulḥan Arukh, Yoreh Deah* 376:4, which rules that *kaddish* may be recited for an apostate who was murdered by gentiles, he discusses the controversy between the *Shakh* and the *Maharsha* and others as to whether this also applies in the case of an apostate who has died a natural death. The weight of authority seems to be that it is permissible to recite *kaddish* even in the case of a *mumar* who died a natural death (and whose sins could not be assumed to be expiated by a violent end).

Further, the *She'elot u Te'shuvot Ḥesed L'Avraham (Yoreh Deah* 84) discusses the case of a Jew who had left his faith, but continued to distribute large sums to the Jewish poor. He requested the Jew through whom he distributed this charity to promise to recite *kaddish* for him after his death. He indicated that if the *kaddish* would be said, he would give even more money to charity. The ruling in the case was that it was permitted to promise to recite the *kaddish,* especially since the great *mitzvah* of charity would be furthered thereby. Support for this point of view was found in the Talmudic account of Rabbi Meir, who sought to rescue Elisha ben Abuyah from punishment after death even though he had denied the Torah and desecrated the Sabbath.

But, says Rabbi Oshry, we have proved only that an apostate who was once a Jew may have *kaddish* recited for him. And even though the acts of generosity of this gentile woman were immeasurably greater than those of the charity-giving apostate referred to in the above case, perhaps there is a difference between one who was born a Jew and left the faith, and one who was never Jewish.

He then proceeds to analyze the basic meaning of the *kaddish.* It is, he declares, simply a petitionary prayer to the Almighty. This is clear from the *Sefer Yuḥasin* (Cracow edition, p. 23) and the *Shevet Yehudah* (Koenigsburg edition, p. 85), in which we are told that when Rabbi Nathan the Babylonian was appointed to the position of *resh galuta,* the *ḥazan,* when he reached the phrase "in your lifetime and in your days," inserted the words "and in the lifetime of our *nasi,* the head of the exile." So, too, in the days of the Rambam they used to say in the *kaddish,* "in your lifetime and in your days, and in the lifetime of our teacher, Moshe bar Maimon." Since such very specific references to God's great name being glorified and sanctified during a particular individual's lifetime were permitted to be introduced into the *kaddish,* it appears evident to Rabbi Oshry that it is a petitionary prayer.

If so, then it is clear that it is permissible to say *kaddish* for this gentile woman, who "saved many Jewish lives from destruction by the cruel and cursed enemy." The *Sefer Hasidim* writes that it is permissible to pray to the Holy One, blessed be He, to judge favorably in the hereafter a gentile who did many favors for the Jews. Certainly, Rabbi Oshry goes on, there could be no greater favor than that rendered by this gentile woman, who saved many Jewish lives from destruction. Therefore it is certainly permitted to recite the *kaddish* for her. To further buttress his position, Rabbi Oshry cites the Palestinian Talmud (*Megillah* 3:6), in which Rabbi Pinhas declares that when Harvonah, the associate of Haman, is mentioned, one must add the expression *zakhur le'tovah* ("may he be remembered for good"), just as one says for Jewish sages, *zikhronom le'berakha* ("may their memory be for a blessing"), since Harvonah helped to save the Jews from destruction.

In *Pirke Avot* 3:2, Rabbi Hanina instructs us to pray for the welfare of the government. The *Meiri* points out that we are required to pray not simply for the Jewish government, but for the welfare of the governments of the people among whom we live, just as the Torah commanded us to bring seventy bullocks as sacrificial offerings in behalf of the "seventy nations of the world."

Rabbi Oshry notes that when he was preparing his work for publication, long after the events described took place in Kovno, he became aware of a *teshuvah* of Rabbi Ahron Wolkin (*Ze'kan Aharon, Yoreh Deah* 87) in which he rules that a convert to Judaism may recite the *kaddish* for his non-Jewish father.

He concludes his own *teshuvah,*

And now, with regard to this gentile woman, without whose acts of great mercy and kindness the Germans would have destroyed these Jewish lives, certainly it is a *mitzvah* to say *kaddish* for her, since, as I have demonstrated, the *kaddish* is simply a prayer. I therefore gave permission to Reb Moshe Segal to recite the *kaddish* for this heroic woman, who had saved his very life.

May He who does loving-kindness to His people Israel, repay with loving-kindness the righeous ones of the nations of the world who risked their lives to save the people of Israel. May the Almighty, who blesses His people Israel with peace, bless them with everything good. May they see when God returns the captivity of Zion and the rebuilding of His chosen sanctuary in which we shall once again offer sacrifices in behalf of the seventy nations of the world, speedily in our days. Amen.

Chapter Five

Bearing Witness

The physical pain and mental anguish of Jews imprisoned in the Nazi ghettos were intensified by the disruption of the religious practices and observances which were such an essential factor in their lives. Insofar as it was possible, they wished to don *tallit* and *tefillin* each day, to observe the Sabbath, to keep the dietary laws—to live as Jews. For many it was simply a matter of continuing to fulfill God's commandments, His *mitzvot,* as they had in the past. For others there was undoubtedly the added dimension of wishing to observe as many *mitzvot* as possible before an almost certain death, so that the *zekhut,* the merit, of these *mitzvot* would accompany them into the *olam haba*—the world beyond.

We have already seen in a previous chapter the tenacious adherence of the Jews of the Holocaust period to the practice of study and prayer. Even more obdurate was their determination to bear tangible witness to their belief in God and their complete loyalty to His commandments by observing the three *mitzvot* associated with the *ke'riat she'ma* (Deut. 6:4–8, 11:13–22; Num. 15:37–42). Not only in the ghettos, where daily living followed a quasi-"normal" pattern, but also in the concentration camps under impossible circumstances, they especially sought to fulfill the *mitzvot* of *tefillin* and *tzitzit.* In the ghettos they were concerned about the *mezuzot* on the doorposts of their houses.

Some of the *she'elot* which arose were occasioned by the sheer physical unavailability of the artifacts necessary for the observance of these commandments. Others concerned the element of risk which the Halakhah permitted or demanded in the attempt to fulfill these religious precepts. Still others addressed the issue of what provisions of the halakhic requirements concerning these *mitzvot* might be temporarily suspended or modified in the circumstances of the Holocaust.

77

Tefillin

I am now intent upon the act of putting on the *tefillin* in fulfillment of the command of my Creator, who hath commanded us to
do so, as it is written in the Torah, "And thou shalt bind them for a
sign upon thine hand, and they shall be for frontlets between thine
eyes." Within these *tefillin* are placed four sections of the Torah
that declare the absolute unity of God, and remind us of the miracles and wonders which He wrought for us when He brought us
forth from Egypt, even He who hath power over the highest and the
lowest to deal with them according to His will. He hath commanded
us to put the *tefillin* upon the hand . . . opposite the heart to indicate
the duty of subjecting the longings and designs of our heart to his
service, blessed be He; and upon the head over against the brain,
thereby teaching that the mind . . . is to be subjected to His service. . . .

(Daily Prayer Book, Meditation
Before Putting on the Tefillin)

The commandment of wearing *tefillin* (Exod. 13:9, 16; Deut. 6:8,
11:18) has always been considered of signal importance by observant
Jews. The epithet *karkafta d'lo manaḥ tefillin* (*Rosh Hashanah* 17a),
"a head which has not worn *tefillin*," was used to characterize the gravest
sinners of Israel. While nowhere was the *mitzvah* of *tefillin* reckoned as
a commandment which must be observed even at the cost of one's life,
during the Holocaust there were many who risked their lives, and some
who died, because of their determination to observe it. The halakhic aspects of putting on the *tefillin* before daylight were clarified by Rabbi
Oshry in a *teshuvah* for those who were impressed into the forced-labor
details in the Kovno ghetto. The amazing resourcefulness and tenacity of
those who donned *tefillin* in the death camps are described in a number
of accounts by survivors.

Rabbi Zvi Hirsch Meisels suggests at least part of the reason for the
importance which this *mitzvah* had acquired:

Understandably there was no way in Auschwitz for us to strengthen
our faith (through the use of reason). For we could not possibly
explain or understand what was occurring and why. The only course
was to become stronger in perfect faith through the mystic symbolic

effect of the *tefillin*. This is why the *mitzvah* of *tefillin* was so beloved in Auschwitz, for it kept broken spirits from losing their complete faith even for a moment, they had no grasp or understanding
of the reason (for their plight).[1]

How was it possible to "bind them for a sign upon the hand and wear
them for frontlets between the eyes" in the concentration camps? Whenever a transport arrived at a camp, the first procedure was the confisca-
tion of all personal possessions and clothing. Religious objects, such as
tefillin, siddurim, and other Hebrew books, were tossed on the enormous
heap of "junk" to be destroyed later because the SS considered them of
no value. Sometimes, because of the leather straps and cases, the *tefillin*
were placed into a pile with other leather objects for salvage. It was from
these sources that they were rescued at great risk and sacrifice by those
to whom the *mitzvah* of *tefillin* was precious. Once acquired, they were
carefully hidden. If one pair was discovered in the frequent searches of
the camp blocks, another was somehow obtained.

Jacob Frankel, an accountant, describes what transpired in Buchenwald:

> Do not think that the most expensive commodity in Buchenwald was
> bread. My experience taught me that there was a much more valua-
> ble kind of merchandise there—a pair of *tefillin.* I myself took part
> in a transaction involving the extraordinary price for a pair of *tefil-
> lin* of four complete rations of bread. To tell the truth, this was a
> partnership venture in which all of us, the *hasidim* of Gur, were
> involved. We who had resided on "tier number four" of the block
> were the purchasers. A Ukrainian *kapo,* a *pogromchik* like all of
> them, was the seller. We had reached Buchenwald in a transport di-
> rectly from Auschwitz. This was in the last stages of the war, when
> people were sent not only to Auschwitz, but also from it to other
> concentration camps. At the *selektion,* which had been made in the
> shadow of the crematoria, everything had been taken from us. There
> was no opportunity to smuggle a single pair of *tefillin.* What were we,
> this *hevrayah* of Gur *hasidim* gathered together on this uppermost
> tier of the wooden bunks, to do now? How could we hold fast with-
> out *tefillin?* . . . God helps! A Ukrainian *kapo* had stolen a pair of
> *tefillin* from the SS storehouse and was prepared to sell them—for
> not less than four rations of bread.

A heated discussion broke out among us. Was it permitted or forbidden to pay this price for them? In Buchenwald, to forgo a few rations of bread was tantamount to committing suicide. Was this permitted according to the *din?* As an accountant I was accustomed to work with figures. My calculations showed very clearly that in Buchenwald, to give up four rations of bread meant dying within a week or at most two. Nonetheless, I went to the *kapo* and informed him I was prepared to give him two rations as a down payment. He refused and wanted the full payment in advance. So another *ḥasid,* Abraham Eliyahu Weiss, an Aleksander *ḥasid* who came from one of the ghettos near Lodz, became my partner. It took several days until the two of us were able to save up four rations of bread. But the *kapo* kept his word and brought us a small pair of *tefillin* wrapped in paper. We quickly inspected them and then prayed in them with an ecstasy which it is impossible ever to experience again in our lives . . .[2]

Rabbi Joshua Aronsohn describes how *tefillin* were put on in Auschwitz:

When we arose in the darkness of the night, we had just managed to wash, the block leaders and their helpers were hurrying us along to the forced-labor details. There were long queues of prisoners waiting in line, not for bread or coffee, but to fulfill the *mitzvah* of *tefillin.* We appointed a special "guard" whose job it was to make sure that no one kept the *tefillin* on for longer than it took him to say the one verse *shema yisrael,* so that more would be able to fulfill the *mitzvah.*[3]

Moshe Brachtfeld writes:

After some time we were taken to another camp, where there were about two thousand Jews from Munkács and other places. They did not have even one pair of *tefillin.* How great was their joy when they discovered that we had brought a pair with us. About five hundred Jews recited the benediction that first day, and so it was every day thereafter. The pressure was so great that we were compelled to divide the set of *tefillin.* One group used only the *shel rosh,* the head *tefillah,* and the other the *shel yad,* the hand *tefillah.*

Understandably, each group recited only the one benediction appropriate in each case. There was no other way; we felt it was better that each one should fulfill at least part of the *mitzvah* than that only some should be able to fulfill it completely. This was really an elixir of life for us.

I recall a Jew from Munkács, Reb Aharon Veider, who arose at two o'clock in the night so that he could pray in the *tefillin.* He was able to pray as much as he desired without interruption. Then at about 3:00 A.M. toward morning, the round of those who put on *tefillin* had already begun. It lasted usually until 5:30, the time of the block inspection. I and my brother were the last to get there. Nonetheless we saw to it that the *tefillin* were brought to the place where we worked. There tens of Jews were able to use the short noon-hour break to put on the *tefillin* in a concealed place.[4]

Moshe Futerman describes how in Dachau, in the "summer block," there were twenty-two men who put on *tefillin.* "Even though we had to put them on in the darkness of the night, we relied on the opinion of the *rav* of Kovno who, when asked by those in the forced-labor detail whether it was permissible to pray before dawn (since they had no alternative), replied in the affirmative and declared, 'Would that my portion (in the hereafter) be with them.' "[5]

The *teshuvah* referred to by the prisoners of Dachau was as follows.

On the twenty-second of Tishre, 5702 (October 18, 1941), Rabbi Oshry was asked a *she'elah* concerning the permissibility of donning *tefillin* at night. The situation was this: The Nazis compelled those Jews who were assigned to forced-labor details to leave the ghetto at 5:00 A.M. while it was still dark. They did not return until after dark in the evening. They could not put on the *tefillin* during their work hours since the Germans might kill them if they were discovered.

In his *teshuvah* Rabbi Oshry discusses the basic issue of whether the wearing of *tefillin* at night is proscribed by the Torah or only by Rabbinic law.[6] After pointing out that the Rambam holds that the Torah proscribes night as a "time of *tefillin,*" he demonstrates that almost all the other codifiers disagree. They hold that it is only forbidden by Rabbinic law. The prohibition is due to the apprehension that if one is allowed to wear *tefillin* at night, he may fall asleep while wearing them, and thus not be able to maintain the state of bodily cleanliness and purity required while wearing these sacred objects.

Now this concern is only valid when one puts on *tefillin* prior to the normal bedtime. But certainly in our present case, where the *tefillin* would be put on after arising, just before going to work, no such fear would arise. There is no question that the forced laborers are unlikely to fall asleep once they have arisen, since their very lives depend on reporting to the work detail. Not only may the *tefillin* be put on, says Rabbi Oshry, but the benediction may be recited as well. He cites Rabenu Peretz *(Tur, Orah Ḥayyim)*, who specifically permits the benediction to be recited when one puts on *tefillin* in the morning (before day) before setting out on a journey. Rabbi Oshry maintains that even those authorities who would normally prohibit the recitation of the benediction where *tefillin* are put on at night, would agree that it might be said under the present circumstances. Since it is impossible to wear the *tefillin* during the day, the *only* time for *tefillin* is the night. This is a permissible time *de'oraita* (as far as the Torah is concerned), and since the reasons for the *de'rabanan* (Rabbinic) prohibition of wearing *tefillin* at night do not apply here, there is fulfillment of a *mitzvah* even as the rabbis defined it, and hence the benediction is appropriate.

As far as the recitation of the morning *shemoneh esreh* is concerned, Rabbi Oshry concludes that it, too, may be recited before daylight while the *tefillin* are being worn. He cites Rashi and the *Me'iri (Berakhot* 2), among others, who permit the recitation of the evening *shemoneh esreh* before dark when there are compelling reasons to do so. Similarly, he suggests, it should be permissible to recite the morning *shemoneh esreh* before it is light when the reasons are as compelling as in the present instance. The morning *ke'riat she'ma,* he suggests, can be fulfilled by the recitation of the first verse sometime after dawn while the men are at work.[7]

In another *teshuvah* Rabbi Oshry considers the case of a man in one forced-labor detail who would covertly and hastily put on his *tefillin* just as dawn was breaking while the men were being marched to their work assignment.[8] He was caught in the act by the Nazis and severely beaten. Moreover, they sadistically tattooed a cross on his biceps, the portion of the arm on which the *tefillin* are bound. Subsequently, when he was no longer in the work detail, he was ashamed to put on his *tefillin* in the synagogue. For when he bared his arm to do so, the cross—to him a mark of shame and disgrace—would be visible. His *she'elah* was whether it was permitted to put a bandage over the tattoo so that it could not be seen, and then put the *tefillah* on over the bandage.

Rabbi Oshry cites in detail the controversy between the *Rosh* (*Teshuvot ha-Rosh* 3:4), who insists that the *tefillin* must be bound on the bare flesh of the arm, and Rashi (*Arkhin* 3b), who apparently does not believe this to be necessary. Since great authorities side with each of them, and the Talmudic passages in question may be interpreted either way, Rabbi Oshry is reluctant to give the permission requested. He suggests as an alternative that the man put his *tefillin* on his bare arm at home, where no one will see the cross, and then go to the synagogue. (It was not an uncommon practice for Jews to don their *tallit* and *tefillin* at home and walk to the synagogue so adorned.) After completing his prayers, he could remove the *tefillah* of the head at the synagogue, and wait until his return home to remove the one from his arm. Thus no one would see his disgrace.

If this is not feasible, Rabbi Oshry suggested, the man might put on his *tefillin* at the synagogue over his shirtsleeve, since there were authorities who permitted this. He was not to recite the benediction when putting on the *tefillah* of the arm, however, but should recite two benedictions when putting on the *tefillah* of the head.

Tzitzit

I am here enwrapping myself in this fringed robe, in fulfillment of the command of my Creator, as it is written in the Torah: "They shall make them a fringe upon the corners of their garments throughout their generations." And even as I cover myself with the *tallit* in this world, so may my soul deserve to be clothed with a robe of spiritual beauty in the world to come . . .

(Daily Prayer Book,
Meditation Before Putting on the Tallit)

During a considerable period of the German occupation of Kovno, Rabbi Oshry taught a group of young men known as the *Tiferet Baḥurim*. On one occasion, a member of the group, Maier Abelov (later martyred), came to Rabbi Oshry with the following *she'elah*.[9] It was impossible to secure either fabric or *tzitzit* to make a *tallit katon*.[10] Most of those from the pre-Nazi days had worn out or fallen apart, or the *tzitzit* had become torn and were ritually unfit. He and his friends, realizing that they might be killed at any moment, wished to fulfill the *mitzvah* of *tzitzit* at all times. Perhaps it would protect them from harm in this world. Certainly it would add to their merits in the world to come. If they were to be slaughtered suddenly and without warning, at least they would be buried, wherever it might be, garbed in a *tallit* as was the ancient custom of Israel.

Maier Abelov was in a forced-labor detail which worked in a warehouse where there were large quantities of wool. He believed he could steal some, with but a slight risk. But his question was twofold. One: Is it permitted to make *tzitzit* from, and recite a benediction over, wool which is stolen? Two: Even if it is permitted to make *tzitzit* from such wool, there was no cloth available out of which to make the *tallit katon,* and thus it would be necessary to cut up a number of *tallitot gedolot* into smaller pieces into which *tzitzit* would be inserted. Is this reduction of the *tallit gadol* to a lesser status permitted?

In his *teshuvah* Rabbi Oshry deals at great length with the difference of opinion among the codifiers concerning the circumstances in which *tzitzit* made from stolen materials are forbidden. One school of thought holds that the *tzitzit* are forbidden only if they were stolen after the wool was woven into the threads, but that they may be used if nothing but the raw wool was stolen. Such use is frowned upon and discouraged, however, and is permitted only in the case of a *fait accompli,* not *ab initio.* Another school of thought (Rambam, *Hilkhot Tzitzit* 1:11) holds that *tzitzit* may not be made from stolen materials under any circumstances, even if nothing but the unprocessed wool was stolen. While the weight of opinion is that *tzitzit* may be made from stolen unprocessed wool *(Shulḥan Arukh, Oraḥ Ḥayyim* 11:6, *Rama),* Rabbi Oshry is reluctant to authorize its use solely on this basis.

However, he points out, in this case the wool was almost certainly not brought from Germany by the Nazis. It was stolen by them either from Jews or from gentiles. Undoubtedly the original owners had long since given up any hope of recovering the wool. In Jewish law, where there has been such *yai'ush,* abandonment, of hope of recovery, and subsequent change of ownership, and there is no possibility of identifying the original owner, the property is no longer treated as stolen property which may not be used in the fulfillment of a *mitzvah (Succah* 31a).

In addition, even if we were to assume the unlikely possibility that the Nazis had brought the wool with them from Germany, they have acquired the legal status of a *rodef*—one who pursues an innocent victim with intent to kill—by virtue of their acts of murder and acknowledged practice of killing Jews without provocation. To save the victim, any bystander may kill the *rodef* (Rambam, *Hilkhot Rotzeaḥ* 1), and under such circumstances the property of the *rodef* may also be seized. Hence, Rabbi Oshry reasons, the wool may be taken from the warehouse, even *ab initio;* it may be woven into *tzitzit;* and a benediction may be recited when the *tzitzit* are donned.

As to the question of whether a large *tallit* may be cut up into smaller sections out of which a number of *tallitot ke'tanot* will be made, Rabbi Oshry demonstrates that *tzitzit* have the technical status of *tashmishei mitzvah*, appurtenances to a *mitzvah* (*Megillah* 26b, *Peri Megadim* 153), and as such their status may be changed from a greater degree of sanctity to a lesser one where there is a demonstrable need to do so.

The wool was obtained; the mother of Maier Abelov wove *tzitzit* for all the members of the *Tiferet Bahurim* and for other Jews; and "great was the joy of the members of *Tiferet Bahurim* when they were able to fulfill the great *mitzvah* of *tzitzit* . . . of which our sages tell us 'he who is diligent in the observance of the *mitzvah* of *tzitzit* will merit to see the very Divine presence itself.' . . ."

Another instance of cutting down a large *tallit* into a *tallit katon* is described by Rabbi Zvi Hirsch Meisels.[11] However, the circumstances in this case were somewhat different. When Rabbi Meisels and his family were taken from their home and dispatched to Auschwitz, he managed to snatch up and carry with him one of his most prized possessions—his large *tallit*, adorned with an *atarah* (ornamental silver collar) which he had inherited from his saintly grandfather. When they arrived at Auschwitz, the *tallit* was taken from him together with all his other belongings. Determined to recover it, he managed to get assigned as a laborer in the warehouse where the Nazis stored garments to be sorted and classified before being sent to Germany. He searched through the garments, ultimately finding his *tallit*, and managed to smuggle it back to the block in which he was an inmate.

Rabbi Meisels writes:

> Under the circumstances in the camp, with the wicked *kapos* guarding us, it was impossible to wear a large *tallit* such as this even under one's outer garments. So I cut it down into a *tallit katon*, which I wore underneath my other clothes. The wearing of this *tallit katon* involved considerable danger. All of us wore the uniform camp garb, and the thickness of the *tallit katon* made my appearance discernibly different from the others. If I were to be caught, it was almost certain that I would be beaten, and even killed.

I was caught. One day, when I left the camp bath-house, the guard Penicks (a German Communist serving a life sentence), who was there to see that no one took more than one set of clothing, noticed the difference in my appearance. He ordered me to come over to him so that he could see the reason. He felt my clothing and discovered the *tallit katon*. Enraged, he demanded to know what this was and why I was wearing it. In order that he should not think I had stolen it, I replied that this was *ein Gottes-Kleid*— a religious garment—which I had brought with me from home. Immediately, he began to rain murderous blows upon my head and body and shouted that I should come to his private quarters, where he would teach me something about this God.

When I heard this terrible order, my hair stood on end, for everyone knew the meaning of this order—certain death through a cruel and merciless beating from his powerful hands. I could do nothing, and was compelled to follow him to his room. He began his beating again, angrily shouting, "You pig! You speak of a *Gottes-Kleid* when you see with your own eyes how every day your people and your family are being destroyed in every cruel and violent type of death. In these circumstances you are still able to mention the name of God and to believe in Him, and that He governs the world. How can you say or think that there is a God who rules the world? Why does he not prevent the Nazis from removing you from the world with tortures and torments the like of which no human beings have ever endured before? . . ." So he continued in this vein while I lay upon the ground like a stone. I was silent, overcome by despair and pain. The blood ran from wounds on every part of my body. He ordered me to get up and give him some satisfactory explanation for my continued belief—otherwise I would not leave his room alive.

I knew that this cruel beast would kill me if I did not find some rational explanation which would quiet his murderous wrath. So I said, "I will give you a parable. Unto what is this like? A famous professor of surgery who is noted for his success in performing a certain difficult operation on critically ill patients. He is called in to perform such an operation on a great nobleman. In order to carry it out successfully, he begins to cut very deeply into the patient's body, and makes a number of incisions which he believes necessary. A shoemaker watching the operation, who does not understand anything about the disease or its cure, will wonder and say to himself, 'To what purpose is the professor torturing this patient? Not enough that he is gravely ill, but this professor is adding terrible torture and pain to his afflictions by cutting this beautiful body to pieces. When I repair shoes, I do not cut the hide where it is strong and good.' But would you think the professor would stop what he was doing because of the ignorant shoemaker's opinion? Even though no one else understands what he is doing, he himself does. He will, therefore, not stop until he completes doing what he knows must be done. So it is with the conduct of the Creator. The truth is that we do not understand His actions at all. We do not grasp why He makes these 'incisions' in the best and most lovely part of the people of Israel. But we must realize that we are flesh and blood, with limited understanding. The fact that we do not understand Him does not diminish Him in our eyes." I explained this parable at length and concluded with a word from the *rebbe* of Yarislov, who said that the reason he lived to such a ripe old age was that he never asked questions about what the *Ribono shel Olam* did—but accepted everything lovingly. He was afraid that if he did ask such questions the Almighty would say to him, "If you don't understand, just come up to Heaven and I'll explain it to you." Since he wasn't quite ready yet to go up to Heaven, he never asked questions. So, I advised Penicks, "Don't ask too many questions or they may invite you to come up to Heaven for the answers." Praised be the All-Merciful, my words found favor in the eyes of the wicked *kapo*. With a little smile he said, "You are a clever Jew; you can leave in peace. . . ."

Rabbi Meisels was able, he writes, to wear his *tallit katon,* unmolested, up until a few days before he was liberated by the Americans. At that time a *kapo,* who was angry because he could not find any valuables to take from Rabbi Meisels while searching him, ripped off the *tallit katon,* tore it in two, and threw it into the flames.

Mezuzah

One of the *she'elot* concerning a matter that was cause for concern to the Jews of the Kovno ghetto was whether or not they were required to have a *mezuzah* on their dwellings.[12] Some of those already in place were discovered to be *pasul* (unfit); other buildings, which were being used for the first time as Jewish dwellings, did not have any *mezuzah*. There was no way of securing or preparing *mezuzot*. The hypothesis was put forth that the entire ghetto should have the legal status of a prison. It was entirely enclosed, an electrified fence surrounded it, and there were watchtowers and guards. If it could be demonstrated that a prison was not required to have a *mezuzah,* then perhaps none of the ghetto dwellings would require one.

In his reply Rabbi Oshry quotes the Rambam, *Hilkhot Mezuzah* 6:1, in which he lists the conditions which make it necessary for a dwelling to have a *mezuzah.* In the absence of any one of these, no *mezuzah* is required. In Rabbi Oshry's opinion the ghetto dwellings lacked two of these qualifications. The first, that the residence be a *dirat kavod*—a dwelling of dignity; the second, that it be a *dirat keva*—a permanent residence.

Certainly a prison is not a *dirat kavod.* Since the entire ghetto is in reality a prison, its houses might not, therefore, require a *mezuzah.* However, Rabbi Oshry returns to the question of the status of any prison later in his *teshuvah.* He proceeds with what to him is the more obvious disqualification—that a ghetto dwelling is not a *dirat keva,* a permanent residence. First he describes how many more people are crowded into a room than it was ever intended to hold. The horrible crowded conditions are impossible to describe. Surely this is not a permanent residence, for if the inhabitants but had the opportunity, they would leave immediately. Moreover, each day the Germans take some of the ghetto residents out to be slain, and no one knew when his own time would come. Every day men would part from each other saying, "We will meet again in the world of truth," for they were not certain that they would see each other in this world. Under such circumstances, what could be considered a more temporary residence than the ghetto? Hence there would be no obligation to have a *mezuzah* for those living in it.

Having established that for this reason alone there is no requirement of *mezuzah,* Rabbi Oshry returns to the question of whether a prison— any prison—does require one. He discovers some authorities who believe that *mezuzah* should be placed in a Jewish prison, others who do not. The *Birkei Yosef,* 286:3, and the *Shaar Efrayim,* 83, are inclined to believe that a prison does not require a *mezuzah,* especially if the prisoner will be confined two months or less.

Since the "prisoners" of the ghetto may have their confinement terminated at any moment, they would be even less obligated than a prisoner with a sixty-day term. However, even though there is no obligation to have a *mezuzah,* Rabbi Oshry encourages those who are able to have one on their door to do so, as a constant reminder of the unity of the Holy One, blessed be He. Thus those who affix *mezuzot* to their doors in the ghettto have a great *mitzvah,* although he cautions that they should not recite a benediction since they are not actually required to have one. As for those who do not have *mezuzot* and are unable to obtain them, "let them be neither troubled nor worried," but rely upon God's assistance.[13]

Chapter Six

The Appointed Seasons

And the Lord spoke unto Moses, saying: Speak unto the children of Israel, and say unto them: the appointed seasons of the Lord which ye shall proclaim to be holy convocations, even these are My appointed seasons.

(Lev. 23:1–2)

The "appointed seasons of the Lord," the Sabbaths and holidays, were also appointed by the Nazis for special acts of cruelty and bestiality against the Jews. They took sadistic pleasure in setting unusually arduous tasks for the forced-labor details to complete on the Sabbaths or the holidays, to add the pain of desecrating these holy days to the sufferings already endured by pious ghetto or concentration-camp inmates. Later, they deliberately singled out the sacred days for "actions" in the ghetto or "selections" in the camps in which Jews were sent to death and destruction, in order that the survivors might then look forward to the approach of each new holiday with dread and foreboding.[1]

Yet somehow the "seasons of the Lord" were kept by the Jews living in the Holocaust kingdom. In no small measure, their observance served as a source of strength and a symbol of defiance, enabling the Jews to confound the Nazi "experts" on Jewish culture, and to thwart their avowed intention of compelling them to give up their Judaism before giving up their lives.

The halakhic questions involved in observing the holidays were of many different kinds. Common to the Sabbath and to all the holidays was the Biblical prohibition of labor. As we have already seen (pp. 47-49), when a Jew is compelled to violate a commandment because the non-Jew wishes to derive some benefit from such violation (e.g., from his labor), and not specifically because he wishes to compel the Jew to abandon his religious practices, the Halakhah declares *ya'avor ve'al ye-horeg,* "transgress and do not be killed." Thus, while it might be maintained that the element of religious persecution was often present in situations of forced labor, yet, since in the overwhelming number of instances, the Nazis were interested in and needed the product of this labor for their war effort, it was held by many that martyrdom was not demanded in such cases.[2] Moreover, as Rabbi Oshry and others brilliantly argued, such labor performed under duress did not fall within the Biblical prohibition of labor (see below p. 93). Still, great numbers of Jews did die rather than work on the Sabbath or *yom tov.* Others managed to avoid or evade such labor at the risk of their lives. Many more contrived to do a minimum amount of work and tried at least to avoid performing *melakhot de'oraita,* Biblically forbidden labors.[3]

But in addition to this common negative prohibition of labor, each holiday has associated with it the performance of one or more positive commandments. For example, Passover has its *mitzvat aseh* of eating *matzah;* Succot, its *mitzvot* of dwelling in the *succah* and taking up the *lulav* and *etrog.* We have already discussed the fact (p. 48) that while many halakhic authorities do not hold that the observance of such positive commandments *(bitul mitzvat aseh)* demands the risk of martyrdom, believing Jews in the thousands opted for the opposite point of view in their lives—and, sometimes, their deaths. Their determination to hold fast to holiday observances extended not only to the Biblically ordained festivals, but even to the Rabbinic ones of Hanukkah and Purim. Observing the commandments forbidding eating and possessing *ḥametz* (leaven) on Passover, as well as that forbidding the eating of any food on *Yom Kippur,* raised extraordinary difficulties. Yet often these were wholly or partially surmounted, as we shall see in the following examination of each of the "seasons of the Lord."

The Sabbath

The problem of working on the Sabbath was considered in a rather special situation by Rabbi Oshry in a *teshuvah* on the subject.[4] Nonetheless, his ruling was applied to other Jews confronted with a dilemma similar to that of the questioner in Rabbi Oshry's case.

One of his students, a certain Reb Ya'acov, came to him during the period when starvation was rampant in the Kovno ghetto with the following *she'elah.* He had the opportunity of working in a forced-labor detail in the ghetto kitchen, rather than in the more arduous construction work at the airfield which the Germans were constructing near Kovno. However, in the kitchen he would be forced to violate the Sabbath by cooking. On the other hand, if he did accept the kitchen assignment, his already weakened body might be strengthened by the opportunity of getting somewhat more of the "black soup" which the Germans provided for the Jewish workers. Would cooking on *shabbat* be permitted under these circumstances? Since the lighter labor and the increased food ration might keep him from dying of starvation, would this not be considered a case of *pikuah nefesh,* saving of life, which overrides the prohibitions of Sabbath labor? He further inquired if he himself might eat the soup which he cooked on the Sabbath, since ordinarily a Jew is forbidden to derive any benefit from the product of labor performed by him on the Sabbath.

In his *teshuvah* Rabbi Oshry cites the passages in the Talmud and the Codes dealing with the prohibition of food prepared on the Sabbath (*Hullin* 15a; *Yad, Hilkhot Shabbat* 23; *Shulhan Arukh, Orah Hayyim* 318). While there is some variation of opinion, the decision of the *Shulhan Arukh* (loc. cit.) is: "That which has been cooked on the Sabbath deliberately [*bemezid*] may never be eaten by one who cooked it (even after the Sabbath); others may eat it, after the Sabbath is over." The *Magen Avraham,* commenting on this passage, adds that if the food has been prepared on the Sabbath especially for a certain person's use, the same law applies to him as to the person who actually cooked it, and accordingly he would be forbidden to eat it at any time. Now, since the food prepared by the Jewish forced laborers in the kitchen was only for the use of Jews, Rabbi Oshry suggests that if we followed the *Magen Avraham*'s reasoning, they should not be allowed to eat the food that was cooked by other Jews on the Sabbath.

However, an array of great authorities rule that if one is *compelled* to perform a forbidden labor on the Sabbath, he is not in violation of a Biblical prohibition, but only of a Rabbinic one. Under such circumstances, the product of the prohibited labor would not be forbidden. Thus, the *Rosh Yoseph, Shabbat* 72, concludes that labor performed under duress on the Sabbath is a *melakhah she' enah tzerikhah legufah* —that is, an act of labor which the performer neither desires nor needs for its own sake, but only incidentally, in the accomplishment of some other purpose—in this case, to comply with the will of those forcing him to perform the act. Such a *melakhah she'enah tzerikhah legufah* does not fall within the Biblical definition of *melakhah,* where there must be volition and intent to perform the specific act for its own sake. Using this reasoning, the *Maharsham,* in the *Orḥot Ḥayyim, Hilkhot Shabbat* 278, declares that Jewish soldiers impressed into the army and forced to work on the Sabbath are only in violation of a Rabbinic prohibition. He supports this position with a citation from the *Maharik, Shoresh* 137, who, commenting on the Talmud, *Yevamot* 122b, rules that in the case therein mentioned of a Jew being forced to cook on the Sabbath under threat of death by an idolator, the Jew is only performing a *melakhah she'enah tzerikhah legufah.*

After ingeniously resolving an apparent contradiction to this point of view from the Palestinian Talmud, *Ḥagigah* 2:1, Rabbi Oshry cites a number of authorities *(Peri Megadim* 328:4; *Ḥavot Ya'ir* 183; *Maharik* 193) who agree that where there is duress of any kind, there is no violation of a Biblical prohibition. The *Yad Sholom,* 57, goes so far as to say that under certain circumstances it may be permissible to violate the Sabbath if the government compels one to do so. In our case, then, which is one not of ordinary duress, but of actual threat of death, Rabbi Oshry concludes that it is certainly permissible to violate the Sabbath. He rules, therefore, that Reb Ya'acov ought to accept the assignment to work in the kitchen on the Sabbath. Especially so since, in any event, the Nazis would make him do some kind of labor on that day at the airfield; and what difference does it make whether he violates the Sabbath by cooking or in some other fashion? There is certainly no violation of a Biblical commandment, because work done under duress on the Sabbath is a *melakhah she'enah tzerikhah legufah.* There is not even the violation of a Rabbinic commandment since danger to life is involved.

> Therefore, it is certainly permissible for him to cook on the Sabbath, especially since this will give him some additional food to restore his strength. Also, there is not the slightest prohibition of his eating the soup he cooks on the Sabbath, since under these circumstances everyone agrees that the product of Sabbath labor is not forbidden. For the eating of this food is a matter of *pikuaḥ nefesh*—the saving of life. It may certainly be eaten by other Jews as well, for *pikuaḥ nefesh* overrides the Sabbath, and the resistance of these unfortunates, wasting away from hunger and want has reached its breaking point. Let them, therefore, eat this soup, though it be cooked on the Sabbath, and restore their strength somewhat. May the good Lord

guard us from error, and say to the Destroyer, "Enough!" and bring us forth from darkness to light, from bondage to redemption, speedily in our days, Amen.

For a time, at least, others in the Kovno ghetto managed to avoid Sabbath labor. Rabbi Elḥanan Person, a survivor of that ghetto, writes,

> Many made great sacrifices in order to keep the Sabbath. They agreed to perform the most difficult labor during the week in order to be given freedom from work on the Sabbath. There were those who gave up the special food rations which were distributed to those who would work seven days (including *shabbat*) at the airfield in order to avoid desecrating the Sabbath—this at a time when hunger was too great to bear.[5]

Similar sacrifices are recorded of the Jews in the other ghettos of Nazi Europe. Even in the concentration camps, some individuals managed to avoid working on *shabbat*. The brushmakers in the labor camp of Plaszow (see p. 55 above) "were particularly zealous in the observance of *shabbat* . . . under circumstances which it is impossible to imagine. The Germans had set for us a production quota for each week. We worked madly to complete the required number during the six weekdays so that on *shabbat* we could appear to be working at full speed whereas in reality we did no work at all. Only when the German manager made a sudden inspection (on *shabbat*) did we turn on the machines, since *pikuaḥ nefesh* was involved."[6]

If they could not avoid working, there were other ways in which the Jews of the ghetto and the camps were able to mark *shabbat*. If *kiddush* could not be recited over wine, it could be over bread. Some did not eat their daily bread ration so that on Friday night they could have two bits of bread *(leḥem mishneh)* over which to recite the *kiddush*. Two teen-age boys who had lost their entire families in Auschwitz, and were in a transport from that camp to a work camp at Nieder-Orschel, were overcome with delight when they were each given a whole loaf of bread as rations for the long journey. Simche Unsdorfer writes, "His delight spread to me. 'Yes, a whole loaf of bread also means that we shall be able to make *kiddush* this evening and tomorrow on a whole bread. That's also worth something!"[7] *Kabbalat shabbat* services welcoming the "Sabbath bride" attracted many camp prisoners who would not or could not come to some of the weekday *minyanim* in the camps.[8]

But to many Jews, particularly to Jewish women, since this is considered to be *their* special *mitzvah,* the most significant and meaningful of the Sabbath symbols was the lighting of Sabbath candles, which are kindled prior to sunset on Friday evening.

In the early days of the Kovno ghetto, the halakhic problem concerning Sabbath candles was not any German prohibition of lighting them, but the inability to obtain any. In 5702 (1942) Rabbi Oshry was asked whether it was permissible to fulfill the *mitzvah* of kindling Sabbath candles by lighting an electric light.[9] They also wished his guidance on whether it was permissible to recite the benediction of "kindling the Sabbath lights" under these circumstances. It was impossible at the time to obtain candles. Electricity, however, was freely provided by the Germans to the ghetto.

Rabbi Oshry cites the *Bet Yitzhak, Yoreh Deah* 120:4, as permitting both the kindling of electric bulbs and the recitation of the benediction. Since the *Orhot Hayyim* 264:3, the *Or Hadash,* and the *Mahzeh Efrayim* agree, he concludes that it is permissible, particularly under the ghetto conditions, to use electric bulbs both for the Sabbath candles and as a substitute for the *havdalah* candle at the end of the Sabbath, as well as to recite the appropriate benediction in each case.

He notes, however, that in *M'orei ha-Esh,* 5, the author makes a distinction between two types of electric bulb, frosted and clear. It is this author's contention that the benediction may be recited only if the bulb is clear, and the "flame" of the filament visible—but not if the bulb is frosted. Rabbi Oshry points out that since the only bulbs used in the ghetto were clear ones, there was no question that they might be employed and a benediction recited for the Sabbath candles and for *havdalah.*

Somewhat later, Sabbath candles in the ghetto of Kovno were associated with a moving and tragic scene, which is described by Rabbi Oshry. On the eve of *shabbat shuvah,* 5702 (September 26, 1941), while the Jews were preparing themselves to greet the Sabbath, the Germans suddenly burst into the ghetto. Screaming, they rained fierce blows upon the Jews and forced them to assemble half-clothed and bewildered in an open field. Among them was Ella Shmulewitz, the head of the *Bais Yaacov* (religious girls' school) in Kovno, and her family. She had managed to snatch up her Sabbath candlestick and candles. Her hands were bleeding from the blows the Germans had given her, but she did not let go of the candlestick. As the sun was about to set, Ella Shmulewitz reminded her fellow Jews that it was *shabbat* and they were obliged to sanctify the Sabbath *(lekadesh et hashabbat)* before they proceeded to sanctify the name of God *(le-kadesh et ha-shem)* in martyrdom. She kindled the Sabbath candles, recited the blessing, and prayed that God would receive under His divine protection the souls of those who had sanctified His name on this day of sanctity.

When the sun had set, these *kedoshim* marched to their death at the Ninth Fort, singing the *Lekha Dodi*. Among them were Ella Shmulewitz and a group of *Bais Yaacov* girls.[10]

In her testimony at the Eichmann trial, Rivkah Kuper describes the lighting of Sabbath candles at Auschwitz:

> When we arrived on the eighteenth of January, 1943 we were put into the blocks at Birkenau. They had previously been horse stables. . . . Among the first things we sought were two ends of candles. Friday night we gathered together on the top tier of our block. There were then about ten or twelve girls. . . . We lit the candles and began quietly to sing Sabbath songs . . . we heard choked sobbing from the tiers of bunks all around us. At first we were frightened, then we understood. Jewish women who had been imprisoned months, some of them years, gathered around us, listened to the songs. Some asked us if they might also recite the blessing over the candles. . . . From then on, every *shabbat* we lit the candles. We had no bread, there was nothing to eat, but somehow we managed to get the candles. And so it was on all the holidays. We fasted on Yom Kippur in Auschwitz. True, we ate no *matzot* on *Pesaḥ,* but we traded our rations with the other prisoners for potatoes so that on *Pesaḥ* we could at least fulfill the commandment of "thou shalt eat no *ḥametz*." [11]

Passover

Observance of Passover, the "Festival of Freedom," by the Jews enslaved in the ghettos and concentration camps of Nazi Europe would appear, at first glance, to be anomalous, if not actually blasphemous. Yet upon reflection it becomes evident that this was the festival in the Jewish religious calendar which spoke most directly to their condition. The familiar phrases of the Haggadah took on new and immediate significance:

This is the bread of affliction. . . . now we are slaves—next year we shall be free men. . . . and also that nation whom they shall serve, will I judge; and afterward they shall come out with great substance. . . . It is this divine pledge that hath stood by our fathers and by us also. Not only one hath risen against us to destroy us, but in every generation have men risen against us to destroy us—but the Holy One, blessed be He, delivereth us always from their hand. . . . Pour out thy wrath upon the nations that have not known thee, and upon the kingdoms that have not called upon thy name: for they have devoured Jacob and laid waste his dwelling place. . . . Pour out thy indignation upon them, and let thy wrathful anger pursue them. Pursue and destroy them in anger from under the heavens of the Lord.

Unquestionably, the recounting of the story of the Exodus strengthened their belief that the Jewish people—if not particular individual Jews—would outlive Hitler as they had outlived Pharaoh. Once again, as He had during past persecutions, the Almighty would bring His people from slavery to freedom and from darkness into great light.

But besides the historic and contemporary symbolic significance of Passover, there were halakhic requirements connected with its observance which were as important—or even more important—to the religious Jew. Among these were the fulfilling of the Biblical commandments of (1) eating a quantity of *matzah* at least the "size of an olive" on the first night of Passover; [12] (2) refraining from eating any *ḥametz,* leavened substance, all during the entire Passover period; [13] as well as (3) not having in one's possession during Passover any kind of *ḥametz,* and (4) telling the story of the Exodus, preferably at a *seder* on the first night of Passover.[14] While the retelling of the story of the Exodus is Biblically enjoined, various other elements of the *seder*—including the *maror,* bitter herbs, the Four Cups of wine, the *ḥaroset,* the salt water, and still other *seder* observances —are, in the opinion of most authorities, Rabbinic enactments.[15]

Undoubtedly many Jews went to great lengths to fulfill these halakhic requirements under the most difficult circumstances, because any observance of Passover, the Festival of Freedom, was considered as an act of defiance against the Nazi tyrant. However, it should also be borne in mind that the eating of *matzah* on *Pesaḥ* traditionally has been considered a supremely important *mitzvah.* The prohibition of eating *ḥametz* on Passover, in terms of the penalty mentioned by the Bible—that is, *karet*—is as severe as that of eating on Yom Kippur. The regulations and ordinances governing the preparation of *matzah,* as well as those defining the nature of *hametz* and the avoidance of its possession during Passover, perhaps because of their very stringency, were among those most scrupulously and universally observed by halakhic Jews.

Incredible as it may seem, some Jews in the labor and death camps, even during the very last stages of the Nazi "final solution," were able to bake *matzah,* avoid *hametz,* and even conduct some kind of *seder.* But for most of them the only element of Passover they could be certain would be present was the *maror*—not the symbolic bitterness of bitter herbs, but the real bitterness of actual slavery. The poignant prayer composed by the rabbis of Bergen-Belsen for those who were compelled to violate the laws of Passover may have assuaged to some degree their sense of guilt. Its poignancy is accentuated by the mold in which it is cast—that of the prayer which the pious Jew ordinarily recites when he is about to fulfill the *mitzvah* of eating *matzah:* "Behold I am prepared and ready . . ."

Prayer before Partaking of *Hametz*

Before eating *hametz* let him say: Our Father in heaven, it is known and revealed before Thee that it is our will to do Thy will and to observe the festival of Passover through the eating of *matzah* and by not violating the prohibition of *hametz.* For this our hearts are grieved—that our enslavement prevents us and we are in danger of our lives. Behold, then, we are prepared and ready to fulfill Thy commandment of "Thou shalt live by them and not die by them"; and to carefully heed the warning, "Take therefore good heed and guard thy life very much." Therefore it is our prayer unto Thee that Thou keep us alive and preserve us and redeem us speedily so that we may observe Thy statutes and do Thy will and serve Thee with a perfect heart. Amen.[16]

While the Jews were still confined to the ghettos, however, and there was still some semblance of "normality," it was possible for at least some of the halakhic requirements of Passover to be complied with—this, of course, provided that halakhically sound answers could be found to the questions raised by the special circumstances which obtained in the ghetto.

There are three responsa by Rabbi Oshry on matters involving Passover observance. One *teshuvah* is concerned with obtaining some sort of *matzah* to be eaten the first night of Passover to fulfill the *mitzvah* of eating un-leavened bread. In the Kovno ghetto this was only conceivable, and then only remotely, during the first Passover of the German occupation in 5702. Another *teshuvah* discusses the method of formally divesting oneself of the possession of *ḥametz* during Passover. Since the Bible declares that no leaven may be found "with thee" during Passover, it is necessary to dispose of all *ḥametz* before the holiday. Where this was not possible, the Halakhah provided for *mekhirat ḥametz,* a transaction in which the owner-ship of such items was legally transferred to a non-Jew since then they were no longer "with thee." After Passover such *ḥametz* could be re-acquired from the gentile and used. *Ḥametz* which was not so sold, and which remained in the ownership of a Jew during Passover, was forbidden by Rabbinic law to be used or benefited from in any fashion, even after the holiday.[17] The third of Rabbi Oshry's responsa concerns fulfilling the *mitzvah* of drinking four cups of wine at the *seder*—in the absence of wine!

With the approach of Passover 5702, many *she'elot* were raised con-cerning what might be done to avoid violating the stringent prohibition of eating *ḥametz* at a time when hunger was growing greater from day to day, and when it was impossible to find *matzah* even "the size of an olive" to fulfill the *mitzvah*. Among the *she'elot*[18] were: (1) Under the circumstances, is it permissible to eat the black beans which the Nazis furnished to the ghettos? (By long-standing custom, European Jews did not eat legumes on Passover, although this practice is not mentioned in the Talmud or early codifiers.) (2) A number of people in the forced-labor details had managed to secure a quantity of dirty potato peelings as well as a small amount of flour. They wished to mix the potato peelings with the flour to extend it; and bake *matzah* to eat on the first night of *Pesaḥ*. This would be permissible, according to Talmudic law, since *mei perot,* the liquid of fruits (and vegetables), when mixed with flour does not cause the flour to become leavened. However, it would be necessary to wash the dirt off the potato peelings, and according to the opinion of the Talmud *(Pesaḥim* 38), as codified in the *Shulḥan Arukh, Oraḥ Ḥay-yim* 462, a mixture of water and the potato liquid could cause the flour to become leavened. However, the authorities do not agree on this mat-ter. While the *Rabenu Tam* and others do not consider the product of such a mixture to be *ḥametz gamur*—Biblically forbidden *ḥametz,* the Rambam and others consider it to be absolutely forbidden. Further, the *Peri Megadim* declares that even *Rabenu Tam* holds his opinion only when there is less water than the *mei perot,* the vegetable juice; and not, as is likely in this case, when there is more water than there is of the other liquid. Is there any permissible way to proceed?

In his *teshuvah* Rabbi Oshry readily disposes of the question of using legumes. While the *Ḥatam Sofer, Oraḥ Ḥayyim* 122, declares that it is not permissible to lift the ban on legumes except by an assembly of all the sages of Ashkenazic Jewry, he admits that in a great emergency, involving the saving of life, an individual rabbi may permit their use after they have been blanched. The *Sedei Ḥemed, Ma'arekhet Ḥametz u'Matzah* 6:1, also agrees that while the general ban cannot be lifted, in an emergency it may be temporarily raised. So too the *Teshuvot Maharshal,* 65, in the name of the *Or Zarua.* The *Sedei Ḥemed* cites the example of Rabbi J. Soloveichik of Brisk, who permitted the use of legumes in a year of famine to rich and poor alike. The *Divrei Malkiel,* 88, also permits their use.

Therefore, there is no question that the Jews of Kovno may eat legumes. If it is possible to blanch them, this is preferable. If not, they may eat them in any fashion.

As to the second part of the *she'elah,* the chief rabbi of Kovno, Rabbi Abraham Shapira, ruled that the potato peelings could not be washed in water, but should be wiped clean with dry cloths. The use of water could cause the mixture of the peelings and the flour to become leavened rapidly. But it would be permissible to mix the cleaned, dry peelings with a little flour, and to bake them into *matzah.* Before the baking a number of holes should be made in the mixture with a fork, so as to allow the air to escape as is done in the baking of regular *matzah.*

Rabbi Shapira instructed that these details be widely publicized so that the community would know that it was improper to proceed in any other fashion.

Just before Passover, 5703,[19] the Germans sent to the ghetto the usual quota of bread which they were accustomed to distribute to the Jews through the *Aeltestenrat.*[20] This ration was for a two-week period. Since observant Jews would attempt to save their bread quota and not eat it during Passover but afterward, Rabbi Oshry was asked what to do in this case about the prohibition of *ḥametz* which had been in Jewish possession during Passover and would thus be forbidden after Passover. It was not possible to arrange the customary sale to a non-Jew, for the Jews were afraid to have any contact with a non-Jew, since this was forbidden under penalty of death, and they were also afraid that even if they did manage to make arrangements with a non-Jew, he might inform the Germans that the Jews were concealing and hoarding bread.

In his *teshuvah* Rabbi Oshry cites the passage and the commentaries in the *Shulḥan Arukh, Oraḥ Ḥayyim* 448:5, which prohibits the use of *ḥametz she-avar alav ha-Pesaḥ* even if the Jew has, before *Pesaḥ,* divested himself of ownership by nullification and declaring the *ḥametz* to be *hefker*—abandoned and free to all comers. Though this procedure frees him from being in violation of the Biblical commandment of "no *ḥametz* be seen with thee," nonetheless, the sages feared that if such *ḥametz* were not forbidden, unscrupulous people would retain their *ḥametz* during *Pesaḥ,* and then simply claim after *Pesaḥ* that they had made the declaration divesting themselves of ownership.

In the *Torat Shelamim, 6,* a case is discussed in which a man who was imprisoned was unable to sell or dispose of his *ḥametz* prior to Passover; he simply nullified his ownership of it by declaration. The *Torat Shelamim* holds that in this case, since he had complied with the Biblical requirements, and since he was under duress and there was no question of his attempting to deceive in the matter, the *ḥametz* might be used after Passover—if not to be eaten, at least to be sold. The *Maharim Mi-rakanti* the *Knesset Hagdolah,* the *Olat Shabbat,* and the *She'elot u'Teshuvot Givat Pinḥas* all concur in this decision. However, the *Nodah Be'yehudah,* 1:19, rules that it is still forbidden even when one is prevented from disposing of his *ḥametz* under complete duress. Rabbi Akiba Eiger and the *Ḥatam Sofer,* 114, concur with him. All these varying opinions are cited in the *Sedei Ḥemed, Ma'arekhet Ḥametz u'Matzah* 8.

The *Mishnah Berurah,* however, concludes in *Oraḥ Ḥayyim,* 448:28, that in the case of a great financial loss, where the owner of the *ḥametz* has not disposed of his *ḥametz* because he is in prison or under some other form of duress, its use may be permitted after *Pesaḥ.*

Further, Rabbi Oshry develops the ingenious point that in any case, the bread ration does not belong to the Jew and is not legally his. For according to the German laws, all Jewish property is legally theirs. Even the bread ration, which they distributed through the *Judenrat (Aeltestenrat),* remained their property, and the *Judenrat* was simply their agent for distributing it. This is so, he points out, for if the Germans were to discover anyone taking some of this bread—they would immediately kill him.

Thus, in this instance Rabbi Oshry believes that even the *Nodah Be'yehudah,* and the others holding his opinion, would agree that if the Jew made the legal declaration of nullification and divestment of ownership of the bread ration before Passover, it would certainly be permitted for him to eat it after the festival.

He advised the Jews of the ghetto to act accordingly, since they were unable to act in any other way without danger to their very lives.

According to the Talmud, "Thirty days prior to Passover, one studies and makes inquiry concerning the laws of the Passover." In the course of fulfilling this obligation before Passover in the Kovno ghetto, Rabbi Oshry was studying the details of Passover observance with the group of young men known as the *Tiferet Bahurim*. One of the inquiries raised was how it would be possible to fulfill the *mitzvah* of the Four Cups of Wine which are essential at the *seder* service. Wine was completely unobtainable in the Kovno ghetto. Nor, for that matter, was there any other beverage except tea, sweetened with saccharin. And many of the ghetto householders did not even have that.

In his *teshuvah* Rabbi Oshry first examined the importance of the Four Cups.[21] He cites the Talmud *(Pesahim 99b)*: "Even the poorest Jew shall not have less than four cups of wine, even if he is supported from the public charity kitchen." The Rashbam, in his commentary on the passage, adds that if the supervisors of the public soup kitchen do not provide him with the wine, he is obliged to sell his clothing, or borrow, or hire himself out in order to get enough money to obtain the wine. While there are some differences of opinion as to the precise circumstances under which he must take these actions to obtain wine for the Four Cups, it is clear that even Rabbi Akiba, who says "make thy Sabbath like a weekday [without special foods, etc.] rather than rely upon charity," would say that this does not apply in the case of the Four Cups, because of the obligation to publicize the great miracle of God's redemption from Egypt symbolized by the Four Cups of Wine.

But, Rabbi Oshry points out, this is all well and good when wine can be obtained. Under such circumstances one must make sacrificial efforts to secure it. But what is one to do when there is no wine? In the *Shulhan Arukh, Orah Hayyim* 483, the Rama observes, "In those places where it is the custom to drink a beverage made from honey, called *mehd,* if he has no wine he may take that beverage for the Four Cups . . ."

The essential quality that any beverage (other than water) must have to make its use permissible for the Four Cups appears to be, therefore, that it must be "the wine of the country," commonly drunk by the masses of the people. This point is made more explicitly in connection with the cup, ordinarily of wine, used in the *havdalah* service at the conclusion of the Sabbath. The *Hayyei Adam* thus holds (8:13) that *kvass* and *borscht* may be used for *havdalah* since they are the "wine of the country." The *Mishnah Berurah*, 296:12, however, rules that they may not be so used since they are in the same category as water.

Rabbi Oshry declares that regardless of their possible impermissibility for use in *havdalah, kvass* and *borscht* would be suitable for the Four Cups since the Rama rules that any beverage which is the "wine of the country" may be used for them. But neither *kvass* nor *borscht* was available in the ghetto.

With regard to *havdalah*, there is a controversy about the use of sweetened tea. The *Minhat Shabbat*, 96:9, holds that it may not be used. However, the *Minhah Hadashah*, 96, cites a number of authorities who ruled that it was permissible to use sweetened tea for *havdalah*.

Therefore, Rabbi Oshry writes,

> I ruled that since sweetened tea might be used for *havdalah* even when it is possible to obtain other beverages, because it is drunk by many as the "wine of the country," how much more so in our case, where it is not possible to obtain any kind of beverage. Certainly since the Rama is lenient in this matter of the Four Cups, more so than in the case of *havdalah,* we may authorize the use of sweetened tea, particularly since great *geonim,* the authorities of the previous generation, permitted it even for *havdalah.*

Logic would seem to dictate that a separate benediction should be recited over each of the four cups of tea, as is done when they are wine. However, since the *Peri Megadim,* cited by the *Mishnah Berurah* 483, holds that only one benediction should be recited when the beverage used is apple cider, Rabbi Oshry ruled that the same practice should be followed in the case of tea.

Rabbi Oshry describes the consequence of his ruling:

> Once I had instructed my students that they could fulfill the *mitzvah* of the Four Cups with tea sweetened with saccharin, they accepted upon themselves the obligation of aiding others to fulfill this great *mitzvah* of the Four Cups, which corresponds to the four expressions of redemption. They distributed sweet tea to all those who did not have even this beverage in order that they, too, should be able to

fulfill this practice, which symbolizes redemption; thereby strengthening their spirits and rejoicing their hearts with the hope that the day was not far distant when they, dwellers in darkness and in the shadow of death, the prisoners of the ghetto, would merit redemption from their enemies who had vowed to destroy them.

Of course, similar halakhic problems were faced by the Jews of ghettos other than Kovno. We have some eyewitness accounts of how they were met in the Vilna ghetto and in that of Warsaw. If, as is unlikely, formal *teshuvot* were ever prepared, they must have perished in the flames together with their authors. In Warsaw, on the very eve of the Great Ghetto Revolt of Passover 1943 (April), the *Piazesner rebbe* convened a *bet din* to declare that legumes were permissible because it was a *sha'at ha-dehak* —an emergency situation. Also on the eve of that Passover, in the midst of the pre-revolt tensions, the *rebbe* of Sokolov, Rabbi Benjamin Morgenstern, came to one of the Jewish officials asking for immediate and urgent help. He had prepared many "bills of sale" for the *mekhirat hametz* of Jews in the ghetto, and now, when it was incumbent upon him to transfer all of it to a gentile, there was none to be found in the ghetto. None of the Poles had come to the Warsaw ghetto that day. The official, Abraham Handel, prevailed upon one of the Polish drivers, one Stanski, himself an anti-Semite, to acquire all the ghetto *hametz* for a substantial bribe.[22]

At the risk of their lives, that same Passover eve a group of Hassidic rabbis, including the *Piazesner rebbe* and the *rebbe* of Sokolov, adhered to ancient custom and drew well water *(mayyim shelanu)* for the baking of *matzah*. As they ascended the steps from the deep pit whence they had drawn the water, they even chanted the *hallel* in muted voices.[23]

Such extraordinary dedication to the observance not only of the *halakhot* (laws) of Passover, but also of its *minhagim* (customs), was, of course, rare. In his Warsaw diary, Chaim Kaplan describes another aspect of the gradations of Passover observance which the fearful conditions of the Warsaw ghetto engendered.

> The war and all its horrible consequences have forced even the most devout Jews to disobey the Torah. The matter of survival alone is what determines their ability to fulfill its injunctions. I know a certain Zionist, a scholar, to whom the national holidays were always a source of joy. This year he secretly provided himself with three

loaves of coarse black bread for the first days of *Pesaḥ*. His wife is more strictly observant; she is religious rather than nationalist in her views. Eating *ḥametz* on *Pesaḥ* was inconceivable to her. All through the *Pesaḥ* week, therefore, the two never once ate together; the husband ate his bread at one table while at another the wife ate not *matzot*, heaven forbid [*matzah* was scarce and beyond the reach of most], but ordinary Passover food prepared in special utensils. This happened in a middle-class home. Poor families remained united— husband and wife sat at one table and hungered together. . . .[24]

There are many accounts of halakhic observances of Passover in the labor and death camps. Most such observances were confined to a *"seder"* of one kind or another. But in not a few instances, Jews were able to maintain, at least in part, the halakhic injunctions concerning *ḥametz* and *matzah*. Here are some typical accounts.

On Friday, March 2, 1945 we reached Mauthausen. . . . in those last few difficult weeks that we spent in the concentration camp, some of us worked in the unloading of cars of grain for the warehouse. A number of times, our small group succeeded in taking a little bit of wheat from the warehouse. The religious Jews among us gave up their bread rations in exchange for that wheat. In this fashion they accumulated a small quantity of wheat for *Pesaḥ*. They crushed the grains of wheat with a hammer into a kind of flour. This they baked into *matzot* and so, some tens of Jews were able to conduct the two *sedarim*.

Late at night, when the guards had left our block, several tables were set up in the washing room. We lit two candles, each participant received one small *matzah*. One of us began reciting the Haggadah in a tremulous voice, the rest repeated it after him weeping, their voices choked with sobs. Thus did a small group of Jews, in the shadow of death, conduct the two *sedarim* in the Mauthausen concentration camp.[25]

Rabbi Samson Stockhamer, one of the well-known rabbis of Warsaw, was taken, after the loss of his entire family, to a work camp in the south of Germany. An eyewitness describes how,

On the Festival of Passover, 5705, the last Passover of his life, he refused to eat any *ḥametz*. I knew that this abstention from *ḥametz* was tantamount to fasting for eight days. It would lead to the complete weakening of his strength and endanger his life. I tried to persuade him to eat something because of *pikuaḥ nefesh,* the saving of life. I said to him, "This is not one of the sins which is in the category of *ye-horeg ve'al ya'avor,* where one must sacrifice his life rather than violate the commandment." He replied, "I know the law. But I have another very important reason. There are 2,500 Jews in this camp. It is only right that at least one of them should refrain from eating *ḥametz*. If you know of another one who lets no *ḥametz* pass his lips, then I will think the matter over. But I doubt if such a person is to be found. Therefore, the obligation rests upon me to be the one Jew out of 2,500 who observes the prohibition of *ḥametz* on *Pesaḥ*. I fulfill this obligation joyously and with love." Indeed, no food entered his mouth all eight days of Passover, except for a little water. It was indeed miraculous to see how his powerful will overcame the weakness of his body and how he continued to work at the forced labor together with his fellows. . . .[26]

The Winter of 5605 [1945] was a difficult one in the Feihingen concentration camp in Germany. We suffered from arduous labor in the stone quarries, cold, and hunger; as well as an epidemic of typhus which killed many. To those who died of typhus were added the victims of the cruel murders of the SS men. The result was despair and apathy and indifference to our fate.

But in this death camp there were some who stubbornly held fast to their Judaism until the last moment. Passover was coming. How does one refrain from eating *ḥametz?* A few days before *Pesaḥ* one of the SS men entered the foundry where I was working as a sign-maker. He asked if I could prepare some targets for rifle practice. At the moment an idea sprung into my mind and I proposed it to him. I would prepare targets with figures of soldiers affixed to them. But I would need a quantity of flour with which to prepare the paste. . . . ultimately I received fifteen kilos of flour. When I got the flour to the foundry I told my friends of the miracle—and it is impossible to describe their joy. The will to live, which was almost extinguished, was kindled anew. We "liberated" some wood, scraped a table with glass, and "kashered" it with hot bricks. . . . we began to bake the *matzot*. . . . On the night of the first *seder* we gathered in the foundry as the marranos did in ancient Spain. We started awesomely. "We were slaves." Each of us had three *matzot*. In place of wine we used water sweetened with sugar. We had potatoes for *karpas,* and white beets for *maror*. Salt and water were not in short supply. We recited the Haggadah from some *siddurim* which we had succeeded in hiding all this time. When we were about halfway through the Haggadah, Azriel began to preach to us not to despair and to withstand the test of affliction, for redemption was near. . . .[27]

Rosh Hashanah and Yom Kippur

Rosh Hashanah and Yom Kippur, the "Days of Awe," have always borne a special significance for Jews. "On Rosh Hashanah it is written, and on Yom Kippur it is sealed, who shall live and who shall die"—so reads one of the most familiar of the liturgical poems in the High Holy Day *mahzor* of Ashkenazic Jewry.[28] In normal times Rosh Hashanah and Yom Kippur brought an increased awareness of the fragile and ephemeral nature of life, calculated to arouse prayer, and penitence, and charity which would "avert the evil decree." During the Holocaust, when Jews, living as they were in the midst of death, were concerned not about the next year of life, but often just with the next hour, the poignancy and intensity of the prayers and observances of the *yomim noraim* defy adequate description.

But apart from the emotional dimensions of prayer on these solemn days, there were halakhic observances associated with them whose fulfillment pious Jews would not easily forgo. On Rosh Hashanah it was a *mitzvat aseh,* a positive Biblical commandment, to hear the sounding of the *shofar*. On Yom Kippur there were Biblical commandments, both positive and negative, enjoining the partaking of food and drink. Regardless of the fact that the Halakhah did not require them to do so, Jews took the most extraordinary risks to pray and to sound the *shofar* on Rosh Hashanah and to pray and fast on Yom Kippur. Some accounts:

In the ghetto of Pietrkov during the *yomim noraim* of 5702 [September 1941] many Jews would not change their accustomed practices. In a number of locations in the ghetto they prayed publicly. They could be seen from the street, through the windows, garbed in *tallit* and *kittel,* standing and praying in loud voices. Jews walked through the streets dressed in holiday attire; there were those who even permitted themselves to walk through the street wearing a *tallit,* as if they were in Jerusalem! One must remember that the previous Yom Kippur Jews had suffered because they had held public services, and many had been transported to Germany in punishment.

It appeared as if they had ceased to be afraid. What would the Germans do to them? Shoot them? What matter! At least they would know where they were going to be buried. . . .[29]

Rabbi Joshua Greenwald tells of his concentration-camp experiences:

I learned that one of the inmates had a *siddur.* I went to him secretly with a bit of paper that I had found . . . I copied the *shemoneh esreh* of Rosh Hashanah and Yom Kippur. On Rosh Hashanah we prayed in one of the blocks without the Germans finding out. I recited the *shemoneh esreh* from my handwritten copy, and the rest of the prisoners, about two thousand men, repeated it after me quietly amidst tears and sighs and sobs. We had barely finished the prayers when we were compelled to go out to that day's forced-labor tasks. . . . On the eve of Yom Kippur, at sunset time, the Germans took us out for an "inspection." Knowing that it was a holy day, they kept us there until it was dark so we were unable to eat the morsels of poor bread which we had hidden and put aside to prepare for the fast. . . . we were worried that we would not be able, God forbid, to fast and to fulfill the *mitzvot* of the day properly. Kol Nidre night we prayed in the same place as we had on Rosh Hashanah. However, on Yom Kippur morning we were unable to finish. In the middle of *shemoneh esreh,* the murderers broke in, their weapons drawn. We tried to run away in different directions, but not everyone was able to escape. Those who were caught were beaten murderously. *Ne'ilah* we were able to pray in a hidden spot without any disruption. . . . After Yom Kippur our hearts were overjoyed that we had had the merit of fulfilling the commandment of fasting. . . . At that time I really understood what *kiddesh ha-shem* was . . . As I observed the sacrificial spirit of even Jews who had been irreligious in the past trying now to fulfill the commandments of God and rejoicing in fulfilling the will of their Creator.[30]

Rabbi Zvi Hirsch Meisels describes his Rosh Hashanah in Auschwitz.[31]

On the day of Rosh Hashanah, I went from block to block with a *shofar* in my hand. . . . This was fraught with great danger if the Nazis or the vile *kapos* should become aware of this. But, praised be the Lord, and praised be His name, that I had the *zekhut* to sound the *shofar* on that Rosh Hashanah some twenty times—each time the prescribed number of one hundred blasts. To some extent this restored the spirits of the people; and it eased their consciences somewhat, to know that at least they were granted the opportunity of fullfiling the *mitzvah* of *tekiat shofar* on Rosh Hashanah in Auschwitz.

The fourteen hundred boys who had been condemned to be sent to the crematorium and were locked up in one of the blocks learned that I had a *shofar*. They began to cry out and plead bitterly that I should enter their block and sound the one hundred blasts for them in order that they should have the precious *mitzvah* of *shofar* in their last moments. I did not know what to do. For it was a very dangerous situation. If the Nazis should come suddenly and find me among them, there was no doubt that they would take me to the crematorium. . . . The lads cried out bitterly, *"Rebbe, rebbe,* come, for God's sake; have pity on us; let us have the merit of this *mitzvah* in our last moments." The entreaties of the boys did not allow me to rest. . . . I decided not to turn them away empty-handed. I began to bargain immediately with the *kapos*. After many entreaties, and for a substantial sum which was gathered together, they agreed to my request. But they warned that if I heard the gate bell sound, the signal that the SS were coming, this would mean that my fate would be the same as that of the boys; for then they would not let me leave the block under any circumstances.

I agreed, and I went in to the boys. I took the precaution of stationing my son outside to watch to see if the SS men were approaching the gate. If he saw them he would run and warn me so I could leave immediately—even if it should be in the very midst of sounding the *shofar*.

The truth be written, this decision did not conform to the Halakhah, for I well knew that according to the Halakhah, I should not have taken even the slightest risk for the sake of sounding the *shofar*. But after we had seen with our own eyes, thousands of people killed and burned, or falling dead in the field from hard labor, like sheaves after the harvest, my life had no worth at all, and this was the reason for my coming to this decision. . . . After the sounding of the s*hofar,* when I was about to leave the block, one boy stood up and cried out, "The *rebbe* has strengthened our spirits by telling us that 'even if a sharp sword rest on a man's throat, he should not despair of God's mercy.' I say to you, we can hope that things will get better, but we must be prepared for them to get worse. For God's sake, let us not forget to cry out *shema yisrael* with devotion at the last moment." . . . When I was leaving a few of the boys came up to me to ask if I could possibly provide them with a morsel of bread in order to fulfill the *mitzvah* of eating on Rosh Hashanah. For from the time they had been locked up in the block, no food or water had passed their lips. And they believed that, according to the Halakhah, it is forbidden to fast on Rosh Hashanah. To my sorrow, it was not possible for me to fulfill their request and to re-enter their block. Thus, that bitter day was a fast day for them, and, fasting, they were taken to the crematorium. May God speedily avenge their blood.

Observance of Rosh Hashanah in the ghettos, while it entailed considerable risk, was not as dangerous as it was in the concentration camps. Most such ghetto observances, particularly in the early days of the Nazi occupancy, were not unlike that described by Chaim Kaplan in his Warsaw diary for Rosh Hashanah, October 2, 1940:

We have no public worship, even on the high holy days. There is darkness in our synagogues, for there are no worshippers—silence and desolation within, and sorrow looking on from without. Even for the high holy days, there was no permission for communal worship. I don't know whether the *Judenrat* made any attempt to obtain it, but if it didn't try, it was only because everyone knew in advance that the request would be turned down. Even in the darkest days of our exile we were not tested with this trial. Never before was there a government so evil that it would forbid an entire people to pray. But never before in our history, drenched in tears and blood, did we have so cruel and barbaric an enemy.

Everything is forbidden to us. The wonder is that we are still alive, and that we do everything. And this is true of public prayer too. Secret *minyanim* by the hundreds throughout Warsaw organize services, and do not skip over even the most difficult hymns in the liturgy. There is not even a shortage of sermons. Everything is in accordance with the ancient customs of Israel. . . . They pick some inside room whose windows look out onto the courtyard and pour out their supplications before the God of Israel in whispers. This time there are no cantors or choirs, only whispered prayers. But the prayers are heartfelt; it is possible to weep in secret, too, and the gates of tears are not locked.[32]

While Jews who lived by the Halakhah might, *in extremis,* forgo hearing the *shofar,* or joining in congregational prayer, or abstaining from labor on Rosh Hashanah, eating or working on Yom Kippur presented greater psychological, if not halakhic, problems. It was sometimes necessary for their religious leaders to persuade or compel them to violate Yom Kippur on the overriding grounds of *pikuah nefesh*—saving of life.

In Kovno, on the morning of the first Yom Kippur of ghetto existence, only a very small number of workers appeared at the airfield for their forced-labor duties. The Germans immediately notified the *Aeltestenrat* that if the required number of workers did not appear within the hour, they would launch severe reprisals against the ghetto. Because of the great danger, Rabbi Shapira, the chief rabbi of Kovno, gave permission to work on Yom Kippur. In order to avoid a severe decree against the ghetto, the rabbi called upon all the worshippers in the synagogues and *minyanim* who were scheduled to work that day, to stop their prayers immediately and report to their work locations.[33]

Y. Kashetzky writes, "In the ghetto of Kletzk, *erev Yom Kippur,* the rabbis of the city went from house to house and directed the Jews not to absent themselves from work on Yom Kippur. However, we all fasted the entire day as we worked at our regular task of building the Nazi barracks."[34]

On Yom Kippur in Stutthauf, the Jews in the camp were made to stand lined up in an open field from dawn until late afternoon. Then the Nazis brought out pots of hot, fragrant stew made with carrots, potatoes, and meat. The inmates had not seen the like of such food for years. Each person could have as much as he wanted. The wonderful smell of the stew so tempted the weary, starving Jews that it was difficult to resist. They encouraged each other to overcome the temptation: "Let us not be seduced. . . . Let us show that even starving as we are in this camp, we will not sell our sacred day." There were some who were so weak and feeble that they were overcome by the intoxicating aroma and could not resist; they looked down at the ground in shame, and ate. The rest of the prisoners, among them Jews who had never before fasted on Yom Kippur, did not succumb. They fasted and stood on their feet until night-fall. Towards evening, at *ne'ilah* time, the men of the camp drew close to each other and conducted the *ne'ilah* prayers, and repeated over and over again to each other, "This year in Jerusalem." [35]

Succot

This is what happened in the camp of Plaszow, the first night of Succot, 5702 [October 5, 1941]. This "month of the great holidays" [*yerah etanim*] had been turned into a month of great slaughter in our camp. The oppressors demanded sacrifices from us for every holiday. On Rosh Hashanah two hundred Jews were slaughtered; on Yom Kippur, ninety; *erev Succot,* they took 150 such sacrifices. In spite of all this, what did the remaining Jews busy themselves with and worry about? They sought to find some plan by which they could fulfill the *mitzvah* of *succah* and recite the blessing of *she-he-heyanu* upon the occasion of Succot, "the festival of our joy."

The first night of the festival there was a covert procession in one of the sections of the camp. To where was it heading? To a *succah,* truly a frail and temporary dwelling, which had been erected in the camp lumber yard. The workers employed in that division had built a little "shelter" designed ostensibly to store their tools. The "shelter" had no roof, and it was covered with *sekhakh* made from odds and ends of boards. This *succah* drew unto it all the camp inmates. The news spread from mouth to ear; the Jews endangered their lives by leaving their blocks to go to the secret *succah.* I also was among those who went in to it. For one moment I stayed in the "shelter," recited the benediction of *she-he-heyanu,* and went out the other door. There was no time to remain longer. . . . the long procession was still coming . . .[36]

Auschwitz was blessed not only with a *succah* but with a *lulav* and *etrog* as well. The use of the *lulav* and *etrog* and the recitation of the benedictions over them required not only unusual courage, but an uncommon familiarity with the Halakhah as well. Rabbi Zvi Hirsch Meisels writes,[37]

It is easy to understand that under the Nazi oppressors in Auschwitz it was not possible to fulfill any *mitzvah* the execution of which required some overt action visible to the eye. For the Nazis were prepared to kill anyone caught in such an overt act. Therefore one can imagine how difficult and dangerous it was to fulfill the *mitzvah* of *lulav* and *etrog* on the festival of Succot. The difficulty was a double one. First, the very obtaining of the "four species" under the conditions prevailing in the camp was an impossible task. Second, even if through some miracle one should succeed in getting them, it would be extremely difficult to fulfill the *mitzvah* without the SS becoming aware of the matter.

But, with the help of God, before Succot I succeeded in getting hold of an old *lulav* and *etrog* from the previous year, which had been brought to Auschwitz by Jews from the ghetto of Lodz who had been transported to Auschwitz. I managed to get three of the "four species." The *lulav* and *etrog* from Lodz; *arovot* [willows] which I picked along the bank of the river which ran by the camp. These three species I secretly brought to other Jews in order that they should be able to fulfill the *mitzvah* of *netilat lulav*. The joy of their hearts knew no bounds, when in their sad circumstances they were, at least, able to fulfill this *mitzvah*. They fulfilled it at the risk of their lives, and with extraordinary courage.

The halakhic problems confronting Rabbi Meisels in attempting to fulfill the *mitzvah* of *lulav* in this fashion were complex. The use of a *lulav* from a prior year is permissible, according to all authorities (*Orah Hayyim* 649:6), *be-sha'at ha-dehak,* in an emergency. While most authorities are dubious about this being permissible in the case of an old *etrog,* there are many who permit such use and allow a benediction to be recited (*Rama,* loc. cit.). However, this applies only when all four species are available. Rabbi Meisels had but three. He points out that while the *Shulhan Arukh* (*Orah Hayyim* 651:12) allows only the "taking" of the *lulav* and the other two species, but not the recitation of the benediction, the *Ba'al Hashelamah,* as quoted by the *Maharik* (*Shoresh* 41:3), rules that if one of the four species is missing, the benediction may be recited over the other three. While this position is disputed by the *Hakham Tzevi* (161) and others, there is much reputable opinion (Rabbi Yehudah of Orleans and the *Or Zarua*) supporting the belief that anyone "taking" three of the four species is fulfilling a *mitzvah*. This is particularly the case on days other than the first day of Succot, when the *netilat lulav* is a

Rabbinic ordinance. So Rabbi Meisels rejoiced that he and others were enabled to fulfill the *mitzvah* of *lulav* as defined by the Halakhah.

He writes further,

> I was also able to fulfill the *mitzvah* of *succah*. In one corner of the camp some Jews worked on the repair of beds and sofas. I asked them for a few boards, which I joined together and covered with *sekhakh*. The sitting in this *succah* involved considerable danger since the SS men passed by the place at all hours of the day in order to supervise the work of the Jews. If they found anyone eating in the *succah* they would beat him murderously. In this fashion they caught my son Zalman eating in the *succah,* and it was only through a miracle that he remained alive after the beating about the head and body which they inflicted on him. Thus, one can see the extraordinary sacrifices which the Jews, even in the dreaded camps of death, were willing to make to fulfill the *mitzvot* of the Almighty, whenever and however a *mitzvah* came their way.

Rabbi Meisels's *succah* was not the first or only *succah* in Auschwitz. Rabbi Joshua Ahronson writes:

> In 5704 [October 1943—a year prior to Rabbi Meisels's account] we built a *succah* in Auschwitz. . . . At the edge of the camp, between us and the residences of the SS guards, there were stored long rows of large barrels. Between the rows there was room enough for a large *succah*. We set up a third wall alongside two rows of barrels [a *succah* with only three walls is *kasher*]; and covered the *succah* with *sekhakh*. No one was aware this was a *succah* except those to whom the secret had been imparted. The first night of Succot we went there secretly, recited *kiddush* over a bit of bread which we had saved from the morning, and ate the required *ke'zayit* [olive-sized amount] hastily. This, because the spot where the barrels were stored was surrounded by an electrified fence; and camp inmates discovered there were punished by death. I was in doubt as to whether I should recite the benediction of *lei-shev ba-succah* because of this danger, since, according to the *Rama* in the *Shulḥan Arukh, Oraḥ Ḥayyim* 640:4, if one sits in a *succah* built in a "place of danger" he may not be fulfilling the *mitzvah* at all. Nonetheless, the blessing spontaneously rose to my lips as well as the *she-he-ḥeyanu* benediction,

joyously, because we were able to arrange a *succah* in the very "jaws of the lion." Many of the camp prisoners ate in that *succah*. . . . one would leave, and another would enter.[38]

In the ghetto of Pietrkov, on Succot of 1941, many Jews built *succot*. Jacob Koretz writes,

> In my courtyard there were two *succot*. In one of them there sat a Jew singing *zemirot* in a loud voice. I entered and asked him if he didn't realize where we were; how he dared sing so loudly as if nothing had happened. He just shook his head and continued with his *zemirot*. When he was finished, he turned to me and said, "What can they do to me? They can take my body—but not my soul! Over my soul they have no dominion! Their dominion is only in this world. Here they are the mighty ones. All right. But in the world to come their strength is no more . . ." [39]

In the Warsaw ghetto on Simḥat Torah, the concluding day of the Succot holiday, in October of 1940, Chaim A. Kaplan made the following observations in his diary:

> In the midst of sorrow, the holiday of joy. This is not a secular joy, but a "rejoicing of the Torah," the same Torah for which we are murdered all day. . . . But we have not shamed our eternal Torah. This was not a raucous celebration, but an inner one, a heartfelt joy, and for that reason it was all the more warm and emotional. Everywhere holiday celebrations were organized, and every prayer group said the wine blessing. The Hasidim were even dancing, as is their pious custom. Someone told me that on the night of the holiday he met a large group of zealous Hasidim on Mila Street, and they sang holiday songs in chorus out in public, followed by a large crowd of curious people and sightseers. Joy and revelry in poverty-stricken Mila Street. When they sang they reached such a state of ecstasy that they couldn't stop, until some heretic approached them shouting, "Jews! Safeguarding your life is a positive Biblical commandment; it is a time of danger for us. Stop this!" Only then did they become quiet. Some of them replied in their ecstasy: "We are not afraid of the murderer! The devil with him!" [40]

Purim

One of the group or *hasidim* who prayed and studied together on "tier four" of the wooden bunks in Buchenwald, Yaakov Frankel, writes about Purim in that camp.[41]

> "One night we recalled the old saying, "When the month of Adar comes, joy is increased." [42] We decided to arrange a secret celebration of Purim as the law requires. With the last remnants of my strength I labored for many days in gathering all sorts of scraps of paper scattered about the camp—a torn order from the Nazi officers, a coarse wrapping from a sack of cement, or a bit of a German newspaper whose margins were blank. All of these I collected with especial diligence because I had decided to write the *megillah* of Esther on them—from memory.
>
> We divided the bundles of scrap paper among the group. Altogether we had only one pencil; more correctly the lead from one broken carpenter's pencil. It was passed from hand to hand. Each one wrote several verses that he remembered from the *megillah*. . . . When the Fast of Esther was completed on Purim eve, we gathered together at the appointed hour on the "upper level" of the block. A number of the unfortunate prisoners who lived on the lower tiers sensed our evident joy. "We, too, wish to take revenge on the wicked Haman!" Their dull eyes glowed with a last glimmer of faith and hope. I suggested that we begin the reading of the *megillah* at 10:00 P.M. or even as late as 11:00 P.M., fearing that if it were earlier the plan would be discovered by the murderous guards.
>
> According to the *din* [law] it was clear to us that we could not recite the benediction *al mikrah megillah,* since the *megillah* had been written on these different scraps of paper by our trembling hands. But the reading itself was marked by an extraordinary exaltation and great enthusiasm. Most important, when we finished reading it, and we began to sing *Shoshanat Yaacov,*[43] the song burst forth from our mouths like a mighty storm. It seemed to us as if all of Buchenwald held its breath for a moment and listened trembling to the words, "Cursed be Haman, who sought to destroy me; blessed be Mordekhai, Mordekhai the Jew." The next morning we got up and went our difficult way, as always. Yet we sensed that something had changed in the atmosphere of the camp. Just because we had the

boldness to cry out aloud, "Cursed be Haman!" and it was clear to everyone just who was meant by "Haman," the terrible pressure was lightened just a little bit.

Hanukkah

In Auschwitz, Rabbi Sinai Adler was part of a group of young religious boys from Central Europe and Greece, imprisoned together in one of the blocks of the camp. He writes,

> Each day we gathered together in one of the corners of the block to pray. Our praying together and our observance of the *mitzvah* created strong bonds of friendship among us in spite of our different countries of origin. The days of Hanukkah drew near. We were lucky enough to be able to get hold of one candle, which for us meant a great deal. The first night of Hanukkah we gathered together on the upper tier of one of the platforms, and we lit the candle which was so precious to us. The burning candle kindled in our hearts new hope for the future and strengthened our trust in the "rock of our salvation . . ." [44]

In Nieder-Orschel (part of the Buchenwald industrial-camp complex), seventeen-year-old Simche Unsdorfer from Bratislava kept

> a little diary in which I entered the Hebrew dates and festivals. I discovered with great delight that Hanukkah . . . was only a few days ahead. I decided that we should light a little Hanukkah lamp even in Nieder-Orschel, and that this would go a long way toward restoring our morale. . . . Benzi [his fellow-townsman and companion] was enthusiastic about my idea. . . . Two problems had to be overcome: oil had to be "organized," and a place had to be found where the lighted wick would not be seen. There was no lack of oil in the factory, but how could we smuggle even a few drops into our barrack in time for Monday evening, December 11, the first night of Hanukkah?
>
> We knew, of course, that Jewish law did not compel us to risk our lives for the sake of fulfilling a commandment. But there was an urge in many of us to reveal the spirit of sacrifice implanted in our ancestors throughout the ages. We who were in such great spiritual

as well as physical distress felt that a little Hanukkah light would warm our starving souls and inspire us with hope, faith, and courage to keep us going through this long, grim, and icy winter. . . . We decided to draw lots. The first name drawn would have to steal the oil; the third would be responsible for it, and hide it until Monday evening; and the fifth would have to light it under his bunk. I was drawn fifth. . . . Grunwald . . . persuaded the hated *Meister* Meyer that his machine would work better if oiled regularly every morning, and that this could best be arranged if a small can of fine machine oil was allotted to us. . . . On Monday evening . . . I put the oil in the empty half of a shoe-polish tin, took a few threads from my thin blanket, and made them into a wick. . . . I made the three traditional blessings, and a little Hanukkah light flickered away slowly, under my bunk. Not only my friends from the "religious" table were there with us but also many others from the room joined us in humming the traditional Hanukkah songs. . . . For a moment nothing else mattered. We were a group of Jewish people, fulfilling our religious duties and dreaming of home and of bygone years.

Unsdorfer and his friends nearly lost their lives because of the Hanukkah menorah. The Nazi *untersturmfuhrer* smelled the burning oil and was about to discover it under Unsdorfer's bunk when an air-raid warning sounded. The search was called off. "In delight I grabbed my little Menorah and ran out with it. . . . Outside, in the ice-cold, star-studded night, with the heavy drone of Allied bombers over our heads, I kept on muttering the traditional blessing to the God who wrought miracles for His people in past days and in our own time . . ." [45]

Chapter Seven

Out of the Depths

A number of the *she'elot* propounded to Rabbi Oshry in the Kovno ghetto are concerned not with ritual observance but with *dinei mammo-not*—property rights. Included in this chapter are three such *she'elot* having to do with the permissibility of using the belongings of Nazi victims, and the propriety of opening a grave in order to rescue property buried inadvertently with a Jew murdered by the Germans. There are questions of *issur* (ritual) as well as *mammon* (property rights) involved in each of these. The very raising of the questions reveals an attempt to adhere scrupulously to the Halakhah under circumstances of dreadful temptation in which one might expect halakhic norms to be ignored. Also included in this chapter is a ruling by Rabbi Oshry, involving the ownership of books recovered after the liberation, in which his decision ignores sentiment and conforms to the rigorous demands of the Halakhah as he sees it.

We have also included in this chapter several unrelated *teshuvot* which shed more light on the cruel and unusual difficulties which the Nazis devised in order to prevent Jews from living, and even from dying, in conformity with the requirements of their faith.

The Property of Martyrs

On the eve of Rosh Hashanah, 5702 (September 21, 1941), the Jews of the Kovno ghetto did not fill their quota for the forced-labor detail. (Each day they had been required to provide about a thousand men for the construction of an airfield near the city.) The Germans vengefully fell upon the ghetto to seize men for the labor detail, and in their anger they shot and killed two men who had risen early for the *erev Rosh Ha-shanah selihot* service. These were Reb Yitzhak Boim, owner of an ironmonger's shop on Linkeve Street in Slobodka, in whose hand was a Rosh Hashanah *maḥzor,* and one Reb Berel Mendelowitz.

The Nazis forced the Jews of the ghetto to dig a pit to bury the dead and made them strip the bodies of their outer garments before burying them. They then left these outer garments for the Jews who had performed the burial. The garments were not bloodstained. Rabbi Oshry was asked, Is it permissible to use the garments or derive any benefit from them?

Rabbi Oshry's *teshuvah* is based on a passage in the *Shulḥan Arukh, Yoreh Deah* 364:4, and the commentaries upon it.[1] The passage reads, "If a Jew is found slain, he is buried in his clothing exactly as he is found, without the usual shrouds. Even his shoes are not to be removed."

The reason for this practice is given by the *Shakh,* 364:11, who cites various authorities who amplify the provision of the *Shluḥan Arukh* to include the burial even of any blood-soaked earth on which the victim of violence has been found, as well as a prohibition against washing or cleansing the body in the usual *taharah*—process of purification. The rationale for this is that burial must include the lifeblood of the deceased, and when he has died by violence, it may be that his blood has been soaked up by his clothes, by his boots, or by the earth under and around his body. Hence all of these must be buried, and then the body is not to be washed, lest the blood be removed in the process.

However, the *Bayit Ḥadash,* on the passage cited, gives an additional reason for the burial in his clothing of a Jew who has died violently. In the case of a Jew who has been murdered by gentiles, even though the flow of blood had stopped, he is buried in his clothing "to arouse wrath [at the outrage] so that revenge will be taken."

Rabbi Oshry declares that since there was no blood whatsoever on the outer garments of the two men slain by the Nazis, there need be no concern about the interment of the "lifeblood." From that point of view their use should be permitted. Before addressing himself to the question of "arousing wrath," he anticipates a number of other halakhic problems which should be considered.

There are cases *(Yoreh Deah* 364:4; *Shivat Tzion* 58) dealing with the preparation by a son of a grave or a monument for his father where, for one or another reason, the grave or monument prepared could not be used, and as a result the father was interred elsewhere or a different grave marker was used. In such cases the son may not sell or otherwise derive benefit from the original grave or monument out of respect to the memory of his father, for whom they had been intended. It might be argued here, too, since it was originally assumed that the victims were going to be buried in their outer garments, that it would be improper and a sign of disrespect to use them for anything else once they had been "designated" *(hazmanah)* for that purpose.

Rabbi Oshry declares, however, that this question of "honor of one's father" applies only in normal times. But in this difficult and unsettled period, when the "sword bereaves from without and in the chambers is terror" (Deut. 32:25), certainly these martyrs could be paid no greater honor and would have no greater satisfaction than that of knowing that their children could use these garments to warm their bodies, or could sell them in order to buy food to save themselves from starvation. Undoubtedly this would be the desire of the dead, and it is "honor" that we pay them in giving their children this clothing so that they may remain alive, and so that their names and those of their children not be blotted out—despite the wrath and anger of the murderers, whose desire and plot it was, to destroy their seed and that of the people of Israel.

Rabbi Oshry further points out that a case cited by the *Birkei Yosef, Yoreh Deah* 349:5, in which shrouds which were removed from one dead body might only be used for another dead body, but not for the benefit of the living, does not apply here, since the outer garments in question were never specifically designated as burial garments while they were being worn, or even immediately after the death of the victims.

As to the matter of "arousing wrath and assuring revenge"—in our case, says Rabbi Oshry, it is certain that the martyred victims would prefer the saving of the lives of their children from starvation to the arousing of wrath against the cursed murderers. Therefore, he permitted the use of the garments for the benefit of the children of the slain victims.

A similar *she'elah* was brought before Rabbi Oshry after the eighth of Heshvan, 5702 (October 29, 1941). On that day some ten thousand Jews were slaughtered in the infamous Ninth Fort of Kovno. Subsequently, Reb Elijah Zhidikov, who was one of the forced laborers in the "Jordan Brigade," came to Rabbi Oshry and told him that in the place of his work in the fort, there was a storehouse of clothing which the Germans had stripped from their victims before murdering them. The pockets of the garments contained letters, pictures, and other personal objects usually found in people's pockets, and hence there was no doubt that these were the clothes of those who had been killed. Moreover, some of the members of the work brigade had found among the photographs, pictures of their own brothers or mothers or other relatives and friends. However, there was not the slightest sign of blood on the garments, which was conclusive proof that the murderers had stripped the victims before killing them. Reb Elijah Zhidikov asked if it was permissible to use any of this clothing.

In his *teshuvah* Rabbi Oshry cites many of the sources referred to in the previous one.[2] In the present case, unlike the earlier one, the garments were taken off before death, and not simply before burial. This is evident from the lack of blood, as well as from the testimony of an eyewitness, who escaped and indicated that the Germans had ordered the victims to strip before being executed. Hence, in this case, there are even less grounds for treating the clothing as garments intended for burial—which, once such *hazmanah,* designation, had taken place, would indeed be forbidden. Further, as was generally the case, the victims were deceived by the Germans until the last possible moment. While they were clothed, they still did not know that they were destined for death. Hence, it did not enter their minds at any time that the clothes they were wearing would be their burial garments.

Accordingly, Rabbi Oshry permitted use of the garments not simply for the benefit of the children of the victims, but also for any surviving Jew. "For certainly these pure martyrs would not object to this; on the contrary this would bring them a measure of satisfaction in the 'world of truth,' and their souls, which are bound up in the bond of life, would rejoice in heaven at seeing their unfortunate brethren, who are found 'in trouble and captivity,' clothed and protected by the garments which they wore during their own lifetimes."

A related *she'elah* was presented to Rabbi Oshry on the tenth of Ḥeshvan, 5702 (October 31, 1941), after the major *aktion* in the Kovno ghetto, when he was approached by one of the survivors. The man was from a prominent Jewish family of Kovno. He and his family had shared living quarters with another Jewish family in the ghetto. On the day of the *aktion,* all the members of that family had been killed. They had no living relatives. Now he and his wife and small children were literally starving. The other family had left a few pitiful possessions in the apartment. Was is permissible for him to take these, sell them, and buy food for his wife and children?

In his *teshuvah,*[3] Rabbi Oshry cites the Talmud *(Baba Kamma* 114a), the Rambam *(Hilkhot Gezeilah* 6:6), and the *Shulḥan Arukh (Ḥoshen Mishpat* 259:7), which agree that he who snatches his neighbor's property from predatory beasts, or draws it up from the bottom of the sea, or seizes it when it is being swept away by a flooding river, or rescues it from pillaging idolators, acquires title to the property. The reason for this, as explained by Rashi, is that the owners, in the face of its apparently certain loss under such circumstances, abandoned all hope of ever recovering it. According to the Halakhah, this *yei'ush* (abandonment), together with the change in actual physical possession of the property *(shinu'i reshut),* is sufficient to transfer ownership.

Hence in our case, even if there were claimants to the property from the family of those slain by the Nazis, undoubtedly they would have abandoned any hope of ever receiving it. For it was known to everyone that after the Nazis had mercilessly slain and slaughtered the Jews, they would plunder any object of value that had belonged to their victims. Whatever was left of insignificant worth, such as the objects about which the inquiry was being made, were left *hefker*—free for anyone to take. Thus there need be no qualms about taking them. Certainly the martyred family would have preferred that their belongings be used to keep a Jewish family alive, rather than be taken by their murderers.

Rabbi Oshry notes that after the liberation from the Nazis, he came across a responsum by Rabbi Shlomoh Tzror, in *She'elot u'Teshuvot Ḥut ha-Meshulash,* concerning a Christian who pillaged Hebrew books, which he subsequently sold to a Jew. Afterwards, the original owner sought the return of the volumes which had been stolen from him. The purchaser maintained that they belonged to him, since he had paid for them, and since, if he had not bought them, they would have been burned, as were so many others, by the gentiles. In this case, because the gentile did not recognize the value of the books and simply sold them for the worth of the paper, Rabbi Tzror ruled that the original owner could regain them if he repaid the money paid to the pillager. But in the case of objects other than books, Rabbi Oshry declares, he would rule that title passes to the person who has rescued objects which the owner would assume to have been irretrievably lost.

Therefore, in the instant case, Rabbi Oshry ruled that it was certainly permissible to take the objects left behind by the martyred family. Even in the unlikely event that relatives of the deceased would appear at some future time to lay claim to the property, there would be no legal obligation to return it to them.

Opening of a Grave

Not the least of the difficulties confronted by the Jews of the Kovno ghetto was starvation. As the food supplies dwindled and the situation worsened from day to day, they sold everything they possessed in order to get a piece of bread to sustain their lives and those of their families. But while there was no lack of those willing to sell their possessions, there were no purchasers.

The ghetto was completely isolated. The condition of all was equally desperate. Every person was willing to sell whatever he had left which had not been taken by the Germans, but there were no Jews able to buy. Without exception none of them had even the wherewithal for a loaf of bread. Moreover, there was practically no contact or communication with the Lithuanian gentiles, for the Germans had forbidden them to enter the ghetto on pain of death, just as they had forbidden the Jews to leave it.

But there was one method still available for some commerce and trading. Each morning the Germans would take a number of Jews from the ghetto for the forced-labor detail. Each evening these would return to the ghetto. While they were outside the ghetto walls, some of them managed to come into contact with the gentiles secretly and to do some trading and bartering with them.

With the aid of these forced laborers, some ghetto residents managed to sell the remnants of their jewelry, such as rings, bracelets, precious stones, and pearls. They could not dispose of larger items because the Germans searched them upon their departure and return. Understandably, the forced laborers who risked their lives in these transactions also received a share of the food which resulted from them.

On one occasion, a ghetto Jew gave to one of the men in the forced-labor detail a precious stone to be sold to a gentile. In order to be able to slip away from his work station to come into contact with the gentile, he needed to remove from his sleeve the yellow *Magen David* which all Jews were forced to wear as identification. Also, in order that the Germans not suspect that he was Jewish, he walked on the sidewalk—a privilege which had been forbidden to Jews, who were compelled to walk in the middle of the street.

As he was walking on the sidewalk to his rendezvous with the gentile, he was recognized by the Germans, who shot him dead. This was his punishment for being outside the ghetto and for daring to walk on the sidewalk, which was reserved for "free" men. After they had killed him, the Nazis brought his body to the ghetto, and turned it over to the Jews to serve as a sign and a warning that they not do as he had done. The Jews buried the man in his clothing, in accordance with the Halakhah governing those who die a violent death, not knowing that he had sewn into his jacket the precious stone belonging to the other Jew. The owner of the stone, learning of the burial, came to Rabbi Oshry asking that the grave be opened, so that he could get his jewel back. He maintained that his very life and that of his starving family depended on his retrieving this stone, his sole hope of surviving. Was it permissible to open the grave?

The basic concern of the Halakhah in this case, as Rabbi Oshry points out in his *teshuvah,*[4] is that of *nivul ha-met.* The viewing of the decomposing flesh of the deceased by the living is considered to be a disgrace to the dead person and to diminish his dignity. There is also a subsidiary issue, that of *hareidat ha-din*—disturbing the peace of the dead, which Rabbi Oshry also discusses. He cites the Talmudic passage in *Baba Batra* 154a, in which Rabbi Akiba, because of *nivul ha-met,* forbade the opening of a grave in order to determine whether the deceased was legally a minor (which would make transactions prior to his death invalid). It is clear, Rabbi Oshry points out, from the subsequent *gemara* and the commentaries that if funds belonging to others were involved—and not merely funds of the deceased's family—those others could insist on the grave's being opened despite the factor of *nivul ha-met.* In the instant case, there are funds belonging to others—that is, the precious stone—and its owner has a right to demand that the grave be opened even though there might be such *nivul ha-met.*

Moreover, Rabbi Oshry finds that the Palestinian Talmud, *Moed Katan* 3:3, implies that there is no *nivul ha-met* until after three days following burial. The request to open the grave in Kovno was within the three-day period. Further, the *Arukh Hashulhan,* 363:8, rules that a grave may be opened wherever it is necessary for the fulfillment of a *mitzvah* and there is a loss of money to others. In the case before him, it was not simply a question of loss of money, but of *pikuah nefesh*—of saving the owner of the stone and his family from starvation. Further, in the *She'elot u'Teshuvot Maharsham,* 2:112, he holds that whenever opening the grave is for the honor of the dead, it is permissible to do so. What greater honor could there be for this dead person, asks Rabbi Oshry than to know that the stone was restored to its rightful owner, and that it should not be said of him that he took with him to the grave that which belonged to others?

After discussing the opinions of other authorities who have reservations about opening a grave, particularly because of *hareidat ha-din*—disturbing the peace of the dead—even under these circumstances, Rabbi Oshry concludes, nevertheless, that where opening a grave, as in this instance, will be of benefit to the living and bring honor to the dead, it is permitted. If we may set aside the question of *nivul ha-met* because of *pikuah nefesh,* so too, he concludes, may we set aside the fear of *hareidat ha-din.*

The grave was opened and the jewel returned to its owner.

The Finder Keeps

On the first of Adar, 5702 (February 18, 1942), the Nazis ordered that every Hebrew book to be found in the ghetto, without exception, whether sacred books, such as prayer books, Bibles, and Talmudic volumes, or secular books, be turned over to them under penalty of death. This special order was given to the Jewish ghetto police for implementation. Understandably, the Jews began to bring the books to the central assembly point which the Germans had designated. Included were the books of all the synagogues, as well as volumes from private libraries belonging to individuals, such as the library of the late great chief rabbi of Kovno, Rabbi Isaac Elhanan Spektor. Among these books were very rare ones of great value, particularly some of those from the library of Rabbi Spektor.

At great personal risk, one of the officers of the Jewish ghetto police, Yitzhak Greenberg, secretly took out some of the rarest volumes, put them into a chest, dug a deep pit, and covered it with dirt. It was his hope that if one day the Jews of the ghetto should be rescued, then the redeemed remnants of his people would once again have these treasures in their possession.

And when the inhabitants of the ghetto finally were freed, those remaining alive began to search and dig for the possessions which some had managed to conceal in the ground from the plundering Germans. One of those who was digging in the ruins of the ghetto found the chest of books which had been hidden there. He recognized their value immediately and exulted over his find, because he believed they now were his property in accordance with Jewish law in the case of anyone who finds ownerless and abandoned articles.

When the news of the finding of the chest of books spread quickly throughout the rescued community, all came to see and to feast their eyes on the precious volumes. Suddenly, one of the men recognized his own property. Among the volumes were several which had belonged to him—inscribed with his name, and the names of his father and grandfather. Since the volumes were valuable, they had been handed down as a family inheritance. He began to demand of the finder that they be returned to him. The finder maintained that he had a legitimate claim to the books, as one who has found an ownerless and abandoned article, or who rescues an article from the bottom of the sea. The two claimants asked Rabbi Oshry to render a decision in accordance with the Torah.

In his decision,[5] Rabbi Oshry cites the Talmud, *Baba Kamma* 114a: "He who saves articles of value, from a river, or from a marauding band or from robbers, if the owners have abandoned hope of recovery, they belong to him." Rashi explains that in all these cases, it is assumed that there has been *yei'ush,* abandonment of hope of recovery, and therefore that the finder has acquired legal ownership through the combination of *yei'ush* and possession (*shinu'i reshut*). The Rambam, *Hilkhot Gezelah* 6:6 and 11:1, and the *Shulḥan Arukh, Ḥoshen Mishpat* 259:7, codify the provision thus: "He who saves valuables from a lion, or a bear, or from the bottom of the sea, or from idolators, they belong to him, even though the original owner stands and protests."

Certainly, says Rabbi Oshry, the original owners of these books abandoned all hope of recovery once the Nazis had taken them. Not only their possessions but their very lives were in the hands of the Germans to do with as they wished. Thus there is no question that there was *yei'ush.* Moreover, the *Rashba* holds that in the case of a conquering army, there is not even a need for *yei'ush,* since the conqueror acquires title to the booty under the laws of war. Anyone who subsequently acquires it from him also has a clear title according to the *Rashba.* The Germans were a conquering army.

However, Rabbi Oshry cites *Tosafot* from *Baba Kamma* 114b, which is of the opinion that in the case of stolen books, even though they may have been taken by a non-Jew, there is no automatic *yei'ush.* This is because the original owner knows that the thief, whether Jewish or non-Jewish, having no other market for them, will inevitably attempt to sell them to Jews, and he, the owner, will ultimately recover them. If this were so, except for the point of the *Rashba,* who requires no *yei'ush,* then the orginal owner of the books in our case should be entitled to claim them.

However, there is a difference in our case. Since all the Jews knew that the intention of the Germans was to grind up the books into pulp for making paper, they could not have had any hope of their ultimately being sold to other Jews and returned to them. After considering several other possibilities which might make it lawful for the original owner to recover the books, Rabbi Oshry nevertheless concludes that in view of the original owner's undoubted abandonment of all hope for recovery, and by virtue of the factor of the finder's possession, the books are now, according to the Halakhah, the property of the finder.

Desecration of Torah Scrolls

Immediately after the invasion of Poland in September of 1939, when the Nazis overran Jewish community after community, they began a pattern of destruction of synagogues and Jewish sacred objects. They made a point of publicly destroying and defiling *sifrei-torah* (scrolls of the Torah) in an apparent attempt to display their contempt for Judaism and the powerlessness of the Jewish God, as well as to undermine the morale of the Jews. *Sifrei-torah* were torn, burnt, tossed into the streets, and covered with filth and excrement. Sometimes the Jews themselves were forced to take part in the work of destruction.[6]

In a number of cases they heroically refused to lay hands on the *sifrei-torah* even though the Halakhah does not demand that human life be sacrificed to save a scroll. Thus in Aleksander, at the end of September 1939, the Germans piled a great number of *sifrei-torah* in the middle of the street and set them afire. One Motel Hochman, a resident of the town, passed by and was ordered by the German commandant to rip one of the scrolls into bits. He refused. The officer beat him. He still refused. The German warned him that he would be shot unless he obeyed the order. Hochman was placed against the wall and the Germans leveled their guns ready to fire. Hochman cried out *"Shema Yisrael!"* and prepared to die. Fortunately, a German manufacturer who was an important citizen of Aleksander was able to prevail on the Nazis to release Hochman and let him off with a severe beating.

In Widowa, Rabbi Abraham Mordecai Maraco did not fare as well. The young rabbi, some thirty years old, was a promising Talmudic scholar and the editor of a rabbinic journal. In that same month of September 1939, a number of German officers entered the rabbi's house in a search for Jewish sacred objects, which they aimed to destroy. They discovered a *sefer-torah* and ordered Rabbi Maraco to tear it. They threatened to burn him alive if he refused. He refused; they poured gasoline over him, set him afire, and tossed the scroll into the flaming pyre which his body had become.

Not all Jews were able to display comparable heroism or to go beyond the demands of the Halakhah in protecting even the most sacred object of the synagogue. In the Kovno ghetto, after the scrolls were defiled, Rabbi Oshry confronted a different halakhic problem.

On the fourth of Elul, 5701 (August 27, 1941), the Germans organized a hunt for stray dogs and cats, rounded them up into the "new *bet midrash*" *(Die Nayeh Kloiz)* in Slobodka, and shot the animals to death in the synagogue. They forced numerous Jews to come and watch this desecration of the sanctuary, and compelled a number of them to tear a *sefer-torah* apart with their hands and use its parchment to cover the bodies of the animals, so that the holy scroll was besmirched with blood and dirt. A *she'elah* was presented to the chief rabbi of Kovno, Rabbi Abraham Shapira as follows: Were those who had witnessed this tragic event, especially those who had actually torn the *sefer-torah,* obliged to undertake some special act of *teshuvah*—of penance—such as fasting? Should a fast day be proclaimed for *all* the inhabitants of the ghetto who had heard of the event and who considered it an evil portent? This, so that through fasting and prayer and repentance they would not only pour out their hearts in prayer to the Almighty to have mercy upon them, but also to strengthen their own faltering spirits. Since Rabbi Shapira was gravely ill at the time, Rabbi Oshry was given the responsibility of determining what should be done.

In his *teshuvah,*[7] Rabbi Oshry cites the relevant Talmudic passage from *Moed Katan* 26a: "Rabbi Ḥelbo says in the name of Rabbi Huna, 'He who sees a scroll of the Torah torn asunder, is obligated to rend his clothing [as a sign of mourning] twice; once for the parchment, and once for the writing' . . ." However, in the Palestinian Talmud the text reads, "he who sees a scroll of the Torah *burned* . . ." The *Alfas* and the *Rosh* follow the reading of the Palestinian Talmud, and in their opinion only he who sees the burning—not the tearing—of a *sefer-torah* is required to rend his garments.

However, although the *Shulḥan Arukh, Yoreh Deah* 340:37, also uses the expression "a *sefer-torah* that is burned," the commentators, such as the *Taz,* the *Bah,* and the *Ba'er Heiteiv,* all agree that while the *Shulḥan Arukh* uses the term "burned," the same consequences would apply if it were torn or otherwise violently destroyed, since the Babylonian Talmud, which is more authoritative than the Palestinian, reads "torn."

Accordingly, Rabbi Oshry declares that while those who actually saw the desecration of the scroll might need to rend their garments, those who merely heard of the incident, but were not personally present, are not obligated to do so, since the Talmud specifically uses the term "he who sees . . ." This point of view is further documented by Rashi on the passage in the *Alfas* in *Moed Katan,* who uses the expression "he who sees with his own eyes," which implies that there must be a personal viewing of the desecration. So too the *Ḥakham Tzvi,* sec. 17, writes that one must be a personal witness to the desecration in order to incur the obligation of mourning, and the *Agudah* on *Moed Katan* also makes this point.

What, however, about the obligation to fast? It would appear at first that all who saw the desecration ought to be obligated to fast; for surely this terrible incident should be taken no less lightly than the case of those who see a *sefer-torah* dropped accidentally, where the practice is to fast. Rabbi Oshry then examines the authority for the very practice of fasting on the part of those who see a *sefer-torah* accidentally dropped. All those cited agree that there is no clear evidence for the practice in the Talmud and the Codes. Some attempt to justify the practice in various ways by indirect and ingenious deductions from Talmudic passages *(Ḥayyim Sh'al* 12; *Divrei Ḥayyim, Yoreh Deah* 49; *Kapot Temarim, Succah* 41; and others). However, there is considerable weight of opinion, even here, that only the person who has himself dropped the *sefer-torah* is obligated to fast—not the onlookers (cf. *Birkei Yosef, Shiyurei Berakha* 382:4 and *Teshuvot Zeikher l'Yehoseif, Oraḥ Ḥayyim* 31).

Rabbi Oshry, therefore, concludes that certainly those who saw the episode should fast, if they are able to, since so many great authorities are of the opinion that one is obligated to fast even if he merely sees a *sefer-torah* fall. However, if it is not possible for them to fast because of bodily weakness induced by the hunger and persecutions which increase each day in the ghetto, they need not do so (since there are authorities who rule that the onlookers need not fast when a *sefer-torah* is dropped).

As to rending the garments—since the *Alfas,* the *Rosh,* and the Palestinian Talmud all refer specifically to "burning" and not "tearing," we may rely upon them under the present difficult circumstances, and we need not impose this obligation on those who were present, even though there are authorities who hold to the contrary.

However, those individuals who actually tore the *sefer-torah* with their own hands, even though they were forced to do so under threat of death, certainly are obliged to fast. As to the rest of those who live in the ghetto, who simply heard about but did not see the desecration, there is no need for them to fast, since the Talmud specifically limits mourning to "those who see." Nonetheless, Rabbi Oshry concludes his responsum, "While I exempted the people from fasting, I rendered a judgment that those who had heard of the event, give charity each in accordance with his ability."

Problems of Dying

On the night of the twenty-fourth of Av, 5701 (August 17, 1941), Rabbi Oshry was teaching his regular class in Talmud in the *Abba Yeḥez-kel Kloiz* in Slobodka. In spite of the persecutions and slaughter, he had endeavored to continue the study and teaching of Torah to strengthen the spirit of his people, as a sign of defiance to the Nazis, who wished to destroy the Torah, and in the hope that through its merit, salvation would come to the Jews.

Suddenly the men sitting around the table heard a terrible shrieking and wailing. The daughter-in-law of Reb Zalman Sher, one of the regular participants in the group, rushed into the *bet midrash* and cried out that the Germans had just taken her husband and their three sons away to be killed. When Reb Zalman Sher heard the news, he suffered a stroke and fell dead on the spot.

One of the other members of the class was Reb Ḥayyim Moshe Kaplan, who was also the *gabbai* of the *hevrah kadisha*—the burial society—and upon whom the responsibility for the funeral arrangements would fall.

He asked Rabbi Oshry a *she'elah*. The Germans had established new procedures and regulations about burial. Contrary to Jewish practice and custom, they did not allow a burial immediately after death, and it would take at least one or two days until they would permit the funeral. By that time it might be impossible to find people able or willing to perform the *taharah*—the rites of physical cleansing and ritual purification of the body before burial. Was it permissible, he asked, to perform the *taharah* then and there in the *bet midrash,* even though some considerable time would elapse before the actual burial? The customary practice was to conduct the *taharah* just prior to the burial. Here in the *bet midrash,* he went on, the task would be performed by Reb Zalman's friends, who had studied Torah together with him. It would be appropriate that these men should perform this last act of true kindness alongside the table at which he had studied *mishnah* and *gemara*.

In his *teshuvah,*[8] Rabbi Oshry cites the *Nodah be-Yehudah, Mahadura Tinyana, Yoreh Deah* 211, who permits the *taharah* to be performed immediately after death when some period of time will elapse until the burial. The *Hatam Sofer, Yoreh Deah* 325, the *Sefer Ḥasidim,* 239, and others also permit this practice when there is reason to believe that the physical condition of the body or other factors will make it impractical to perform the *taharah* just prior to burial.

Rabbi Oshry, therefore, permitted the *taharah* to take place immediately; and further instructed Reb Ḥayyim Kaplan that in the future, whenever anyone died in the ghetto, the *taharah* should be performed immediately after death, since there was no certainty that it would be possible to do so prior to burial.

In the Presence of the Dead

During the course of the Nazi attempt to destroy the Jews of Kovno, they gradually narrowed the confines of the ghetto and drove the inhabitants from their former residences into a much smaller area, to which they were restricted. Toward the very end, the ghetto, which had originally included all of the suburb of Slobodka, was actually outside that area in a location where Jews had never lived before. As a result, there were conditions of terrible crowding, and large numbers of families were forced to live in quarters which were too small even for one family.

At that time Reb Efrayim Mordekhai Yaffe approached Rabbi Oshry with the following *she'elah.* In one of the houses, a Jew had died during the night. He could not be buried until the next day. In the same room as the dead man, there lived a number of Jews who had to report early the next morning for their forced-labor detail. If they did not eat their meager meal, weakened as they were, they would be unable to work and would be severely punished or killed by the Germans. They could not eat their food outside because of the bitter cold. Even though the Halakhah does not ordinarily permit eating in the same room with a deceased person, under these circumstances, may they eat their morning meal in that room?

In his *teshuvah,*[9] Rabbi Oshry cites the Talmudic passage *Berakhot* 17b: "He whose dead lies before him, eats in another house; if he has no other house, he eats in the house of a neighbor; if no neighbor's house is available, he erects a partition between himself and the corpse and eats; if he has nothing of which to make a partition, he turns his back and eats . . ."

He explores the opinions of various authorities who attempt to give the reason of the law. Rashi *(Berakhot* 17b) suggests that it is forbidden to eat in the presence of the dead, just as it is forbidden to perform a *mitzvah,* because this would seem to be *lo'eg la'rosh*—taunting, so to speak, the dead, by engaging in pleasurable activities which he can no longer do. The *Nimukei Yosef* suggests that the reason for the law is that one may do only those things in the presence of the dead which are necessary for his benefit—for example, burial arrangements and the like, since it is unseemly to be concerned with the needs of the living in his presence.

While some authorities hold that the prohibition of eating in the presence of the dead applies only to his relatives and not to others, Rabbi Oshry points out that according to the other reason—that given by Rashi, or that of the *Nimukei Yosef*—the prohibition would apply even to those who were not mourners. Accordingly, he commends the widespread and common practice in Lithuania of forbidding eating and drinking in the presence of the dead, even by those who are not related to the deceased. However, one authority, the *Ḥokhmat Adam,* 153:1, rules, "Only the mourners are forbidden to eat in the room where the deceased is present, but one who is not a mourner may do so." The *Ḥokhmat Adam* accepts the reason given by Rashi for the prohibition, that is, *lo'eg la'rosh*—mocking the dead, but he maintains that only the performance of a *mitzvah*—praying, putting on *tefillin,* or the like—constitutes *lo'eg la'rosh*—mocking the dead, who can no longer fulfill these Divine commandments. Eating, however unseemly it may be, does not fall into the same category of actions which the soul of the departed longs to engage in. The *Arukh Hashulḥan, Yoreh Deah* 346, also holds this point of view.

Therefore, Rabbi Oshry rules, in the present case, where these unfortunates are not relatives of the deceased and have no other place to eat except the room where the deceased body is, they may rely upon the *Ḥokhmat Adam* and the *Arukh Hashulḥan,* and, if it is not possible to erect a separation between them and the body, may eat in the same room.

Pikuaḥ Nefesh

One of the immediate and inescapable problems which confronted observant Jews in the ghettos and concentration camps was that of *kashrut.* The dietary laws prohibit the eating of the flesh of all animals which do not chew the cud and do not have split hooves (e.g., pig, rabbit, and horse), of water creatures which do not have scales and fins (e.g., shellfish and crustacea), and of many kinds of birds of prey. In addition, animals whose flesh is permitted (e.g., cattle and sheep), as well as permitted fowl, must be slaughtered in special *kasher* fashion and the meat from them soaked and salted to draw out available blood, which is also forbidden by the Bible. Even *kasher* food cooked in vessels which have been used to cook *terefah (non-kasher)* food is under most circumstances considered prohibited. Mixtures of dairy products and meat are forbidden, as well as food cooked in pots which have been used for such mixtures.

In both the ghettos and the concentration camps, the Nazi policy was one of maintaining the Jews in a condition of semi-starvation. Yet in order to keep their slave-labor force operating, some food had to be provided. Such food consisted primarily of very slim rations of very poor quality bread, margarine, and sometimes potatoes, beans, or other vegetables. Generally these latter were cooked in a kind of soup in which some quantities of meat or meat products were included.

For a brief period, in some of the ghettos, *kasher* slaughtering continued.[10] But very soon the supply of *kasher* meat was exhausted. It was necessary to eat the *terefah* food provided by the Nazis in order to maintain strength barely to stay alive, let alone to work. While some Jews managed all during the Holocaust period to survive by eating only bread or potatoes, obtaining extra rations of these by bartering their portions of *terefah* food with others, most were unable to do so.

However, there was clear guidance in the Halakhah for conduct in these circumstances. *Pikuaḥ nefesh,* the saving of life, supersedes all commandments of the Torah, with the exception, of course, of the prohibitions against idolatry, sex crimes, and murder (see pp. 47-49). This principle is clearly enunciated in connection with the Sabbath, which may be violated in order to save life *(Shabbat* 132a and *Oraḥ Ḥayyim* 328:10–17), and in the case of an ill person who must eat some *terefah* product in order to be cured.[11]

In the opinion of many authorities *(Paḥad Yitzḥak,* s.v. *Pikuaḥ Nefesh; Shibolei ha-Leket* 117), a person who might save his life by eating *terefah* food and does not do so is guilty of a capital sin. Generally, in the situation under the Nazis, eating *terefah* food was not something the Germans were compelling Jews to do in order to force them to abandon Judaism. There simply was no other kind of food available. Thus the rules requiring martyrdom for violating any commandment in time of religious persecution did not apply (see pp. 47-49). Accordingly, the Rabbinic authorities permitted, even ordered, Jews to eat in order to live. Rabbi Oshry, very early in the period of the Nazi occupation, addressed himself to this question. The *she'elah* propounded to him was complicated by the fact that the situation was not yet critical. However, his ruling in this instance applied not only to those who sought his guidance, but also had wider application to other observant Jews during the Holocaust.

On Elul 27, 5701 (September 19, 1941), the Germans ordered the

Jews of Kovno to provide one thousand men each day for a forced-labor detail to assist in the construction of an airfield outside the city. Each man in the detail was given a bowl of *terefah* soup as his daily food ration. Many refused to violate the laws of *kashrut* and refrained from eating the soup. But after a few days they became weak from hunger and from the arduous labor. So, sometime between Rosh Hashanah and Yom Kippur of 5702 (about a week later), a group of men came to Rabbi Oshry and asked if they could be permitted, according to the Halakhah, to eat the soup. If they continued to reject it, they might endanger their very lives.

There was no question that the prohibition against eating *terefah* food would be set aside if there were an immediate and present danger to life. But in their case there was no such immediate threat. It was, rather, that over the course of a period of time they would become weak and perhaps fatally ill. Should the Halakhah view the situation as of only the present moment, and prohibit the soup? Or should it take into account the likely course of future events, and permit its use immediately?

In his *teshuvah*,[12] Rabbi Oshry draws upon the Talmudic and Rabbinic sources dealing with the analogous case of a sick person on the fast day of Yom Kippur. There, the decision must be made as to whether the Biblical prohibition of eating on Yom Kippur should be set aside to preserve the well-being of the patient. There is no question that if his life is threatened not only may he eat—but he must! However, a problem arises when there is a difference of opinion between the patient and his physician as to the element of danger, or when the experts themselves disagree. In this situation, as in the one confronted by Rabbi Oshry, one must consider whether an action taken, or not taken, in the present may have dangerous consequences in the future.

After citing the relevant Talmudic passages in *Yoma* 83a, and the implications which the *Rosh* and other early commentators draw from the text, Rabbi Oshry quotes the *Tur (Orah Hayyim* 618), whose ruling is: "[On Yom Kippur] in the case of a patient who may need to eat, if there is an expert physician present who says it is possible if he is not fed that his illness will be intensified, and he may be endangered, we follow his advice and feed the patient." Rabbi Oshry notes that it is not necessary that the physician say "it is possible that the patient will die." If he but says that it is possible his illness will be intensified and he may be endangered, we feed the sick person on Yom Kippur. The physician does not even have to say "it is certain" that the illness will be intensified, only that "it is possible." For it is a basic and important principle of the

Torah that *safek nefashot l'hakel*—where there is even a possibility of danger to life—we rule leniently.

From this it is clear to Rabbi Oshry that the law of *pikuah nefesh* (saving of life) is not defined by the present status of the patient. For even if there is no immediate danger at the present moment, the case falls into the category of *pikuah nefesh* since it is possible that later his illness may be intensified, and we feed him on Yom Kippur—in the present moment.

Accordingly, in the instant case the men in the forced-labor detail should be permitted to eat the *terefah* soup, especially so since expert physicians declare that it would be impossible for a person to survive very long under the conditions in which these people were placed. This, then, is not a case of *safek sakanah*—of possible danger to life; but of *vaday sakanah*—certain danger. And as we know from the Talmud, *Baba Batra* 8b, death from starvation is worse than death by the sword.

Rabbi Oshry concedes that all the passages dealing with Yom Kippur speak of a "patient," that is, someone who is already ill. Perhaps, one might say, only in such cases do we follow this lenient approach; but not, as in the case before us, where the men have not yet fallen ill. However, he adduces additional support for his position from another Talmudic case, which deals, not with an ill person, but with a well one. In *Shabbat* 69b, the case is discussed of a person who is lost in a wilderness and does not know on which day the Sabbath falls. He is required to arbitrarily count six days and observe the seventh one as the Sabbath. Rava says that on each of the six days he may work only enough to sustain his life (since perhaps that day is really the Sabbath), and on the seventh day he may not work at all. The question is raised, "And what should he do [if he does not work enough to get food] on that seventh day? Die?" The conclusion of the *gemara* is that he may work even on on the seventh day just enough to sustain his life. How then does he distinguish the seventh day from the others? By reciting *kiddush* and *havdalah*. The Rambam, in *Hilkhot Shabbat* 2:22, and the *Shulhan Arukh, Orah Hayyim* 344:1, rule accordingly.

Commenting on this decision, the *Tevuot Shor* suggests that if the lost traveler can fast on the seventh day without endangering himself, he ought to do so, and it is forbidden for him to labor on that day since no immediate *pikuah nefesh* is involved. However, the *Bigdei Yesha,* with whom Rabbi Oshry concurs, vehemently disagrees with this point of view. He writes that it is not necessary for him to afflict himself by fasting, even though he will not injure himself through such a fast. It is incumbent upon him to attempt to get out of the dangerous wilderness as quickly as possible. To do this, he will need all his strength. It is clear from this opinion that even though now (on the seventh day) there is no immediate question of *pikuah nefesh,* nonetheless, we permit him to possibly violate the Sabbath by working for his food, since if he does not get out of the wilderness quickly he will be in danger, even though that danger may come later. Similarly in the present case, Rabbi Oshry maintains, the men should be permitted to eat the *terefah* food immediately, since if they did not do so, they would ultimately be in danger.

He further proves his point from a *Tosefta* of *Shabbat,* 16:13, and a passage in Rashi on *Yoma* 85b.

Rabbi Abraham Duber Kahana Shapira, the *av bet din* of Kovno, concurred in Rabbi Oshry's granting of permission to eat the *terefah* soup.

The Status of a Repentant Convert

Among the first victims of the Germans in the period just after they entered Lithuania on the twenty-eighth of Sivan, 5701 (June 23, 1941), were a man and wife who were slain on the same day. Their gentile maid, who lived with them, successfully hid their only son, a lad of about sixteen, for some time. She was fearful, however, that she would be unable to conceal him much longer and that the Germans would kill her if they discovered him. She therefore brought the boy to her church and turned him over to the priest, so that he might not only save the boy's body, but also his soul, through baptizing him into her religion. This the priest did. He converted the lad and arranged for him to be absorbed into the gentile community so that no one would know that he was Jewish. He lived and worked among the gentiles as one of them, wanted for nothing, and might have continued to live in peace and security.

However, the boy knew no inward peace. He saw before his eyes the vision of the vicious murderers killing his mother and father; he could take no pleasure in eating or drinking all the while he was aware of the evil and destruction that his people were subject to each day. He was melancholy and unable to sleep.

He mustered up his courage and his strength, left the gentiles among whom he was living, and made his way to the Kovno ghetto. He resolved to be with his Jewish brethren in trouble and captivity, to share their destiny, even though it might bring him to the gates of death itself. Truly, the boy repented and returned to the worship of God with all his heart and with all his soul. He suffered much anguish at having previously consented to be with the gentiles and to live as one of them.

Rabbi Oshry was asked, in view of the fact that the boy had been formally converted to Christianity, whether he could still be counted as a member of a *minyan.* Since he was a *kohen,* could the boy be honored by being called to the first portion read from the Torah and be allowed to participate with the other priests in blessing the congregation with the priestly benediction?

In his *teshuvah,*[13] Rabbi Oshry points out that the question of whether a *kohen* who has apostatized may regain his priestly privileges if he returns to Judaism, is of great antiquity. Differences in the interpretation of the Talmudic passage in *Menahot* 109a, prohibiting priests who served in the Temple of Onias in Egypt [14] from serving in the Temple at Jerusalem, result in varying opinions. One school of thought, represented by Rabbenu Gershom and Rashi, holds that an apostate priest who has returned to Judaism may be allowed to be called to the Torah first and to participate in the priestly benediction. In addition to the interpretation of the passage in *Menahot,* which leads him to this conclusion, Rabenu Gershom adds, "If you do not say this, you will discourage those who wish to repent and return; for the shame and disgrace of being denied their priestly status will weaken their resolve to repent."

Rav Ahai Gaon in the *She'iltot* and *Tosafot* in the name of the *Sefer Hazahir* are the exponents of a point of view which declares that a *kohen,* once having apostatized, can no longer recapture his priestly status. There are some authorities—for example, the *Tur (Orah Hayyim* 125)—who would allow the *kohen* to be called to the Torah, but not to recite the priestly benediction.

After analyzing all these opinions, Rabbi Oshry cites the *Bet Yosef, Orah Hayyim* 125, who concludes that even according to those who forbid a priest from resuming his status *(Rav Ahai* and the *Sefer Hazahir),* this would apply only if he voluntarily abandoned Judaism for another faith and then wished to return. But if he were *forced* to convert to another religion, the *Bet Yosef* maintains, even they would agree that he could be returned to his priestly status.

Inasmuch as in the *Shulhan Arukh, Orah Hayyim* 128:37, the *Bet Yosef* cites this opinion as the Halakhah, Rabbi Oshry concludes that the boy in the instant case may certainly be included in a *minyan,* be called to the Torah as a *kohen,* and participate in the priestly benediction. For in his case he did not become a Christian voluntarily; but only to save his life and in order that there remain a remnant alive of his family, the rest of which had been totally destroyed by the Nazis.

Rabbi Oshry cites other authorities to buttress his position, among them the *Mordekhai* (manuscript), *She'elot u'Teshuvot Besomim Rosh,* 387, and *Ḥemdat Shelomo,* 8, who hold that where the *kohen* was forced to abandon Judaism he regains his former status.

Rabbi Oshry writes at the end of his responsum,

> In truth, this lad fulfilled the *mitzvah* for which the great Rabbi Akiba longed, when he said, "When will I be able to fulfill the *mitzvah* of thou shalt love the Lord with all thy soul—even if he takes thy soul" [15]—the commandment of sanctification of the name. When he fled the gentiles, and joined his brothers in the ghetto, this boy knew full well what might lie in store for him. Yet he determined to throw his lot in with them and not to be separated from them in life or in death. And in the day of the destruction of the ghetto in 5704, when the Germans took out to the slaughter those who still remained from their earlier destructions, this lad was among the *kedoshim*—the martyrs. In him and his fellow martyred Jews were fulfilled the words, "who were lovely and pleasant in their lives, and in their death were not separated; swifter than eagles, stronger than lions to do the will of their Master and the desire of their Rock. May our God remember them for good with the other righteous of the world and render retribution for the blood of his servants which hath been shed." [16]

Chapter Eight

Aftermath

After the liberation of Europe from the Nazi tyranny, many *she'elot* were directed to the remaining halakhic scholars in Europe, as well as those in Israel and America, concerning problems raised by the Holocaust. Most of these are concerned with finding halakhically acceptable ways to grant permission for survivors of the Holocaust to remarry in the absence of the conventional proofs of the death of their spouses. This material, a literature in itself, is beyond the scope of the present volume.

However, a number of the issues which were treated by Rabbi Oshry after the liberation of Kovno throw light on the mental attitude and religious spirit of the Jews who lived by the Halakhah during the Holocaust and survived it with their faith intact. These *teshuvot* are set forth in this chapter.

Honorable Burial

After Kovno was liberated, when the Jews who remained alive emerged from their hiding places, their eyes beheld a terrifying scene. Human skeletons, skulls, bones, and limbs were strewn about on every side, and in every corner of the concentration camp into which the Kovno ghetto had been converted. Underneath the ruins of the ghetto houses, which the Germans had set afire in order to burn and suffocate the Jews hiding in tunnels and cellars, one could see projecting here and there the singed hands or feet of those who had burned or suffocated to death in those hiding places. At the infamous Ninth Fort, where the Germans had killed some fourteen thousand Jews, who had been brought there for that purpose from every part of Europe, there were piles of corpses on top of stacks of wood saturated with gasoline which the Germans had not had time to burn before they were defeated. One could not turn over a shovelful of earth there without finding human bones and limbs.

The immediate question which confronted Rabbi Oshry was what should be done about the burial of these remains in accordance with the Halakhah. On the one hand, a *met mitzvah,* one who is found dead and who has no relatives to bury him, should be buried on the spot where he is found. This, according to the Talmud (*Baba Kamma* 81a), was one of the enactments of Joshua when the Jews entered the Promised Land. On the other hand, since the bodies were shamefully strewn all about, like "dung on the face of the field"; since they were being eaten by birds of prey and wild animals; and since, even if they were buried where they had fallen, there would subsequently be no way of preventing the bodies from being disturbed by wild animals who root and dig in the earth, perhaps it would be preferable to remove the remains to the Jewish cemetery of Kovno. A second halakhic question, in the event the remains were reburied in the cemetery, was whether or not it was necessary to dig up and remove for burial with the bodies the *tevusah* (three finger's-breadth of the earth underneath the corpse, which is presumed to contain some of the blood and other substance of the disintegrating body).

Rabbi Oshry demonstrates in his *teshuvah,*[1] from the Mishnah in *Ohalot* 16:5, the Mishnah in *Eduyot* 8:5, and the commentaries thereon, that the Halakhah does not require the *tevusah* (the surrounding earth) to be interred with the corpse where bodies of those who have been violently slain are found, and where the corpse is not complete. (Presumably this is because part of the body is already missing and thus there still will not be a complete interment even if the *tevusah* is buried—see *Avnei Tzedek, Yoreh Deah* 146.) In addition, in spite of the enactment of Joshua, it seems clear from these *mishnayot* that the bodies of those who were violently slain may be removed from the place of their death for burial. The *Divrei Malkiel,* 4:95, explains that Joshua's enactment that a *met mitzvah* should be buried where he was found was for the benefit of the deceased—so that this friendless person should not be put to shame while strangers were seeking here and there for a place of burial.

It is, therefore, clear that if the *met mitzvah* is found in an unsuitable and inferior place, where his body may be brought to disgrace, and where removal to a Jewish burial ground is certainly for his honor and dignity, that whoever does so performs a great *mitzvah.*

Further, Rabbi Oshry notes, the enactment of Joshua applied only in Eretz Yisrael (*Bah* on *Ḥoshen Mishpat* 274). The *Maharshal* (*Baba Kamma* 81a) also writes, "All fields where we live in the lands nowadays belong to the gentiles, and they are not subject to the enactment of

Joshua. And if one finds a *met mitzvah,* it is a *mitzvah* to bring him to Jewish burial."

While Rabbi Oshry had demonstrated to his satisfaction that it was not necessary to inter the *tevusah* with the corpses and skeletons found strewn about in the Ninth Fort and elsewhere, and while, very likely, the same might apply to the bodies found in place under the ruins of the burned houses, he had some reservations about the latter situation. These were based on the *Tosefta* of *Ohalot* 4, as interpreted by the Vilna Gaon, and by the Rambam, *Hilkhot Tumat Met* 3:8.

Accordingly, he instructed that each body found under the houses be buried together with the loose earth around it in an individual grave in the Jewish cemetery. The bodies, skeletons, and limbs from all other areas were gathered together and buried (without the *tevusah*) in one large grave, "the grave of brothers, lovely and pleasant in their lives and not separated in death. "Even though it is forbidden ordinarily to mingle the remains of one person with those of another (*Perisha, Yoreh Deah* 450; *Ḥatam Sofer, Yoreh Deah* 352; *Maharam Schick, Yoreh Deah* 356), this applies where it is possible to recognize the individual corpses and to know to which particular corpse the various bones belong. In these circumstances, of course, this was not possible, so Rabbi Oshry ruled that they be buried all together.

He writes that the survivors of the ghetto were so physically weak that they did not have the strength to themselves bury the thousands of bodies. The military government assigned a number of German prisoners of war to assist in the physical labor of removing and transporting the dead. He concludes, "In the six weeks from the fifteenth of Av, 5704, to the twenty-eighth of Elul, we fulfilled the great *mitzvah* of bringing to Jewish burial some three thousand people. May their memory be for a blessing, and may He that rendereth retribution for blood remember them and render retribution to his enemies."

Scarlet Letter or Sign of Honor

It is a principle of Jewish law that if a woman has voluntarily had intercourse with a man other than her husband, the husband may no longer live with her once he becomes aware of the fact. If, however, she was *forced* to have intercourse with another man, her husband may live with her afterwards. A case involving this principle was brought to Rabbi Oshry. After the German defeat, a young man and a young woman, who had lost all their children in the Holocaust, were reunited and determined to resume their wedded life and rebuild their destroyed family. However, to his horror and dismay, the man discovered, tattooed on his wife's arm, the words "Prostitute for the Armies of Hitler." The husband, concerned that it might be assumed that his wife, in her role as prostitute, willingly had intercourse with the Germans, asked if it was permitted for her to live with him once again as his wife.

In his *teshuvah*,[2] Rabbi Oshry cites the classic sources, which distinguish between an *anusah*—a rape victim, and a *mefutah*—one who has been seduced. These sources make a distinction (based on Deut. 22:23–25) between the event's having transpired in the city or in a field. In the city it is presumed that the woman was seduced—otherwise she would have called for assistance and been rescued. In the field it is presumed that she cried out, but that no one was there to answer her call. The Rambam, in *Hilkhot Na'arah Betulah* 1:2, adds that "in the city she may be presumed not to have been forced unless witnesses testify that her attacker brandished a sword and threatened her with death if she cried out."

Rabbi Oshry declares that the unfortunate girls who were impressed into the Nazi army brothels had lived under a constant threat of death that was equivalent to the "brandishing of the sword" mentioned by the Rambam; therefore, the woman in the instant case may live with her husband. He adds,

> There is not the slightest shadow of suspicion that she might have been seduced into voluntary intercourse with the Germans, since she herself saw what they had done to her fellow Jews, men, women, and children, murdered and slaughtered without mercy or compassion. Certainly these oppressors were so disgusting, abominable, and detestable in her eyes that it is inconceivable they could have seduced her.

Rabbi Oshry gives great weight to the opinion of the *Nodah be-Yehudah* (*Mahadura Tinyana* 201) that even in the city the woman is believed if she maintains that she resisted the man, even if there are not witnesses to support her testimony. Since this point of view is also held by such eminent authorities as the *Ketav Sofer* (*Even ha-Ezer* 17), the *Mishpatei Uziel* (*Even ha-Ezer* 23), and others, Rabbi Oshry uses this as additional support for permitting the woman to resume her married life with her husband.[3]

He rejects the additional possibility that she might have voluntarily and actively participated in sexual intercourse, not out of lust or emotion but to save herself from death (a circumstance which would once again have raised the question of permissiblity to her husband—cf. *Shulḥan Arukh, Even ha-Ezer* 7:1), since she knew that in any case the usual fate of the Jewish girls in such brothels was death, particularly once they had been marked with the tattoo.

> It is therefore the *din* that this unfortunate, and all her sisters whose bitter fate it was to be seized for such shameful purpose, are permitted to their husbands (if they are not *kohanim*), and there is not the slightest reason to forbid them to their husbands. Shall we treat our unfortunate sisters as harlots? Are they then worse than Rahab the harlot (Josh. 2:1), who [repented] and ultimately married Joshua the son of Nun! . . . In the *Tanna de-vei Eliyahu* we are told that . . . Rahab became the ancestress of eight prophets. . . . Dinah the daughter of Jacob was defiled by Ḥamor (Gen. 34), and yet the Holy One, blessed be He, Himself avenged her humiliation and restored her honor as it was before. . . .
>
> I am of the opinion, therefore, that there is no need to attempt to efface the tattoo; on the contrary, it should be viewed not as a sign of shame and disgrace, but rather as a sign of honor and strength, to show how we suffered for the sanctification of His blessed name. This tattoo, through which the murderers wished to degrade the pure and upright daughters of our people, and to brand them with everlasting shame; this tattoo has become a sign of honor to them and to our people, as a sign that we shall yet see the destruction of those who lost all semblance of humanity, who were like beasts of the forest and ravening wolves. . . . this tattoo will remind us always of what is written in the Torah of Moses the man of God, "Sing aloud, O ye nations of His people; for He doth avenge the blood of His servants, and doth render vengeance to his adversaries" (Deut. 32:43).

The Sanctity of the *Parokhet*

After the Germans had fled from Kovno, the surviving Jews of the ghetto sought to find a place in which they could once again worship. They discovered that the synagogues and houses of study had been destroyed by fire, or were otherwise unusable. The one synagogue which had the remotest possibility of being made fit for worship was the *Hoizman Kloiz*. Even it was full of filth and waste, which the Germans had deliberately disposed of in this holy place. However, after much labor and toil, the Jews succeeded in cleaning and refurbishing it, so that it might once again have its glory and sanctity restored through prayer and study. They were unable, though, to find a *parokhet* (curtain) to hang in front of the holy ark. It was impossible to find any kind of cloth out of which to fashion one, since the Nazis had plundered all such materials.

At that time, one of the Jews came and said that he had seen a *parokhet,* which had belonged to the *bet ha-knesset* of the merchants, in the house of a gentile who was using it as a bedspread. Rabbi Oshry was asked whether it was permissible to reacquire this *parokhet* and return it to its former sanctity by hanging it before the ark in the *Hoizman Kloiz,* the one place which they had succeeded in making fit for public prayer. Or had the *parokhet* become defiled and lost its sanctity by virtue of the use to which the gentile had put it?

In a brief responsum,[4] Rabbi Oshry writes that it is permitted to use the *parokhet,* and to return it to its former role of sanctity and glory. The use to which the gentile had put it did not profane its sanctity. As his authority he cites the *Maḥneh Ḥayyim* 1:135, who was presented with a similar case and ruled that such a *parokhet* might be used.

In still another *teshuvah* regarding a *parokhet,*[5] Rabbi Oshry goes into further detail concerning the absence of religious artifacts after the liberation.

On 13 Av, 5704 (July 2, 1944), the rescued remnants of the Jews emerged from behind the walls of the ghetto. They discovered that most of the synagogues and houses of study for which Kovno had once been noted had been completely destroyed. The few that were still standing had been converted into stables and cattle barns. There were no *sifrei-torah* or other religious articles available, except for Rabbi Oshry's own small *sefer-torah,* which he had carefully guarded and kept with him all during the German occupation. Several weeks after the survivors of the ghetto were freed, two of them wished to be married. However, nowhere was there a *ḥupah* (wedding canopy) to be found. Rabbi Oshry was asked if it was permissible to use a *parokhet* which had been found in the attic of the *bet hamidrash* of the *Hoizman Kloiz* (subsequent to the incident referred to earlier).

In his *teshuvah* Rabbi Oshry cites two opposing points of view concerning the permissibility of using a *parokhet* for a *ḥupah*. The *Bet Yosef,*

Orah Hayyim 154:3, includes the "curtain which hangs before the ark" among the articles which acquire a degree of sanctity requiring them to be "hidden away" (*genizah*) when they are no longer used, and which may not, therefore, be converted to other, less sanctified purposes. The *Mishnah Berurah* (154:11) points out that the *Bet Yosef* is referring to circumstances which obtained in Talmudic times, when the ark curtain was also used to cover the *sefer-torah,* or for it to rest upon. Nowadays, however, when this is no longer done, the *parokhet* does not have the same degree of sanctity as *tashmishei kedushah* (appurtenances to the performance of a *mitzvah),* which must be "hidden away"; but a lesser one of *tashmish detashmish* (an appurtenance to an appurtenance). The *Taz* and *Rabenu Nissim* also hold this view. However, Rabbi Oshry maintains, the *parokhet* would still be considered as having the general degree of sanctity of a synagogue, and, hence, it would be improper to use it for a *hupah,* a non-synagogue purpose. He cites the responsum of the *Bah,* 17, who specifically forbids the use of a *parokhet* as a *hupah* for this reason.

However, the *Magen Avraham* (154:13) writes that such use may possibly be permitted, since it may be assumed that when the *parokhet* was first installed, there was an implicit understanding by the community religious leaders that it might at some future time be put to any other worthy use they might determine. When such a condition is made, *ab initio,* variations from the original function or purpose of synagogue components are permitted. The *Elyah Rabbah,* 154:11, also writes that "it is our custom to permit such use."

The *Sedei Hemed* (*Ma'arekhet Bet ha-Knesset* 39) writes that "in the city of Jerusalem, the leaders and rabbis of the city adorn the walls of their *succot* with the *parokhet,* and (on the occasion of a *berit*) it is spread on the 'chair of Elijah' and the *sandek* sits upon it." He writes further that eminent authorities investigated these practices, as well as that of using the *parokhet* as a *hupah,* and concluded that there is not the slightest doubt that it may be so used, because all who contribute a *parokhet* to the synagogue do so with the understanding that it may be put to any use determined by the religious leaders of the city; and they, in turn, have implicitly approved the use of the *parokhet* for these worthy purposes.

In the light of the above opinions, and in view of the fact that no other appropriate covering for a *hupah* was available, Rabbi Oshry permitted the use of the *parokhet* for this purpose.

The Ransom of Sacred Pages

After the Nazis were defeated and the Jews of Kovno liberated, those remaining alive found that the enemy had not only wreaked havoc on the bodies and material possessions of the Jews, but had sought to destroy their spiritual belongings as well. When Rabbi Oshry first emerged into freedom, he could not find a single *siddur, gemara, ḥumash,* or *naḥ* in all of Kovno. But after several weeks of continual searching, he found some chests of Hebrew books in the warehouse of the customs office. These books had belonged to the Jews of Hamburg. When the Germans drove them out, the Jews of Hamburg, who had lived there for generations, were deceived into believing that they were simply going to be resettled in areas of Eastern Europe, such as Lithuania. To maintain the deception, the Germans said it would be necessary for them to take all their belongings along. The Hamburg Jews, in all innocence, believed the Germans and packed all their possessions for the journey. They soon discovered that they had been cruelly misled, for they were all brought to the infamous Ninth Fort near Kovno, where the Nazis spilled Jewish blood like water. At the same Ninth Fort, not only were the Jews of Hamburg destroyed, but also those who were brought from many other places. The Nazis, of course, plundered all the objects of value which had been brought from Hamburg; but they left the chests of sacred books in the customs warehouse.

Rabbi Oshry rejoiced at finding the books and brought them to the Hoizman *bet hamidrash,* where they were made available to all who wanted to use them. At that time, the *shamash* of the *bet hamidrash,* Reb Reuven, tearfully told Rabbi Oshry that in the fish-market, the gentiles were using loose pages of sacred volumes—Talmud, Rambam, *Shulḥan Arukh, Tur*—which had been taken from the warehouse of the Romm Printing Company in Vilna, to wrap herring and other objects.

The *she'elah* was asked whether there was any obligation upon the Jews of Kovno to redeem—that is, to purchase—these pages from the gentiles so that they not continue to be used for such demeaning purposes. Further, if they did redeem them, what ought to be done with them, since as isolated pages from different works they could not be used for purposes of study? Was it necessary to place these leaves in a *genizah,* and, if so, how should this be done?[6]

Rabbi Oshry responded that it is evident from the Talmud, *Shabbat* 115a, and from the commentary of the *Rosh* on this passage, that the obligation to save sacred writings from destruction includes not only books of the Bible, but also books containing the Oral Law—that is, the Talmud and Rabbinic literature. The *Shulḥan Arukh, Oraḥ Ḥayyim* 334:12, specifically states that we must rescue sacred volumes not only from destruction but also from "every place of ignominy." The *Magen Avraham,* 154:9, makes it clear that this clause also includes volumes of the Talmud and the like.

Therefore, Rabbi Oshry rules, there is a definite obligation to redeem these pages, for, since the gentiles are using them for every kind of shameful purpose, there could be no greater "place of ignominy" than this.

Since the leaves could not be used for study, they must be put in a *genizah,* "hidden away," where they would not be subject to destruction or desecration. The reason for the practice of *genizah* is the fear that the name of God, which might be included in writings on sacred subjects, may be obliterated or effaced. (So the Rambam, *Hilkhot Yesodei ha-Torah* 1:8; and Rashi in *Shabbat* 71.) While the *Shakh,* in *Yoreh Deah* 276:12, holds that the name of God is not considered sanctified if there was no specific intention to sanctify it when it was written (this would be the case with all printed books, as well as with manuscripts other than a *sefertorah*), and there is no Biblical prohibition against effacement, even, he would agree that there is a Rabbinic prohibition against effacing such a "non-sanctified" name. This also is the view of the *Meshiv Davar,* 2:80, as well as of the *Melamed Leho'il.*

Rabbi Oshry considers the opinion of a number of authorities that effacing the Divine name is prohibited only when it is done by direct action, and not (as in the instant case) when one simply allows it to take place or indirectly causes it (*gerama*); but he rejects these views. According to Rabbi Isaac Elḥanan Spektor, the former chief rabbi of Kovno, the proper *genizah* procedure is to place all the worn and torn fragments of sacred books in sacks and bury them with honor and dignity in the Jewish cemetery. So Rabbi Oshry directed that to be done.

He concludes his *teshuvah,* "The Children of Israel are truly holy. After I ruled that it was a *mitzvah* to redeem the pages from the gentiles, the rescued remnant, those who had been saved from the ghetto, denied food to their mouths, and with their last few pennies purchased the pages from the gentiles in order that they might be buried as the law requires."

Kapos and Collaborators in the Halakhah

The role of the Jewish police in the ghetto and the *kapos* in the concentration camps is one that has generated intense controversy. A number of post-liberation *she'elot* concerned their status in the Halakhah. In one such *teshuvah* Rabbi Oshry discusses in some detail the motivations of those Jews who, in one fashion or another, assisted the Germans in subjugating and destroying their brothers.

> The story of those Jews who voluntarily or unwillingly collaborated with the Germans, thinking that thereby they would avoid sharing the tragic destiny of their fellow Jews, forms a unique chapter in the history of the Holocaust. Invariably, though, they came to a bitter end. When the time came, nothing prevented them from sharing the fate of their brothers. While it is true that most of them were compelled to work for the Germans against their will, there were others who naively believed that they might employ their close association with them and their status with this ruling power for the benefit of their oppressed brethren. They thought they would be able to plead on their behalf with the cruel enemy to lighten the yoke of their bondage. But the one thing that all who were close to the Germans had in common was that they were detested and hated by the rest of the Jews. They were viewed as traitors who had rejected the Jewish community and refused to share its destiny.
>
> I was asked a *she'elah* concerning one such collaborator who was ultimately killed by the Germans. Just before he was taken out to his death, he confessed to his sins and evil deeds in the presence of his fellow Jews and tearfully entreated them and his Creator for forgiveness. I was asked if it is permitted to mention the name of that man when his son is called up to the reading of the Torah in the manner customary among us, "let so-and-so the son of so-and-so stand up . . ." For since he was a wicked person, his name ought not even to be mentioned, as it is said, "the name of the wicked shall be blotted out" (Prov. 10:7). Certainly, at the time of the performance of a *mitzvah,* such as the calling up of his son to the Torah and his reciting the benedictions thereof, it might be improper to mention the father's name. Or perhaps there are no grounds at all for such concern, and we ought not to change the customary practice and his son ought to be called up to the Torah just as everyone else is called up, and it is permissible to mention his father's name.

In his *teshuvah*[7] Rabbi Oshry first cites the Tamudic passage in *Succah* 56a, which relates that the ancient priestly family of Bilgah had its privileges and perquisites in the Temple curtailed because of the wicked actions of one of its daughters, Miriam. One might infer from this that in our case, too, the son might properly be singled out publicly in the manner of his being called to the Torah because of the sins of his father.

Yet the *Shulḥan Arukh* (*Oraḥ Ḥayyim* 128:37) rules that "an apostate is not allowed to recite the priestly benediction; but there are those who hold that if he has repented he may do so. And if he was forced to apostatize, everyone agrees that he may recite the priestly benediction." We see, Rabbi Oshry declares, how great is the power of repentance, which makes it possible even for an apostate to raise his hands in the priestly blessing. Moreover, the *Rama* notes that "this point of view is essentially the correct one." Therefore, in our case, since the father repented publicly before his death, there is no question whatsoever about mentioning his name when the son is called to the Torah. For the son's being called to the Torah reading is certainly of no greater sanctity than the recitation of the priestly blessing, which is permitted for the apostate himself, provided he has repented.

Besides this, the *Shulḥan Arukh* ruled that "if he was *forced* to apostatize, everyone agrees he may recite the priestly benediction." This means that even those who are strict in their ruling, and do not believe that the repentance of an apostate is adequate reason for allowing him to recite the blessing, would nonetheless agree that if he had been compelled to apostatize, he would be permitted to do so. In our case, there is some evidence to suggest that the father collaborated with the Germans only because he was compelled to do so. He often tried to do favors for the Jews and saved a number of them from death. Certainly, therefore, one ought not to be strict in this case and to punish his son. Particularly since the father repented publicly before his death; whereas in the case cited in the *Shulḥan Arukh* it appears there was no such public confession and repentance, and the ruling is still that the transgressor's repentance restores him to his full priestly status.

In addition, Rabbi Oshry notes, the son is an observant and pious Jew, and it would be wrong to shame him when he is called to the Torah by differentiating him from all others. We find that we may sometimes render honor to a wicked father for the sake of the honor of a righteous son, as in the case of Amon and Josiah (2 Kings 21:20). Further, since the father was killed violently by the Germans, his death is his atonement, and accordingly one ought to mention his name at the time the son performs a *mitzvah,* so that this may accrue to the merit of the father in the "world of truth."

In still another *teshuvah* Rabbi Oshry considers the case, not of the son of a collaborator, but of a collaborator himself.[8] He first describes the manner in which some of the Jewish ghetto police attempted to curry favor with the Germans by carrying out to the letter, and even exceeding, their orders concerning forced-labor quotas. He writes with burning indignation of their craven cowardice before the Germans and their arrogant behavior toward their fellow Jews. They spared them neither tongue-lashing nor whip-lashing in their attempt to display their own subservience to their German masters.

After the ghetto was liberated, Rabbi Oshry writes, the synagogues once again were filled with worshippers and students of the Torah. At that time he was asked a *she'elah* about one of the former ghetto policemen who had made life difficult for the Jews working at forced labor. He now declared that he regretted his former evil deeds and completely repented of the harmful acts he had done to his brethren while the Germans were in power. Moreover, he now wished to be appointed as a *she'liah tzibur,* a synagogue reader, to stand before the Holy Ark in prayer and petition before the Almighty on behalf of His people Israel. Is this fitting?

In his *teshuvah* Rabbi Oshry cites the *Shulhan Arukh, Orah Hayyim* 53:4, "A *she'liah tzibur* must be fitting; 'fitting' means that he must be free from sin and not have had an evil reputation even in his youth." He then quotes the *Rama,* who in *Hoshen Mishpat* 34:4 declares (in defining what constitutes a *rasha,* an evil person who is disqualified as a witness), "He who just lifts up his hand as if to strike his fellow man is disqualified by Rabbinic law." What shall we say then, asks Rabbi Oshry, about this man who did not simply lift up his hand to strike, but repeatedly struck his fellow Jews in order to find favor in the sight of the Germans? Certainly he is a *rasha.* Who can really know if his repentance is sincere? And even if one does indeed believe that his contrition is complete and earnest, he still continues to have a *shem ra* (an evil name—i.e., reputation), which has not ceased. There can be no greater *shem ra* than the publicly known and acknowledged fact that he was a ghetto policeman. After considering many different cases cited by other authorities concerning the qualifications of a *she'liah tzibur,* Rabbi Oshry concludes that in our case the erstwhile policeman must not be allowed to lead his fellow Jews in prayer. Even where the rulings were lenient in the cases examined by Rabbi Oshry, this was only where the man in question was already serving as a *she'liah tzibur,* and the issue was whether or not he should be removed from his position. But in this instance, where we are being asked *ab initio* to appoint him, the answer cannot be other than an emphatic no. Even where there is only unverified rumor that a prospective *she'liah tzibur* has sinned, the authorities rule that he not be appointed. How much more so here, where "it is widely known how vicious was his past conduct; how he would torment his brother Jews with oaths and imprecations, with threats and blows." In this case he must not be appointed even though he says he has repented. For this is no better than the case we cited earlier, where having a "bad reputation *(shem ra)* in one's youth is enough to disqualify him."

Rabbi Oshry concludes his *teshuvah* with a reference to the *Divrei Hayyim* (2:12), who points out that many Jews are compelled to stray from complete observance of the *mitzvot* by virtue of their occupations or the society in which they live. Oftentimes the only purity of observance that remains for them is their participation in congregational prayer with pious and God-fearing people led by a pious *she'liah tzibur*. If, Heaven forfend, he is not God-fearing, he defiles the hearts of those who hear him and causes untold harm. Therefore, even on a temporary basis, we cannot allow this former ghetto policeman to serve as a *she'liah tzibur*.

NOTES

CHAPTER ONE: HOLOCAUST AND HALAKHAH

1. *Encyclopaedia Judaica,* s.v. "Holocaust." See also *Entziklopedia Shel Galuyot* (Jerusalem, 1966), vol. 4, pt. 1, in which N. M. Gelber, the editor of the section on Lvov, writes, "I have seen this time and again in the hundreds of memorial volumes which ignore the truth, that the great majority of Jews in the destroyed communities were believing Jews."

2. For an excellent and succinct summary of the relationship of the responsa to the sources of Jewish law, the general reader is referred to David Feldman, *Birth Control in Jewish Law,* pp. 3–18. Solomon Freehof's *The Responsa Literature* (Philadelphia, 1959), pp. 21–45, may also be of interest.

3. *Einzatzgruppen* were special-action units entrusted with the mobile killing operations of Jews. See Raul Hilberg, *The Destruction of the European Jews,* pp. 183 ff.

4. Zvi Hirsch Meisels, *Mekadeshei ha-Shem,* vol. 1, p. 8.

5. A *kapo* was a prisoner in charge of a group of inmates in the concentration camps. According to some the word derives from the Italian *capo,* "boss." Others derive it from *Kameradschaftpolizei. Kapos* were appointed by the SS to carry out its orders and insure absolute control over the prisoners. They were initially appointed from the ranks of German criminal prisoners. Jews were appointed kapos only in camps where the prisoners were primarily Jewish. The majority of them were cruel and repressive and imitated the conduct of the SS. A few did help their fellow prisoners.

6. Rabbi Meisels reveals the halakhic considerations which did not permit him to render a clear-cut decision under the circumstances prevailing at Auschwitz to be as follows: In the *Shulḥan Arukh, Ḥoshen Mishpat* 388:2, the *Rama* rules that if a man sees impending danger to himself, he may save himself even if by so doing he endangers his neighbor. However, the *Sema* quotes the *Nimukei Yosef* as holding that this applies only when the danger is potential and not actual. However, once he is in the actual situation of damage or danger, he may not save himself by diverting the threat to his neighbor. In his commentary to *Hoshen Mishpat* 163:11, the *Shakh* cites a

158   *The Holocaust and Halakhah*

teshuvah of the *Maharival* to the effect that if a man has been seized and is being held for ransom, and it is known that if he is rescued another will be seized in his place, it is forbidden for others to attempt to rescue him. However, the prisoner himself may certainly attempt to extricate himself from the impending or certain danger of harm from those who have seized him. This is the opinion of the *Yad Avraham, Yoreh Deah* 157. Now Rabbi Meisels's concern was whether or not a father's relationship to his son is so close that he is considered "the same person." If so, then he would be permitted to rescue his son even though another would be seized in his place. For a man may rescue himself even though another will suffer. However, if a father is considered "another person," he has no right to save the son at the expense of a third party. There is no clear opinion as to which is the correct halakhic evaluation of this situation. This same source material was cited by Rabbi Oshry (see p. 29) in a somewhat different context.

It is interesting to note that Shlomo Rozman, an eyewitness to the episode involving Rabbi Meisels and this *she'elah*, gives a more detailed account in *Zikhron Kedoshim*, pp. 380 ff. Rozman's version, however, differs in one essential particular. As he recalls it, after Rabbi Meisels's unsuccessful attempt to persuade the father to follow the dictates of his own conscience, "the father insisted; he had the golden coin with which he could quickly ransom his only son, but he wanted to know whether he could do this according to the Halakhah. Both shed bitter tears, and the rabbi rendered the *pesak din* [quoting the Talmud, *Sanhedrin* 74a], 'Who can say that your blood is redder? How do you know that your son's blood is redder than that of the other child [who would be taken in his stead]?' " Whether, in fact, Rabbi Meisels meant this reference as a *pesak din,* as Rozman assumes, or was simply musing aloud about the various halakhic considerations involved in the tragic situation, did not, of course, affect the outcome. In either event, whether Rabbi Meisels specifically ruled that the son could not be ransomed, or whether the father assumed from his silence that this would be what the Halakhah required, he felt he had no other course but to obey that Halakhah willingly.

7. Gen. 18:26.

8. *Kiddushin* 39b; *Hullin* 142a.

9. Joseph H. Hertz, ed., *The Authorized Daily Prayer Book* (New York, 1948), p. 179.

10. Ibid., p. 162.

11. Ibid., p. 195.

12. Ibid., p. 511.

13. H. Adler, ed., *Service of the Synagogue:Day of Atonement* (New York), p. 180.

14. This description of the stages in the Nazi program for the "final solution" is based on Hilberg, op. cit.; *Encyclopaedia Judaica,* s.v. "Holocaust"; and *The Holocaust and the Resistance* (Jerusalem: Yad Vashem, 1972).

15. Jehiel Weinberg, *Seridei Esh,* vol. 1, pp. 4–8.

16. Ibid., vol. 2, p. 22.

17. Menahem Kirschboim, *Tziyyun le-Menahem,* p. 361. In 1939, just

before the outbreak of World War II, Rabbi Kirschboim fled to Brussels. On *shabbat shuvah* of 1942 (September 19), during the Nazi occupation of Belgium, he was arrested by the Gestapo. Since it was the Sabbath, he had not been carrying his identification pass. He was sent to Auschwitz, where he perished.

18. *Seridei Esh,* vol. 1, p. 2.

19. For a description of the situation in Hungary, see Hilberg, pp. 509 ff., and Eugene Levai, *Black Book of Hungarian Jewry* (Zurich, 1948).

20. "Santification of life"—this term was coined by Rabbi Yitzhak Nissenbaum in the Warsaw ghetto. "This is the hour of *kiddush ha-ḥayyim.* . . . the enemy demands the physical Jew, and it is incumbent upon every Jew to defend it: to guard his own life." Also related to this concept was "confronting death with an inner peace, nobility, upright stance, without lament and cringing to the enemy." Cf. Peter Schindler, "Responses of Hassidic Leaders and Hassidim during the Holocaust," p. 138.

21. Students of the Halakhah who may have reservations or questions concerning the reasoning or conclusions in the cited responsa should, of course, consult the full text of the *teshuvah* in question. The study of each step in the argument should, in most cases, resolve their difficulties. It must be remembered that all these rulings were rendered *be'sha'at ha-dehak,* in emergency situations, where a great deal of flexibility is possible in selecting the earlier and later authorities whose views lead to a halakhic decision which best meets the emergency conditions. The emotional and physical pressures which existed at the time these responsa were formulated should also be borne in mind.

22. Shimon Huberband, in *Kiddush Hashem,* p. 94, reports that while there were few *she'elot* concerning the dietary laws in the Warsaw ghetto (because of the virtual absence of kosher meat), there were a great many relating to other problems engendered by the Nazi persecutions. Most of those he lists are quite similar to the ones encountered by Rabbi Oshry in the ghetto of Kovno. Among them are questions concerning the observance of mourning and the recitation of *kaddish* for victims of the Nazis; the manner of conducting a *seder* without the Four Cups of Wine or *matzot;* permission to eat on Yom Kippur for those who were weak or sick; the permissibility of eating *terefah* meat for those who were ill or weak; the permissibility of using leavened bread which had not been legally sold before Passover, after the Passover was over. Unfortunately, these *she'elot u'teshuvot* were not committed to writing or were destroyed in the ghetto uprising.

CHAPTER TWO: MATTERS OF LIFE AND DEATH

1. *Yoma* 82a.
2. See chap. 1, p. 5.
3. Oshry, *Mi-Ma'amakım,* vol. 2, p. 7.
4. The Seventh Fort and the Ninth Fort were areas near Kovno used for the mass executions of Jews.

5. *Gittin* 56b.

6. The treatment of this very theme by Aḥad Ha-Am, the great essayist and seminal thinker of the Zionist movement, using the same Talmudic sources, is worth noting. In 1910, in an essay entitled "Between Two Opinions," reprinted in part in *Ahad Ha-am: Essays, Letters, Memoirs* (Oxford, 1946), p. 133, he wrote: "Every man's life is entrusted to his keeping, and to preserve your own charge is a nearer duty than to preserve your neighbor's. But when a man came to Raba and asked him what he should do when one in authority threatened to kill him unless he would kill another man, Raba answered him: 'Be killed and kill not. Who hath told thee that thy blood is redder than his? Perhaps his blood is redder.' And Rashi who generally gets to the root of the matter with his instinctive understanding of Judaism, correctly explains thus: 'The question arises only because you know that no religious law is binding in the face of danger to life, and think that in this case also the prohibition of murder ceases to be binding because your own life is in danger. But this transgression is not like others. For do what you will, there must be a life lost ... How do you know that your life is more precious than his in the sight of God? Perhaps his life is more precious? ... But suppose the case was reversed: suppose the question to be whether I can save another from death by giving my life instead of his. Raba would reply: 'Let the other be killed and do not destroy yourself. For do what you will there must be a life lost; and how do you know that his blood is redder than yours? Perhaps yours is redder.' From the standpoint of Judaism every man's blood is as red as any other's; every soul is precious in the sight of God be it mine or another's. ... Jewish history of course records many cases of martyrdom, which will remain precious and sacred memories for all time. But these are not cases of one life given for the preservation of another similar life; they are sacrifices of human life for the 'sanctification of the Name.'. . ."

7. *Sanhedrin* 37a.

8. Rabbi Simeon ben Lakish was the leader of a band of gladiators, or robbers, before he became a student (*Baba Matziah* 84a).

9. Cited in Niger, *Kiddush Hashem,* pp. 161–62.

10. Oshry, *Divrei Efrayim,* p. 95.

11. See chap. 6, n. 20.

12. See Rabbi Meisels's use of the same source in chap. 1, n. 6.

13. The details of this episode are described by Leib Garfunkel in *Kovno ha-Yehudit be-Ḥurbanah,* p. 72: "This decision [to post the notices concerning the *selektion*] was accepted amidst great anguish after a long and grueling session lasting many hours, and after a late-night meeting with the venerable rabbi of Kovno, Rabbi Shapira. When he heard the words of the *Aeltestenrat,* he became overwrought and fainted. After he had recovered somewhat, he asked that he be given a few hours to search in the source books for guidance as to what course of action the ethics of Judaism demanded under these terrible circumstances. The next morning, Rabbi Shapira notified the *Aeltestenrat* that if they believed that by fulfilling the order ... it would be possible

to save even a small number of the Ghetto community—they must gird themselves with strength and take upon themselves the responsibility of fulfilling the German command."

The rabbinate of Vilna disagreed with this interpretation of Jewish law and forbade the *Judenrat* of that city to deliver any Jews to the Germans for the purpose of saving others. *Encyclopaedia Judaica*, s.v. "Holocaust" (p. 898).

14. Efrati, *Mi-gai ha-Haregah*, p. 23.

15. For an interesting parallel, see the case in Joseph Fletcher, *Situation Ethics* (Philadelphia, 1966) p. 124, "Ponder this: Along the Wilderness Road, or Boone's Trail, in the eighteenth century, westward through Cumberland Gap to Kentucky, many families and trail parties lost their lives in border and Indian warfare. Compare two episodes in which pioneers were pursued by savages. (1) A Scottish woman saw that her suckling baby, ill and crying, was betraying her and her three other children, and the whole company to the Indians. But she clung to her child, and they were caught and killed. (2) A Negro woman, seeing how her crying baby endangered another trail party, killed it with her own hands, to keep silence and reach the fort. Which woman made the right decision?"

16. "And the battle went sore against Saul, and the archers overtook him; and he was in great anguish by reason of the archers. Then said Saul to his armor-bearer: 'Draw thy sword and thrust me through therewith; lest these uncircumcised come and thrust me through, and make a mock of me.' But his armor-bearer would not; for he was sore afraid. Therefore Saul took his sword and fell upon it. And when his armor-bearer saw that Saul was dead, he likewise fell upon his sword and died with him."

17. Oshry, *Mi-Ma'amakim*, vol. 1, p. 45.

18. The post-Talmudic tractate *Semaḥot* is the first to use the term *m'abed atzmo la-da'at* for a suicide. It is the provisions in this tractate (2: 1–5) which form the basis of the halakhic definition of suicide in regard to burial and mourning practices. The passage reads: "We do not occupy ourselves in any respect with the funeral rites of one who committed suicide willfully [*la-da'at*]. Rabbi Ishmael said: 'We exclaim over him, "Alas for a lost life. Alas for a lost life."' Rabbi Akiba said to him, 'Leave him unmourned; speak neither well nor ill of him.'. . . With anything that makes for respect of the living we occupy ourselves, but with anything that does not make for the respect of the living, the public do not in any way occupy themselves. Who comes within the category of 'one who commits suicide willfully'? He does *not* who climbed to the top of a tree and fell down and died, or he who went up to the top of the roof and fell down and died. But he who calls out, 'Look, I am going to the top of the roof or to the top of the tree, and I will throw myself down that I may die' comes within the category. . . . If a person was found strangled or hanging from a tree or lying dead on a sword, he is presumed not to have committed suicide willfully, and none of the rites are withheld from him. . . . It is related of the son of Gorgias of Lydda that he ran away from school and his father pointed to his ear [threatened to punish him]. In fear of his

father he went and destroyed himself in a pit. They went and inquired of Rabbi Tarfon, who ruled: 'We do not withhold anything from him.' "

19. It might justifiably be maintained that many of the sources which Rabbi Oshry cites as permitting suicide under duress, address themselves only to the question of how the Halakhah judges the suicide *ex post facto* with regard to funeral rites and mourning. They do not unequivocally indicate that under such circumstances an advance permission may be given to commit suicide. In a number of the citations, however, there are reasonable grounds for making this assumption.

20. The Rambam more specifically mentions suicide in *Hilkhot Rotzeaḥ* 2:3.

21. This dictum is nowhere to be found in the Talmud or Midrash. Hence the efforts of the *Maharil* to find an allusion to it in *Ketuvot*. However, the *Torah T'mimah* (Gen. 9:5) suggests that it is implicit in the Biblical verse itself. See also J. M. Tukacinsky, *Gesher Ha-Ḥayyim*, vol. 1 p. 270, who describes it as a self-evident logical proposition.

22. Rabbi Oshry also alludes to still another view, which asserts that Saul's suicide was totally unjustified and was viewed with disfavor by the sages. This is cited in the *Da'at Zekenim* on Gen. 9:5 as follows: ". . . from there [Saul's suicide and the Midrashic interpretation in *Genesis Rabbah* 34:19] they bring evidence that it is permissible to slaughter the children at the time of the persecutions. But there are those who forbid it and explain the Midrash thus, 'You might think that the prohibition of suicide does not include the case of Saul: therefore the Torah tells us by the use of the word *akh*' [a limiting particle] that under no circumstances is it permissible to kill oneself; and Saul did so without the permission of the sages.' And there was an episode with a certain rabbi who slaughtered many infants at the time of the decree (of forcible conversion) for he was afraid that they would be forced to apostatize. Another rabbi was violently angry with him and called him a murderer. But he paid him no heed. The accusing rabbi then said, 'If I am correct, may that rabbi come to a violent death.' And so it was. He was seized by the gentiles, flayed, and tortured to death. Afterwards, the decree was annulled, and if he had not slain the children, they would have been saved."

23. "Open then thy mouth so that the fire enter into thee. He replied, 'Let Him who gave me my soul take it away, but no one should injure himself.' "

24. Garfunkel, *Kovno ha-Yehudit be-Ḥurbanah*, p. 248.

25. Chaim Kaplan, *The Warsaw Diary of Chaim A. Kaplan*, ed. Abraham Katsh, p. 131.

26. See Samuel Gringauz, "The Ghetto as an Experiment in Jewish Social Organization," *Jewish Social Studies* 11 (1949): 17.

27. Oshry, *Mi-Ma'amakim*, vol. 1, p. 111.

28. Ibid., p. 126.

29. Ibid., vol. 2, p. 53.

30. Ibid., vol. 1, p. 102.

31. Rabbi Oshry records (in *Divrei Efrayim*, p. 50) a somewhat related *she'elah* which came before him during the early stages of the Nazi occupation

of Kovno. In this case, a Jew wished to purchase the passport of a gentile, substitute his own photograph for that of the original owner, and use the document to escape the ghetto. Rabbi Oshry once again cites the Rambam's prohibition, in *Sefer ha-Mitzvot,* of deceiving a gentile into believing that one has abandoned Judaism. However, the gentile from whom he purchases the passport certainly knows that he has not left his faith, but is simply using the document to save himself. Therefore, the purchase of the passport would be permitted. However, the difficulty arises when he shows the passport when he is stopped by the authorities. Is he not, by showing the passport, indicating that he is not a Jew, thereby violating the commandment of *kiddush ha-shem?*

Not necessarily, says Rabbi Oshry. For in the *Yoreh Deah* 157:2, we rule that while even at the risk of his life a Jew may not say that he is a Christian, he may wear Christian garb so that others will think he is a Christian. The distinction is, perhaps, that in the case of saying he is a Christian, it was known that he was a Jew, and therefore there is a *ḥillul ha-shem* in the awareness that he had apparently converted. But in the case of wearing the garments, the Christians never suspected at any time that he was a Jew. Therefore there is no *ḥillul ha-shem,* since no one, except he himself, knows that he is Jewish. The *Shakh,* in *Yoreh Deah* 157:17, clearly makes this distinction: "Even in time of persecution . . . to wear a Christian garb is permitted, for then there is not *ḥillul ha-shem,* since the Christians do not know who he is." So, too, Rabbi Oshry believes, the showing of the passport may not be forbidden, since those to whom it is shown do not know or suspect that the bearer is Jewish. However, he is not completely certain of this position and does not give a definitive ruling. The distinction between the passport and the baptismal document, the use of which he strictly prohibited, is that in the latter case, the very document itself is evidence of abandonment of Judaism.

Still another matter involving passports was brought to Rabbi Oshry. A Jew with a name which sounded non-Jewish had a passport that had been issued before the war. All he needed to do was add the letters "R. K." (*Roimisch Katolisch*), which was the manner in which the passports of Roman Catholics were initialed. With such a passport he might be able to save his life. Rabbi Oshry pointed out, as indicated in the previous *teshuvah,* that when a statement is ambiguous, and the gentile believes it to mean that the Jew is a Christian, but the Jew does not so mean it, it is permitted in time of persecution. So, he suggests, if the passport bearer in his mind interprets the initials "R. K." as meaning *kein Roimer,* "not a Roman Catholic," and the viewer of the document takes them to signify "Roman Catholic," it is permitted to make the change in the passport. A comparable case is mentioned by Rabbi Ḥayyim Shor in his *Torat Ḥayyim,* 17, in which he writes, "I have heard about one of the great scholars of earlier times that when he was asked, during the time of persecution, 'Are you a Jew?' he replied, '*Kein Jude.*' Now in German this means 'I am not a Jew,' and this is what the wicked persecutors understood him to say. But what he meant was the Hebrew expression *kayn, yud,* which means 'yes, I am a Jew.' In this fashion he was saved."

Mordekhai Eliav, in *Ani Ma'amin,* p. 126, describes an actual case during the Holocaust when a group of religious students in the ghetto of Cracow implored a young Jew, Mordekhai Shklartzik, who was passing as a Christian and moving freely among the Germans, that if he was asked by them whether he was Jewish, he should reply *"kein Jude"* but really mean *"kayn, yud,"* thereby avoiding the sin of denying his faith.

32. *Yerushat Peletah,* p. 75. A similar *she'elah* was directed to Rabbi Samuel Ungar of Neitra on August 3, 1942 (cited in *Mekadeshei ha-Shem,* p. 214).

CHAPTER THREE: PRAYER, STUDY, AND MARTYRDOM

1. The Talmud, *Sanhedrin* 74b, determines that *kiddush ha-shem be-farhesya,* publicly, requires a minimum number of adult Israelites to be present. That number is ten, the same as is required for a service of public prayer. The use of the word *tokh,* "among," in both Leviticus 22:32, and Numbers 16:21, is used to support this conclusion.

2. *Sanhedrin* 74a; *Avodah Zarah* 27b; *Yoma* 82a; *Pesaḥim* 25b.

3. Cf. *Kesef Mishneh, Yesodei ha-Torah* 5:1.

4. Oshry, *mi-Ma'amakim,* vol. 2, p. 59.

5. So named from the verse in Proverbs 20:29, *"tiferet baḥurim,* the glory of young men, is their strength.

6. *Berakhot* 54a.

7. Ps. 145:18.

8. After Jer. 31:17.

9. The relevant portion of the passage, which Rabbi Oshry cites in full, reads: "When Rabbi Yose ben Kisma was ill, Rabbi Ḥanina ben Teradyon went to visit him. He said to him: 'Brother Ḥanina, knowest thou not that it is Heaven that has ordained this [Roman] nation to reign? For though she laid waste His House, burnt His Temple, slew His pious ones, and caused His best ones to perish, still is she firmly established! Yet I have heard about thee that thou sittest and occupiest thyself with the Torah, dost publicly gather assemblies, and keepest a scroll of the Law in thy bosom!' He replied: 'Heaven will show mercy.' 'I,' he remonstrated, 'am telling thee plain facts, and thou sayest "Heaven will show mercy"! It will surprise me if they do not burn both thee and the scroll of the Law with fire.' . . . It was said that within but a few days . . . they found Rabbi Ḥanina ben Teradyon sitting and occupying himself with the Torah, publicly gathering assemblies, and keeping a scroll of the Law in his bosom. Straightaway they took hold of him, wrapped him in the scroll of the Law, placed bundles of branches round him, and set them on fire. . . ."

10. "All the presidents of the kingdom, the prefects and the satraps, the ministers and the governors, have consulted together that the king should establish a statute and make a strong interdict that whosoever shall ask a petition of any god or man for thirty days, save of thee, O king, he shall be cast into the den of lions. . . . And when Daniel knew that the writing was signed, he went to his house—now his windows were open in the upper cham-

ber toward Jerusalem—and he kneeled upon his knees three times a day, and prayed and gave thanks before his God as he did aforetime. . . . Then the king commanded and they brought Daniel and cast him into the den of lions."

11. The reaction of the Jews of Kovno to the Nazi prohibition of prayer is described by Leib Garfunkel, *Kovno ha-Yehudit be-Ḥurbanah,* p. 133. "To the credit of the religious Jews of the ghetto, it should be noted that but a short time after the decree was issued, they gathered their strength and opened the closed synagogues once again. They prayed publicly, studied *mishnayot* and *gemara,* paying no heed to the dangers this involved. It is worthwhile mentioning one episode that took place in the ghetto. That year, as in the prior one, various *minyanim* were organized for prayer on the High Holy Days. One of these was in the hospital. On Yom Kippur in the middle of *musaf . . .* word spread that two officers of the German *Stadt-Kommisariat* had entered the ghetto and were headed in the direction of the hospital. Exactly as in the days of the Inquisition in Spain, they obliterated in a matter of moments all the evidence of the 'great crime.' They concealed the ark, extinguished the candles, hid the *Maḥzorim;* the worshippers also hid in one of the hospital rooms. The two Germans walked around the hospital for a short while, and after finding nothing suspicious, left the building. After they left, everything was put back in place, and they continued the *musaf* service to its end."

12. Eliav, *Ani Ma'amin,* pp. 78 ff.

13. Ibid., p. 92.

14. Ibid., p. 97.

15. *Emunot ve-Deot* 933:3.

16. A familiar and beloved tale was the *aggadata* in *Berakhot* 61b: "Once the wicked [Roman] government prohibited the study of Torah. Poppus ben Yehudah came and found Rabbi Akiba publicly gathering assemblies and occupying himself with the Torah. He said to him, 'Akiba, are you not afraid of the government?' He replied, 'I will tell you a parable. To what is this like? To a fox who was walking along the banks of a river and spied fish scurrying from one place to another. The fox said to them, "From whom are you fleeing?" They said to him, "We flee the nets which men have spread for us." The fox said to them, "Would you not wish to come up to the dry land so that we might live together as did our ancestors long ago!" The fish replied, "Are you he who is reputed to be the cleverest of all beasts! You are not clever, but a fool, If we are afraid of being caught here in the water, which is our natural habitat, how much more so should we be afraid on the dry land, where we would die!" So, too, if when we study the Torah, which is the source of our life, we are in such straits, how much worse it would be if we abandoned it.' "

17. Eliav, p. 130.

18. Ibid., p. 132.

19. Prager, *Eleh She-lo Nikhne'u,* vol. 2, p. 122.

20. Ibid., vol. 1, p. 112.

21. Seidman, *Yoman Getto Warsha,* p. 141.
22. Schindler, "Responses of Hassidic Leaders," pp. 234–35.
23. Oshry, vol. 1, p. 93.

CHAPTER FOUR: "HOW DOES ONE BLESS?"

1. *Berakhot* 54a.
2. Schindler, "Responses of Hassidic Leaders," p. 137.
3. Ibid., pp. 139–41.
4. For a wide-ranging discussion concerning the authenticity and antiquity of the benediction for *kiddush ha-shem,* see Professor Shraga Abramson's article in *Torah She-be'al Peh* (Jerusalem: Mosad Harav Kook, 1972), p. 156. His conclusions are somewhat different from those in Rabbi Oshry's *teshuvah.* Also included in the same volume are a number of significant articles on many halakhic aspects of the subject of *kiddush ha-shem.*
5. Rabbi Oshry, in *Ḥurban Lita* (New York, 1952), describes the martyr's death of Rabbi Elḥanan Wasserman. "On the eleventh of Tamuz, 5701 (July 6, 1941), he was sitting with a group of rabbis and *roshei yeshivah,* great Torah scholars, who were gathered in the Kovno ghetto, giving his *she'ur* in the tractate *Niddah.* All present were so deeply engrossed in the subject matter that they did not react for a moment when a band of Lithuanian fascists broke into the room. The Lithuanians were enraged and began to fire their rifles; then the rabbis rose from their places, trembling. One of the Lithuanians taunted them, 'You were organizing a revolt in order to go to Israel. But we caught you! You will not escape! Come with us!' They were lined up ready to be marched away when Rabbi Wasserman turned to his follow prisoners and said, in his quiet and tranquil voice, 'It appears that in Heaven they view us as *tzaddikim* [righteous men] worthy to atone with our lives for the people of Israel. We must, therefore, immediately repent here and now, for the time is short and the Ninth Fort [the place of execution] is near. We must remember that we will in truth be *mekadeshei ha-shem,* those who sanctify God's name. Let us therefore go with heads erect, let us, God forbid, have no unworthy thoughts, which like *pigul,* unfit intention, in the case of a sacrifice rendered it invalid. We are now about to fulfill the greatest commandment—that of *kiddush ha-shem.* The fire which will destroy us is the flame out of which the Jewish people will be rebuilt.' " Rabbi Oshry concludes: "And so they marched proudly to their death, thirteen of the great sages of Israel with Rabbi Elḥanan Wasserman at their head. That day they were slain in the Ninth Fort."
6. Oshry, *Mi-Ma'amakim,* vol. 2, p. 28.
7. Ibid., vol. 3, p. 56.
8. Ibid., vol. 1, p. 53.
9. The inclusion of the name of God for the ascribing of sovereignty to Him are held to be essential for a benediction (*Berakhot* 12a). The objection to reciting an unnecessary benediction derives from the prohibition of taking the

name of God in vain. Where there is no *shem*, no name of God, included, there is less objection to reciting a benediction of dubious necessity.

10. *Rama, Yoreh Deah* 376:4 and the commentaries thereon.
11. Oshry, *Mi-Ma-amakim*, vol. 2, p. 36.
12. Ibid., vol. 1, p. 104.
13. Ibid., vol. 3, p. 69.

CHAPTER FIVE: BEARING WITNESS

1. Meisels, *Mekadeshei ha-Shem*, vol. 1, p. 24.
2. Prager, *Eleh She-lo Nikhne'u*, vol. 2, p. 132.
3. Eliav, *Ani Ma'amin*, p. 102.
4. Ibid., p. 96.
5. Ibid., p. 99.
6. Oshry, *Divrei Efrayim*.
7. See also the *teshuvah* by Rabbi Aharon Walkin in *Zekan Aharon* (New York, 1958), vol. 2, where a similar problem, which arose in the Soviet Union, is discussed.
8. Oshry, *Mi-Ma'amakim*, vol. 1, p. 146.
9. Ibid., p. 77.
10. The "small *tallit*" worn underneath the outer garments by observant Jews who wish to fulfill the *mitzvah* of *tzitzit*.
11. Meisels, p. 15.
12. Oshry, *Mi-Ma'amakim*, vol. 1, p. 88.
13. In the ghetto of Lodz, during the years 1940–41, there was a special society known as the *Shomrei Mezuzot*, "Keepers of the *Mezuzot*," which conducted a campaign to see that every doorpost in the ghetto had a *mezuzah*. One of the founders of the organization was convinced that the Jews were compelled to wear the "yellow badge" because they had rejected the *mezuzah* as their mark of identification—measure for measure. (Yitzhak Katzenelson, as quoted in Eliav, p. 84).

CHAPTER SIX: THE APPOINTED SEASONS

1. Eliav, *Ani Ma'amin*, p. 137.
2. *Yerushat Peletah*, pp. 9–10.
3. In Prager, *Eleh She-Lo Nikhne'u*, vol. 1, p. 115, Shmelke Lifshitz writes that in the camp of Gross-Rosen he worked assiduously on the six days of the week so that he would be able to get by with stratagems on *shabbat* to avoid *melakhot de'oraita*. "Each *shabbat* I was extremely careful about every kind of work.... as I worked I reviewed in my mind the *dinim* of *shabbat*. If we were digging trenches on *shabbat,* I complained that my arm was sore and I could not dig, but I volunteered to push carts of material instead. If

we were laying water pipes, I showed a bruised finger and offered to work at sorting the pipes. . . . in this fashion I taught myself a *she'ur* in the laws of *shabbat.*" See also a similar situation described on p. 123 of vol. 2.

4. Oshry, *Mi-Ma'amakim,* vol. 1, p. 39.
5. Eliav, p. 147.
6. Prager, vol. 1, p. 112.
7. Unsdorfer, *The Yellow Star,* p. 118.
8. Eliav, p. 138; Unsdorfer, p. 103, 117.
9. Oshry, *Mi-Ma'amakim,* vol. 1, p. 75.
10. Eliav, p. 146.
11. Ibid., p. 147.
12. Rambam, *Hilkhot Hametz u'Matzah* 6:1.
13. Ibid., 1:1.
14. Ibid., 4:1, 7:1.
15. Ibid., 7:9–11.
16. Cited in Eliav, p. 186.
17. *Rambam, Hilkhot Hametz u'Matzah* 1:4.
18. Oshry, vol. 1, p. 109.
19. Ibid., p. 129.
20. "Council of Elders," leaders of the Jewish community appointed by the Nazis to carry out their directives. Also, and more commonly, referred to as *Judenrat,* "Jewish Council." For a discussion of the conflicting views concerning these councils, see *Encylopaedia Judaica,* s.v. "Judenrat," and the bibliographical references cited there.
21. Oshry, vol. 3, p. 51.
22. Prager, vol. 2, p. 177.
23. Ibid., p. 178.
24. Kaplan, *Warsaw Diary,* p. 308.
25. Eliav, p. 192.
26. Ibid., p. 185.
27. Ibid., p. 183.
28. H. Adler, ed., *Service for the New Year* (New York)
29. Eliav, p. 148.
30. Ibid., p. 149.
31. Meisels, *Mekadeshei ha-Shem,* vol. 1, p. 11.
32. Kaplan, p. 203.
33. Garfunkel, *Kovno Ha-Yehudit be-Hurbanah,* p. 257.
34. Eliav, p. 163.
35. Ibid., p. 165.
36. Prager, vol. 1, p. 113.
37. Meisels, p. 14.
38. Eliav, p. 102.
39. Ibid., p. 148.
40. Kaplan, p. 214.
41. Ibid., p. 180.
42. *Taanit* 29a.

43. J. Hertz, ed., *Authorized Daily Prayer Book* (New York, 1948), p. 956.
44. Eliav, p. 176.
45. Unsdorfer, p. 148.

CHAPTER SEVEN: OUT OF THE DEPTHS

1. Oshry, *Mi-Ma'amakim,* vol. 1, p. 17.
2. Ibid., vol. 2, p. 31.
3. Ibid., vol. 3, p. 48.
4. Ibid., vol. 2, p. 69.
5. Ibid., p. 44.
6. Shimon Huberband, *Kiddush Hashem,* pp. 27–29.
7. Oshry, vol. 1, p. 7.
8. Ibid., vol. 2, p. 25.
9. Ibid., p. 80.
10. See Huberband, op. cit., for a description of illegal *shehitah* in the ghetto. There are numerous accounts of Jews who observed the laws of *kashrut* in whole or in part in the ghettos and concentration camps. Some of these are included in Mordekhai Eliav's *Ani Ma'amin,* pp. 78–117. Moshe Prager, *Eleh Shelo Nikhne'u,* also describes such situations. An example (vol. 2, p. 121): Yaakov Pick, in the Gerlitz camp, not only refused to eat the non-kosher soup, but also refused to trade this soup for bread, since this would give him personal benefit from the *terefah* food. If it contained mixtures of milk and meat, a likely possibility, the Halakhah would prohibit deriving any benefit from such food.
11. Rambam, *Hilkhot Yesodei ha-Torah* 5:6.
12. Oshry, vol. 1, p. 13.
13. Ibid., vol. 2, p. 16.
14. A shrine built by the high priest Onias IV, who fled to Egypt in the second century B.C.E. It maintained an order of sacrifice and worship similar to that of the Temple in Jerusalem, although it was regarded by the Halakhah as unlawful.
15. *Berakhot* 61b.
16. See chap. 1, n. 12.

CHAPTER EIGHT: AFTERMATH

1. Oshry, *Mi-Ma'amakim,* vol. 1, p. 131.
2. Ibid., p. 151.
3. For additional insights into this subject, see Rabbi A. Kook, *She'elot u'Teshuvot Ezrat Kohen* (Jerusalem, 1969), pp. 11–18.
4. Oshry, vol. 2, p. 134.
5. Ibid., vol. 1, p. 137.
6. Ibid., p. 172.
7. Ibid., vol. 3, p. 90.
8. Ibid., p. 100.

BIBLIOGRAPHY

General Works on the Holocaust

Hilberg, Raul. *The Destruction of the European Jews*. Chicago: Quadrangle, 1967.
Levin, Nora. *The Holocaust*. New York: Crowell, 1968.
Robinson, Jacob. *The Crooked Shall be Made Straight: The Eichmann Trial, The Jewish Catastrophe and Hannah Arendt's Narrative*. Philadelphia: Jewish Publication Society, 1965.

Articles and Pamphlets

Encyclopaedia Judaica. Jerusalem: Keter, 1971. s.v. "Holocaust".
Yad Vashem. *The Holocaust and Resistance*. Jerusalem: Yad Vashem, 1972.

Eyewitness Accounts and Anecdotal Material

Eliav, Mordekhai, *Ani Ma'amin*. Jerusalem: Mosad Harav Kook, 1965.
Huberband, Shimon. *Kiddush Hashem*. Tel Aviv: Zachor, 1969.
Kaplan, Chaim A. *The Warsaw Diary of Chaim A. Kaplan*. Edited by Abraham Katsh. New York: Collier, 1973.
Niger, S. ed. *Kiddush Hashem*. New York: CYCO, 1948.
Prager, Moshe, *Eleh She-lo Nikhne'u*. 2 vols. Bnei Brak: Netzah, 1963.
Rozman, Shelomo. *Zikhron Kedoshim*. Rehovot: Published by the Author, 1968.
Schindler, Peter. "Responses of Hassidic Leaders and Hassidim during the Holocaust." Ph.D. dissertation, New York University, 1972.
Seidman, Hillel. *Yoman Getto Warsha*. New York: Die Yiddishe Woch, 1957.
Unsdorfer, S. B. *The Yellow Star*. London: Yoseloff, 1961.

Responsa Concerning the Holocaust *

Breisch, Mordekhai Yaacov. *Helkat Ya'akov*. Vol. 1, Jerusalem, Mahzikei ha-Dat, 1951. Vol. 2, London, 1959.

171

Brisk, Mordekhai. *Ma-ha-ram Brisk.* New York: Talmidei Yeshivat Ma-ha-ram Brisk. 1963.
Efrati, Shimon. *Mi'gei ha-Haregeah.* Jerusalem: Yad Vashem, 1961.
Kirschboim, Menahem Mendel. *Tziyyun le-Menahem.* New York: Makhon le-Heker Ba'ayot ha-Ya'hadut ha-Haredit, 1965.
Meisels, Zvi Hirsch. *Mekadeshei ha-Shem.* Vol. 1. Chicago: Published by the Author, 1955.
Oshry, Ephraim. *Divrei Efrayim.* New York: Published by the Author, 1949.
———. *Mi-Ma'amakim.* 3 vols. New York: Published by the Author, 1949, 1963, 1969.
Stern, Betzalel. *Be-Tzel ha-Hokhmah.* Jerusalem: Published by the Author, 1959.
Walkin, Aharon. *Zekan Aharon.* New York, 1958.
Weinberg, Yehiel. *Seridei Esh.* 3 vols. Jerusalem: Mosad Harav Kook, 1961–69.
Weiss, Yitzhak Ya'akov. *Minhat Yitzhak.* 3 vols. London: Published by the Author, 1955–62.
Yerushat Peletah: Kovetz Teshuvot mi-Gedolei Medinat Hungariyah. Israel: Hevrah Shas de-Kehal Yerai-im, 1971.

*The initial words of the title *She'elot u'Teshuvot* are omitted in all entries.

PRINCIPAL
AUTHORITIES CITED

Abudraham. R. David Abudraham (d. 1345).
Alfas. R. Isaac Alfasi (d. 1103).
Arukh (Arokh) ha-Shulhan. R. Yehiel Epstein (d. 1908).
Bah. Bayit Hadash. R. Joel Sirkes (d. 1640).
Bedek ha-Bayit. R. Aharon ha-Levy (13th cent.).
Bet Yitzhak. R. Isaac Schmelkes (19th cent.).
Bet Yosef. R. Joseph Karo (d. 1575).
Birkhei Yosef. R. Hayyim Yosef Azulai (d. 1805).
Divrei Hayyim. R. Hayyim Halberstam (19th cent.).
Divrei Malkiel. R. Malkiel Tannenbaum (19th cent.).
Elyah Rabbah. R. Elijah Shapiro (d. 1712).
Ha'amek She-alah. R. Naftali Zvi Berlin (d. 1893).
Hagahot Maimuni. R. Meir ha-Kohen (13th cent.).
Hakham Tzvi. R. Tzvi Ashkenazi (d. 1718).
Hatam Sofer. R. Moshe Sofer (d. 1839).
Hemdat Shelomoh. R. Solomon of Posen (19th cent.).
Hokhmat Adam. R. Abraham Danzig (d. 1820).
Issur va-Heter. Author uncertain (14th cent.).
Kesef Mishneh. R. Joseph Karo (d. 1675).
Ketav Sofer. R. Abraham Sofer (19th cent.).
Kol Bo. Author uncertain (14th cent.).

Lehem Mishneh. R. Abraham di Boton (d. 1609).
Levush. R. Mordecai Jaffe (d. 1612).
Magen Avraham. R. Abraham Gumbiner (d. 1683).
Mahaneh Efrayim. R. Efrayim Navon (18th cent.).
Mahaneh Hayyim. R. Hayyim Sofer (19th cent.).
Maharam Schick. R. Moses Schick (19th cent.).
Maharatz Hayyes. R. Zvi Chajes (d. 1855).
Maharik. R. Joseph Colon (d. 1480).
Maharil. R. Jacob Moelln (d. 1427).
Maharsha. R. Samuel Edels (d. 1631).
Maharshal. R. Solomon Luria (d. 1573).
Maharsham. R. Sholom Schwadron (20th cent.).
Meiri. R. Menahem ben Solomon (d. 1306).
Melamed lé H'oil. R. David Hoffman (d. 1921).
Meshiv Davar. R. Naftali Tzvi Berlin (d. 1893).
Mishnah Berurah. R. Israel Meir ha-Kohen (d. 1933).
Mishneh la-Melekh. R. Judah Rozanes (d. 1729).
Mishpetei Uziel. R. Benzion Uziel (d. 1954).
Mordekhai. R. Mordecai ben Hillel (d. 1298).
Netziv. R. Naftali Zvi Yehudah Berlin (d. 1893).
Nimukei Yosef. R. Joseph ibn Habib (15th cent.).
Noda be-Yehudah. R. Ezekiel Landau (d. 1793).
Or Sameah. R. Meir Simha of Dvinsk (20th cent.).
Or Zarua. R. Isaac of Vienna (d. 1260).
Pahad Yitzhak. R. Isaac Lampronti (d. 1756).
Peri Megaaim. R. Joseph Teomin (18th cent.).
Pithei Teshuvah. R. Abraham Eisenstadt (d. 1868).
Radvaz. R. David ibn Zimri (d. 1589).
Rama. R. Moses Isserles (d. 1572).
Rambam. R. Moses ben Maimon (Maimonides) (1135–1204).
Ran. R. Nissim Gerondi (d. 1380).
Rashba. R. Solomon ben Adret (d. 1310).
Rashi. R. Solomon Yitzhaki (d. 1105).
Ritva. R. Yom Tov ben Abraham. (d. 1340).
Rivash. R. Isaac bar Sheshet. (d. 1408).
Rosh. R. Asher ben Yehiel. (d. 1327).
Sedei Hemed. R. Hayyim Hizkiah Medini. (d. 1905).
Sefer ha-Hinukh. R. Aharon ha-Levi. (14th cent.)
Sefer Hasidim. R. Judah he- Hasid. (12th cent.)
Sema. (Sefer Meirot Einayim) R. Joshua Falk. (d. 1614).
Shakh. R. Shabbetai ha-Kohen. (d. 1662).
She'iltot. R. Ahai Gaon. (d. 670).
Shenei Luhot ha-Brit R. Isaiah Hurwitz. (d. 1626).
Shulhan Arukh. R. Joseph Karo. (d. 1575).
Yosef Ometz. R. Joseph Hahn. (18th cent.)

INDEX